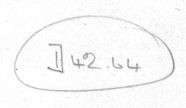

42.64

F

Pate
18/6
25.6

60/40236

The County Books Series

GENERAL EDITOR: BRIAN VESEY-FITZGERALD

SUFFOLK

THE COUNTY BOOKS SERIES

A series comprising 57 volumes. It covers every county in England, and there will be five books on Scotland, two on Ireland, two on the Hebrides, and one each on Orkney, Shetland, Wales, the Isle of Man, and the Channel Islands.

PLEASE WRITE TO THE PUBLISHERS
FOR FULL DESCRIPTIVE PROSPECTUS

SUFFOLK

by

WILLIAM ADDISON

Illustrated and with a Map

London
Robert Hale Limited
18 Bedford Square W.C.1

First published 1950

PRINTED IN GREAT BRITAIN BY
NORTHUMBERLAND PRESS LIMITED
GATESHEAD ON TYNE

"There was an alternation of meadow land for pasture, and of cultivated fields; and, it is easy to see, that this county of Suffolk, enjoys not only a salubrious air, but also a rich and fertile soil; nor is anything wanting, which can contribute either to pleasure or profit; hence it is considered the most fruitful and the most agreeable of all the counties of the kingdom, and such it continued as far as the limits which divide the county of Suffolk from that of Cambridge."

Travels of Cosmo III, Grand Duke of Tuscany, through England, during the reign of King Charles the Second

ACKNOWLEDGMENTS

It is with pleasure that I acknowledge my indebtedness to Mr. R. F. Buckley, Captain Eric Bush, R.N., Lord Cranworth, Mr. C. H. Clarke, Mr. C. R. Cole, Rev. H. Tyrrell Green, Mr. Raymond Keer, Mr. G. N. Kent, Mr. G. P. Lempriere, Mr. H. W. Lewer, Mr. S. H. Lewer, Mr. L. W. Liell, Miss M. M. Raven, Major H. P. Raven, Mr. E. J. P. Raven, and others too numerous to name, for supplying information and checking data, and to Mr. Arnold Kent for cooperation throughout.

CONTENTS

CONTENTS

ILLUSTRATIONS

xi

ILLUSTRATIONS

ACKNOWLEDGEMENT

All the illustrations above are reproduced from photographs supplied by Mr. Arnold Kent of Norwich.

xii

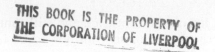
CHAPTER I

SUFFOLK LANDSCAPE

SUFFOLK is the heart of East Anglia. In aspect and character it is softer and kinder than Norfolk, its hard-headed, practical neighbour. Its distinctive beauty is in its tranquil valleys, its churches and homesteads; and equally in its wild heaths: Breckland, and the breezy coast. Without its heaths the scenery of Suffolk might be thought tame—and with them there is nothing startling or magnificent about it. Suffolk has no stage effects. But with its lack of the spectacular it is relieved of the faults that commonly go with it. Exceptionally beautiful counties, like exceptionally beautiful women, often seem spoiled by flattery. They become temperamental. Think of the Lake District or the West Country. They are to be admired, but not trusted. They smile on you one minute and scowl on you the next. Just when you are ready to lose your heart to their beauty a deluge descends upon you, and you would give all you possess for a warm hearth and a bite of bread and cheese. If you like this kind of country and cannot admire any other, Suffolk is not your county. Its charms are of a homelier and friendlier kind. It is a county to settle down with—a county to wed.

Such are the first thoughts that pass through my mind as I sit down to write about this fine English county. They are the kind of thoughts a man might think of Suffolk with his feet on the fender on a winter's night. They suggest the atmosphere of the county in a general sort of way; and in a book designed to interpret its life and character in a broader, freer manner than that employed in the straightforward guide-book, generalisation is inevitable.

Many books have been written on Suffolk as on every English county. Many more will be written. Writers have been describing and artists have been painting the most familiar objects for untold centuries, and will continue to do so as long as writers and artists continue to be born. The scene may be old; but man's delight in it is constantly being renewed as every moment earth and sky enter into new relationships with each other. Here in Suffolk the scene may be as commonplace as a group of elms or a row of willows, yet Constable's willows did not disturb John Nash in painting the same trees by the same river, and disclosing something entirely new and interesting about them. As many pages have been written on Suffolk as canvases painted; but there is still much to be said, and there are many old tales that are worth re-telling. I write as one whose delight it has been, and still is, like Edie Ochiltree " to daunder along the green lanes " of Suffolk, to lie on its heaths, to loiter in its ancient towns, and to be reminded of the course of English history in visiting its churches, its abbeys, and its fine old manor-houses. For men of this mind Suffolk is a rare county.

The man who sits down to write about East Anglia as a whole will probably bite his pen for a few minutes before deciding where to place his western and southern boundaries. There is no such difficulty in writing about Suffolk. It is separated from Norfolk on the north by the Waveney and the Little Ouse, and from Essex on the south by that long and beautiful river, the Stour. The North Sea, which forms the eastern boundary, has been a greedy neighbour, stealing much and returning little, and Cambridgeshire on the west has reason to be uneasy when the eighth commandment is mentioned. Suffolk is obliged to guard itself both east and west, and this acquired instinct for longitudinal defence has become so strong that East and West Suffolk now guard themselves against each other. It is fortunate, therefore, that the longest boundaries are north and south, for with Norfolk on the one hand and Essex on the other, Suffolk lives on the friendliest terms.

River boundaries are easily traced; so I was surprised a short time ago when a friend told me that his father, who was born at Hoxne, never knew whether he was a Norfolk or a Suffolk man because the county boundary ran through the bedroom in which he was born. On first hearing, the story sounds improbable; but there are several places along both the Waveney and the Little Ouse where the county boundary follows an old bed of the river. Many small towns and villages are partly in one county and partly in the other, and amusing stories could be told about difficulties that used to arise in local administration when the location of a particular property was in dispute. Most of these problems, however, were amicably solved several years ago.

On the south, Bures spreads itself across the river, and Nayland folk, who live in Suffolk, have Colchester, which is in Essex, as their postal address. These two counties even agree to share one of their greatest sons between them, for though Constable was born at East Bergholt in Suffolk, Dedham, so closely associated with his developing genius, is in Essex. In our own day, Sir Alfred Munnings, the first President of the Royal Academy to come from Suffolk, has gone even further by intimately associating himself with all three counties. He was born at Mendham in the Waveney valley, and was often over the Norfolk border with the gipsies as a youth, painting their ponies; to-day he lives at Dedham, just over the Essex border. So Norfolk, Suffolk, and Essex live together like three neighbours who are constantly in and out of each other's houses. In such a relationship the one in the middle must always play the most important part. So it is with these three counties, for Suffolk being naturally tactful—not to say wily—has cultivated characteristics that agree equally well with both her neighbours, at the same time retaining an unmistakable character of her own.

There are fewer ways leading into Suffolk than there are into most counties, and most of them go straight through and out again. If you enter Suffolk on the west side, the signposts seem determined to get you through to Norwich instead of to Bury St. Edmunds, which was formerly the end of most pilgrimages in that direction. East Suffolk does get you into Ipswich whatever your destination may be, but you are soon put on the way to Yarmouth or Norwich again.

This determination to wave the traveller forward cannot be set down to any lack of hospitality in Suffolk. Its inns are almost as famous as its churches, and much more popular. But somehow Suffolk seems to assume that the traveller is

3

going to Norwich or Yarmouth if he is travelling north, and
to London or Colchester if he is travelling south. Perhaps,
however, this characteristic is not peculiar to Suffolk, but is
merely part of the general restlessness of the age, and of its
desire for a continually receding destination. However this
may be, it is certain that the road which leads to the heart of
the county is less used than the roads that go straight through
it. The road that leads to the heart, surely, is the one that
enters at Sudbury, for there is a sense in which Sudbury is to
Suffolk what Norwich is to Norfolk. One is the southern
burge, the other is the northern *wick*. Even in the middle of
the eighteenth century, when Arthur Young made his *Six
Weeks' Tour in the Southern Counties*, this road was in a
neglected condition. He wrote: "I was forced to move as
slow in it [the turnpike from Bury St. Edmunds to Sudbury]
as in any unmended lanes in Wales. For pounds of liquid
dirt, and a scattering of loose flints just sufficient to lame every
horse that moves near them, with the addition of cutting vile
grips across the road under the pretence of letting the water
off, but without effect, altogether render at least twelve out
of these sixteen miles as infamous a turnpike as ever was
beheld." The surface is good to-day, and the scenery as
pleasing as ever it was, but surprisingly little traffic passes
along this ancient highway.

There are several other roads for the traveller who is not
in a hurry. There is the one through Bures, for example.
But these are now like private doors for which a man must
carry his own latch-key. Other ways of gaining admittance
to this carefully guarded county seem almost like climbing
through windows, so that if you attempt them you are half
afraid that a policeman's hand will be on your shoulder and
a gruff voice demand your business.

The character of Suffolk roads being such, we may assume
that most people who use them enter from the Colchester by-
pass and reach Suffolk at Stratford St. Mary. This is the
quickest road in the county, and is an excellent road from
every point of view except that of Edie Ochiltree. Within
six miles of Colchester an invigorating wind is felt, blowing
from the broad estuary of the Stour, and an old rhyme comes
to mind:

4

North for grandeur
South for wealth;
West for beauty,
East for health.

I am not sure that I remember it correctly; but I know that I have got the last line right!

While the traveller is filling his lungs with invigorating East Anglian air, the road drops sharply down Dedham Gun Hill, and at once he is called upon to observe a Suffolk peculiarity. Inns are not called by such names as the "Gun" at Dedham or the "Crown" at Orford, but "Dedham Gun" and "Orford Crown." The man who asks for them by any other name will be known at once for a foreigner.

At the foot of Dedham Gun Hill is the Stour itself, and Suffolk is entered at the very centre of the Constable country. But the fact is hardly noticed. The massive brick building on the left, at present only a shell, is not the building Constable painted. This was his country, but only for commercial purposes can anything on the main road be associated with him to-day. There still is a Constable country in Suffolk, to be discovered at leisure later. It is not on the main road. Yet it was from Dedham Gun Hill that his best known "Dedham Vale" was painted. The vale has had a sad history since then. For a time its beauty increased as the willows he loved were allowed to grow freely instead of being pollarded. The Stour was then kept free from weeds, so that the barges could pass freely through the water to Sudbury. Now the barges lie derelict at Sudbury and the river is choked with weeds. Other disturbing agencies have been at work, with the result that the water coming down the river-bed is not strong enough to hold back the tides, and those lovely willows have been killed by the salt water that has bitten into their naked arms. It is a sad sight. Constable's paintings are silent witnesses to the price Nature has had to pay for the water we have drawn from the Stour to supply our Essex industries. But there is one Constable story we must recall at this point. It was while travelling along this road that he called the attention of two strangers who shared the coach with him to the beauty of the surrounding countryside.

"Yes, sir, this is Constable's country," said one, and Constable engagingly confides that he promptly revealed his identity lest the next words should spoil the compliment.

Stratford St. Mary itself retains as much of its old-world character as is consistent with its situation on this busy road. Its flint and stone church, a short distance from the road, is a fine building, with memorials to the Mors family who flourished here as wool merchants in the fifteenth and sixteenth centuries. In some respects, therefore, this is an authentic bit of Suffolk on the very threshold. But it is not a place to linger in, for the highway is broad and the current of traffic swift. For those who can take their eyes off the road itself, the country between Stratford and Ipswich is full of character —of Gainsborough rather than Constable character—and the road itself is rich in associations. From the *Paston Letters* we may recall how John Paston's rival was escorted along this road by a hundred retainers armed with bows and arrows, their heads and bodies well protected and their eyes watchful for a movement in the foliage that might disclose an ambush of the Pastons. At that time the woods closed thickly over the road, and for hundreds of years this was a dangerous hill. The coaches moved slowly in making the ascent, and the guards always had their blunderbusses ready for action.

Later, a pleasant sight might be seen along this road towards the end of the year. Thousands of turkeys were reared annually in Suffolk for the London market, and when Christmas drew near great droves of from three hundred to a thousand birds each were driven daily over Stratford Bridge. Now that sight also is forgotten. Turkeys are no longer seen everywhere in Suffolk as they were in Defoe's day. But everyone entering Suffolk for the first time should keep his eyes open for that sturdy animal, the Suffolk punch, as the Suffolk breed of horse is called. Not that there will be any difficulty in finding him. It is possible to travel far in the county before seeing a good herd of Suffolk red poll cattle or a flock of black-faced sheep, but punches are everywhere, with their sleek, chestnut bodies and friendly faces. Something about the shape of the nose always gives a Suffolk punch the appearance of serene good-humour, and it is an appearance that does not belie its character. The tail is almost sure to be whisking in the friendliest manner; the head tossing a greeting, or nodding approval of some secret thought or sensation that presently sends a quiver of well-being along its sturdy flanks. The Suffolk punch is a fine animal, as Dickens knew when he made William the coachman say to David Copperfield, "And the Punches! There's cattle! A Suffolk Punch, when he's a good 'un, is worth his weight in gold."

Again we are back with the coaches. It is hardly possible for a man who has done much reading to travel along this road without thinking of the many distinguished men and women who have looked across these fields as their great lumbering coaches tossed and creaked along this historic highway. There were riders, too. There was Cobbett for one, whose character suits the county so well, and to whom it was "the crack county of England." Many of their names have been repeated in other books on Suffolk. There is one that is not so well known: Celia Fiennes, who travelled through England on a side-saddle in the time of William and Mary. She entered Suffolk by this road, and recorded that she found Ipswich a clean town and bigger than Colchester. On market day she was interested to find butter being sold by the pint, a pint weighing approximately twenty ounces. The price of the best butter was sixpence, she noted, and inferior grades could be bought for fivepence, and even fourpence. She found also what every observant traveller finds in Suffolk: very good wood-carving. There was a carved figure of Justice, ornamented with gilt, on the market-cross at Ipswich. Christchurch Mansion in that town has many interesting examples of this Suffolk craft, and others can be found in almost every old village and country town. Celia Fiennes, inevitably in her day, saw a great deal of knitting and spinning being done in East Anglia, and it is interesting to learn from her that many of the women carried their spinning-wheels into the streets in sunny weather. A village street must have been a pleasing sight with the women sitting at their wheels by the cottage doors.

When Ipswich is reached, roads branch out in all directions, arteries that distribute the strength of the county from its vigorous county town. One goes over the heath to Felixstowe, another by Woodbridge, Wickham Market, Saxmundham, and Blythburgh with its great church to Lowestoft and Yarmouth. This is the busiest road past Ipswich, leading to the many resorts along the coast, yet it is quiet enough, for in an area of approximately two hundred square miles between Felixstowe and Lowestoft, and between this road and the sea, there is not one town with a population of five thousand, though almost the whole of the area is within a hundred miles of London. Another road goes by Debenham to Eye and Norwich; another to Norwich by a more direct route; and yet another along the Gipping by Needham Market and Stowmarket to Bury St. Edmunds. Lastly, there is the road through Hadleigh to that part of Suffolk that I personally know and love best, the Suffolk of the old weaving towns between Hadleigh and Sudbury.

To name so many towns and villages in one paragraph may seem like making a mere catalogue of Suffolk place names, but there is not one of these that does not bring to the mind of the man who knows his Suffolk, images of quiet market towns and crooked streets that are English to the very core, of sunny squares with wind worn crosses at the centre, noble churches, each towering above a cluster of cottage roofs, and inns that have the history of England written on their stout timbers, and all its hospitality symbolised in their great fireplaces.

When we look at the map and see these old names spread out across it, we see the county fall naturally into three principal divisions, each with its own peculiar characteristics. The soil determines the agriculture of a region, and Suffolk is primarily an agricultural county. It has its industries, but most of them are in Ipswich. Many smaller industries that formerly flourished in the villages are declining. The work of the land goes on, and here Suffolk is in better heart to-day than ever before.

Apart from Mildenhall Fen in the north-west corner of the county, the solid stratum underlying the whole of West Suffolk is a layer of chalk, tilted to the east and south-east. From Sudbury to Ipswich there is a broad belt of London clay, which is found also along the valleys of the Stour, the Orwell, and the Deben. Norwich and red crags, and Chillesford clay, lie under the heaths of East Suffolk, with peat and fen gravels along all the rivers, particularly along the Waveney, which suffers so much from floods. The whole of the chalk formation, except in Breckland, round Newmarket, and less extensively round Bury St. Edmunds, is covered with boulder clay, while along the coast the crags are overlaid with sand and gravel, producing light soils, which leave much crag exposed. Along the coast, then, run the heaths, with light sandy soil, rich in colour from early spring to late autumn, for there is an old saying, " When the furze is out of blossom, then is kissing out of fashion," which is seldom! The same wild and wind-swept characteristics are found again—somewhat unexpectedly by the stranger—in the unique region called Breckland. Along the west runs a ridge of chalk, part of the line extending from the Yorkshire Wolds to Dorset, and it is along this ridge that the county's highest levels are found. They are nowhere considerable. The highest point is Rede, in the south-west, which is 420 feet above sea-level. Two-thirds of the county is clay land, the northern part of which is called " High Suffolk," a wide plateau with little shelter from the cold east winds that sweep across it in early spring. Formerly this region was dense forest, and to this day most of the villages are grouped round a central green, once a clearing in a forest and a common for pasturing cattle. Many of these have their origin indicated by the suffix " field." At the north-western tip there is a small area of fenland more like Cambridgeshire in character.

This variety in the Suffolk soil has influenced the buildings as well as the lay-out of the villages. Most of the flint cottages will be found along the coast and on the Norfolk border. In the valleys nearer Essex, plastered and thatched cottages, and low, gabled farmhouses prevail, many of them dating from the fifteenth and sixteenth centuries. There the roads twist and turn like the rivers, and have an entirely different aspect from the long straight roads of Breckland, or the high road from Bury St. Edmunds to Newmarket, where the fields are flat like a green sea, often with flying clouds above, and where the landscape has few remarkable features. Like the sea itself, this part of the county is inviting under a sunny sky, but repellent under storm clouds or in grey drizzle. Fortunately its monotony is relieved by large parks surrounding many of the finest mansions of the county, and by great avenues of trees, many of which have now achieved stately proportions. But this district has not the homely, friendly atmosphere characteristic of the rest of Suffolk.

Almost everywhere else the Suffolk scene is enlivened by windmills, which somehow symbolise the cheerful, workaday character of the county. Some of these are "post" mills, the oldest European form, so-called because they have a post or tree trunk through the centre, on which the entire building turns in the manner of a weather vane when the wind catches the long tail-piece. These are now comparatively rare in England. Suffolk has several in good preservation. The other kind is the "smock" or tower mill, built of brick instead of timber, with a rotating cap to which the great hurtling sails are fixed. Windmills are always fascinating objects. No other building seems so much a living thing, or gives such an impression of determined energy, and appears at the same time so roguish and variable. No wonder the miller has so often been represented as a merry rascal who might be relied upon to cap even the butcher's tale in the bar-parlour on a Saturday night. The millers of to-day, however, are not always of this character. As likely as not one will turn out to be a Sunday-school superintendent or a churchwarden.

The magnificent Suffolk churches are unquestionably the most remarkable features in the county's landscape, with their great towers dominating every valley and crowning every low hill. The term "silly Suffolk" is said to be derived from the Anglo-Saxon word which in Middle English becomes *sely*, and which originally meant blissful, and also blessed. It was a word rich in associated meanings, carrying a sense of something holy, and at the same time simple, defenceless, and deserving of pity. In course of time this developed into our own word, silly, or foolishly simple. It seems probable that this term came into use from the great number of religious foundations that formerly flourished in Suffolk. In no other part of England were churches so numerous. There were upwards of four hundred when the Domesday Survey was made.

The reason for this religious character of the county was

the immense influence of the great abbeys at Bury and Ely. These two foundations came to have two-thirds of the county under their surveillance, and in addition there were buildings attached to numerous religious orders, such as those of the Black monks at Eye, with cells at Dunwich, Felixstowe, Hoxne, Sudbury, Snape and Rumburgh. The Benedictine nuns were established at Redlingfield and Bungay. The Cluniac monks had priories at Wangford and Mendham. The Cistercians had an abbey at Sibton. The Austin Friars had no fewer than thirteen priories, and the mendicant friars had ten centres in the county. Nor is this a complete list.

Suffolk is a county of the land, the sea, and the Church; but this particular use of the word *sely* seems inappropriate in application to the people who worship to-day in churches with massive towers, symbolising something strong and forthright in the character of villager and townsman alike. There is no suggestion of foolishness in buildings so dignified and noble, and, to be truthful, there is no nonsense in the Suffolk character anywhere. Its wit is shrewd and keen; it is never folly. Indeed, if there is a theological criticism of these Suffolk towers it is that they symbolise so little of the gentleness of Christ. They express nothing of the strength that is perfected in weakness, or of the apparent foolishness of God which confounds the wisdom of men. In appearance they suggest a martial rather than either an ecclesiastical or a commercial civilisation. Yet most of these glorious churches were built either by the rich merchants who flourished in this county from the fourteenth to the sixteenth century, or were directly inspired by the churches the wool merchants had built elsewhere in the county. Their size is a mystery. Many of these old Suffolk villages were formerly larger than they are now, but they were never large enough to justify these village cathedrals. The late distinguished Provost of Eton, Dr. M. R. James, in his book *Suffolk and Norfolk,* assures us that "it was not the population that dictated the size of the church, but higher motives of thankfulness and devotion." It is an agreeable explanation, though we may not feel quite so convinced as he was that these high motives were so prominent in the minds of these rich men. It does not seem unduly cynical to suspect that their desire to glorify themselves was as strong as their desire to glorify God. Dr. James hints that this feeling was no doubt present, but I am inclined to suspect that it was stronger than he appears to suppose. However that may be, there could be few better ways for a rich man to spend his money, even if again we must temper our praise when we see some of the petitions from the poor weavers employed in this once prosperous industry. The rich gave of their profits; but we should remember, too, that the poor gave their labour and skill to produce those profits. Weaving was a hard trade.

Important as the churches are in the Suffolk scene, they are secondary features when the county is viewed as a whole. The two great primary features are the heaths and the rivers. What mountains are to Westmorland and towering cliffs to Cornwall, rivers and furze-covered heaths are to Suffolk. If you are a man of the hills you must go north or west in England. Suffolk is for the man who can lean on a bridge or wander through gorse and heather. It is a friendly and smiling rather than a challenging county. As you come upon these heaths and valleys only one by one, you have to know the county thoroughly to appreciate how much they mean to it. In the valley you pass through first, whether you enter by the Stour or the Waveney, it will be the church that catches your eye. The next thing, I imagine, will be the trees. In Suffolk these are allowed to reach perfect formation unmolested. Their lower branches are seldom lopped off. They often grow singly in a field or hedgerow where their beauty can be appreciated fully, especially against a background of blue sky, for trees are always seen to best advantage in a flattish county.

The distribution of trees in Suffolk I cannot claim to have studied carefully, but I am assured that beeches are extremely rare outside private parks and the south-west corner of the county. Certainly I have noticed few myself. The great beech tree at Stoke-by-Nayland has gone. I can think of no prominent beeches except the fine avenue at Newmarket and the more recently planted beeches in Breckland. Magnificent oaks are to be found everywhere, but the two trees that contribute most to the beauty of Suffolk are the elm and the poplar. I remember an artist friend calling my attention to the tranquillising effect of the vertical cypresses in Tuscany, and I realised that the poplars in Suffolk had precisely the same effect. I had not been conscious of it before, though I knew that they always brought me a sense of satisfaction. Yet they themselves are always in motion, yielding confidingly to the wind, and with laughter in their leaves at the whisper of every breeze. An upright stem in a landscape gives a sense of strength and a focal point on which the eye can rest. Now I never see them consciously without being aware of that particular quality in them. If any one of his landscapes is studied it will be seen how fully Constable appreciated this feature. He emphasised the prevailing horizontal lines in the Suffolk landscape, which have a soothing effect at first, but later make the eye as restless as Noah's dove, then introduced a tall elm or poplar, or a church tower, to bring balance and repose. This upright is usually found one-fifth of the way along a Constable canvas.

With the church towers there is the additional value of all they symbolise. Theirs is the perpendicular of upright faith and stable security. They must have contributed to the local character qualities that might otherwise have been lacking, for Suffolk is a county without rock. A Suffolk man can never have that grand feeling experienced by a Yorkshireman when he stands on a rocky escarpment on Ingleborough or Whernside. It may be suggested that some of the rock has got into the Yorkshireman's brain. There can be no doubt that configuration of landscape does affect character. I remember a Yorkshire postman telling me that people on the side of a dale facing south were much more genial than those on the side that faced north. On the one side he was frequently invited to come indoors for a cup of tea, never on the other side. I imagine that characteristic will be disappearing now, but his story was quite credible twenty years ago. Similarly, a Suffolk man is subtle in his ways. His thoughts wind like his valleys before he reaches a conclusion, and the pace can never be forced. A Suffolk man can be led, but never driven. And the men of East Suffolk have the breeziness of their bracing coast.

All this is not fancy but fact, and it seems reasonable to believe that these solid stone towers, so stalwart and enduring, must have left their mark on the character of the people. Families could not live in daily sight of Lavenham or Long Melford church without being sturdier for it.

Some people resent the slight air of suspicion commonly shown by a Suffolk man on first meeting. It is not so noticeable now as formerly. The two great wars of our own day have almost completely transformed the character of the people. The old idiosyncrasies are quickly disappearing. Though the dialect may be used between natives it is rarely heard by a stranger; but the well-known sing-song intonation is as common as ever. I think you would recognise the speech of any other English county outside the Home Counties more easily than that of Suffolk if you heard several spoken together on a London bus. This may be because Suffolk people are born actors. Those who have produced plays in village institutes have been struck by this characteristic. The Suffolk cottager plays a part admirably and with ease. This, surely, is in keeping with his artfulness in dealing with strangers, and attributable to the county's history. For centuries the Suffolk coast was the most threatened in England. Nelson expected Napoleon to land in Hollesley Bay. The fear of invasion has never been absent long from Suffolk, so a stranger always had to be proved before he could be trusted. Even in time of peace there was danger, for many Suffolk rivers were navigable, and foreign agents always to be watched. There was also the local skeleton of smuggling in the cupboard. Suffolk was a county with a secret.

It is always wise to look for a logical reason for an East Anglian characteristic, because East Anglians are a logical race, even if the south folk are less obtrusively logical than the north folk. East Anglians live in highly cultivated country with no great mountains where mysterious rites have been performed, no deep glens where visitors from other worlds might be met, and no rocky valleys where wild outlaws might have their secret lairs, from which to ride out at night to raid the pastures of quiet farming folk. The seafaring life of the coast has produced adventurous types, but inland there has been a long tradition of patient landwork, most of it in heavy clay, which kills any nonsense that might develop in a man's character. Little superstition survives

14

under these conditions, though it must not be thought that Suffolk is entirely free from it. Barton Mere, near Bury St. Edmunds, is a sheet of water varying so much in size that sometimes it is a small pond and at other times covers twelve or fourteen acres. There is an old belief in High Suffolk that the price of corn rises and falls with Barton Mere, and an old farmer I once heard of used to ride out to the mere before offering his corn for sale at Bury market.

The character of a county has a marked effect on its vocabulary. You will not have to listen long to a Highland Scot, a Welshman, or an Englishman from a romantic countryside, before an expression that contains some element of the poetic or imaginative is used. You will hear few such expressions in Suffolk. Its poet is George Crabbe. Geography can even affect religion. This county that was long a stronghold of the ancient Church soon turned to Puritan realism. The eastern counties were the first to champion Parliament against the King. Even earlier, peasant risings had been strongest in this part of the kingdom. But the Parliamentary allegiance is particularly interesting because the Church had always been so influential here. It was, I think, this loss of Catholicism in East Anglia that was responsible for the disappearance of much of the attractive folk-lore the region had acquired. Roman Catholicism has always been favourable to fables and legends, and Suffolk must formerly have had more of these than it has to-day, though it is by no means poor in them. That scholarly man, Canon J. J. Raven, carried this association of religion with soil rather further than most would be prepared to go in a passage in his *History of Suffolk* that I take great pleasure in quoting to my Nonconformist friends. In writing of the religious bodies in the county, he says: "High Predestinarian doctrine, chiefly of the Particular Baptist type, seems to flourish more on the heavy soils, while the sudden conversions of various forms of Methodism have been more frequent on the sands and gravels."

Some may think this belief in the effect of soil on character a little far-fetched. There can, however, be no doubt about the effect of soil on flora and fauna. This will be introduced in different chapters, but in this discursive, generalising chapter it may be pointed out that the variety of soils in Suffolk

15

makes a cross-county run an interesting excursion for both the botanist and the ornithologist. Breckland is particularly interesting because there may be found such seaside plants as the dwarf-tufted centaury, the golden dock, and the sand sedge, which must have survived from days when an arm of the sea reached the Suffolk fens from the Wash. The ringed plover, which only nests on the coast, according to the textbooks, returns each year to Breckland. Similarly, appropriate plant and bird species are found in the chalk lands of the west, the sandy wastes of the coast, and the heavy clay of the centre. Mr. W. A. Dutt, in his Suffolk volume in the County Geography Series, says that Suffolk has eighty-five wild flowering plants not found in more than twelve of the one hundred and twelve divisions into which Great Britain is divided by botanists. It has twenty-six different orchids, some of them extremely rare.

Though trees contribute so much to the beauty of every Suffolk landscape, when we examine the large scale maps we find that, apart from the plantations of the Forestry Commission, the county has few large woods. In Staverton Forest there is some fine old timber, but outside it most of the woods are in parks or on large estates, which now tend to be broken up. Small groups of trees, however, are numerous, and rookeries are found in every part of the county, where the hungry birds do a considerable amount of damage to the young grain, though farmers now doubt whether they do more harm by the grain they eat than good by the wireworms they take. Robert Bloomfield, a true Suffolk poet, wrote:

> But still unsafe the big swoln grain below,
> A fav'rite morsel with the Rook and Crow.
> From field to field the flock increasing goes
> To level crops most formidable foes
> Their danger well the wary plunderers know
> And place a watch on some conspicuous bough.

When the rooks build high, the village folk will tell you, a fine summer is sure to follow.

In a county where broad rivers are so prominent a feature, we should look to find the heron a familiar sight, and so it

is, for there is a heronry on each of the principal rivers. Many of our rarer birds have their haunts in Suffolk, and the Great Bustard, extinct in the rest of England for the last hundred years, had its last stronghold here. Along the estuaries, with their broad mud flats exposed at low tide, waders and ducks are found in great numbers.

Yet for all its interest and charm, Suffolk is a little-known county. Nor is it particularly anxious to be known. More than one well-known Suffolk man whom I have approached for information has told me frankly that he has no wish to tell the rest of England what good things there are between the Stour and the Waveney, and between the Devil's Dyke and the sea. Suffolk people like to keep things to themselves, and that, no doubt, was why a well-disposed neighbour from Essex was called in to write this book.

Seventeenth-century pargeting on fifteenth-century cottage at Clare

CHAPTER II

THE RISING STOUR

IN spite of the salty humour and occasional brusqueness of most East Anglians, who above all things like to "dew different," Bishop Hall summed up the character of Suffolk admirably when he described it as a "sweet and civil county." Nowhere are these engaging qualities more evident than in the Stour valley, where Essex, let it be conceded, has been extremely generous, for she has allowed all the most attractive towns and villages to be built on the Suffolk side of the river. The only place where she has entered into competition is at Dedham, and there she has shown what she might have done on her own behalf if she had been so minded.

In this part of Suffolk there is no evidence of the striving spirit either across the river or along it, though competition must have been keen enough at one time. Perhaps these kindly old towns would be more progressive if rivalry were keener. In places there are signs of a late awakening from the sleep of centuries, and we must hope that as they have missed the ugly developments of the Industrial Revolution the Stour towns and villages will find their prosperity without sacrificing their beauty. They have a warning, for near the head of the river something of this sacrifice has, in fact, been made. Haverhill, though the winding main street is pleasant enough, lacks the beauty of its neighbours. It is a small industrial town with a ready-made clothing factory employing many of its people, and it has also a modern mill for grinding flour. Recently a tooth-brush factory has been established. With these and other small industries Haverhill flourishes, though it has lost the use of its once busy corn-market. Only the cattle sale-yard behind the "Rose and Crown" brings the farmer and his stock to Haverhill now.

To the north lies the gently rolling country characteristic of the whole of the Stour valley, where so many small streams diversify the scene as they make their way at leisure to the principal river. In this country the low hills are covered in summer with ripening wheat and barley, and neat villages with plastered and timbered cottages in sunny apple orchards give a smiling welcome to the traveller. One of these, Withersfield, is less than two miles away from the drab, huddled little streets of Haverhill, where uniform red-brick houses roofed with grey slate rise sheer from the pavements, or are separated from them only by narrow, town-like gardens. In Withersfield there are no hard pavements. Instead, there are wide grass verges where goats are tethered, and cream-washed cottages with thatched roofs that stand along the high banks through which the road winds. Like so many Suffolk villages Withersfield is grouped along the two slopes of a narrow valley, with a stream crossing the road in the middle.

From Withersfield the road to the Thurlows goes through open corn-fields with wide, unobstructed views. At Little Thurlow, Sir Peter Soames's almshouses are of interest. They are dated, like the mellow old Dower House below them, 1614, though the figures are now effaced from the almshouses. There are eight of these single-roomed dwellings, with a larger one in the middle giving distinction to the design. One of the eight is intended to be used for storing fuel, as a cheerful old pensioner informed me when I stood in the road admiring their symmetry.

"They may be beautiful to look at," she said, "but one room doesn't give you much space to get about in, and you can't hide anything. When the door is open everything can be seen. You can't have no secrets. And you can't fall out of the window because it doesn't open," she added as an afterthought, laughing again. "Not that you can have much to hide," she concluded with a grin. "You can't afford many luxuries on one and twopence a week and your pension."

I told her the pension was to be raised shortly, but she had heard before of good times coming, and was an old lady with a long experience of hard work for little reward, which made her cautious in her optimism.

"The date has gone," I observed, scrutinising the tablet that had once shown it. "They were probably built at the same time as the Dower House."

" Is that what you call it? " she said. " It was a school when I first knew it, and a pretty sight it was to see the children being driven up in their pony-traps. Donkey-carts, too, I remember," and her voice rose and fell in the sing-song Suffolk way. Then, anxious that I should not have a wrong impression of her income, she told me that the old pensioners got a few faggots each year for winter fuel. " But we don't keep them in the other house," she said with a knowing glance round the houses. " We might get them mixed up with somebody else's."

Her smiling, weather-beaten old face, so full of character and shrewd good-humour, was with me as I went forward, past bright cottage gardens, full of sweet-william and Canterbury bells, and hedgerows fragrant with meadow-sweet.

It is easy to feel sentimental about the countryside on a warm July morning, but a later conversation that same day reminded me that life in the country is not all sunshine. In a village that shall not be named there were comely old cottages in ruins, and when I asked why they were not made habitable I was told that labour was scarce and costs high. Some of these cottages were let at two and six and three shillings a week even in 1946. The rents were controlled, so the landlord could not afford to repair them. One pair had been re-thatched recently at a cost of forty-seven pounds ten shillings. Their combined rents amounted to two and nine-pence a week, so the landlord had no hope of recovering his outlay in making them weather-tight. I learned, too, that the young people who had come out of the army wanted new cottages with modern conveniences. At long last they saw promise of the wages to which the labour and skill of farm-work entitled them, and with these wages they were demanding better living conditions. Many of these old cottages would no longer serve. This problem of rural housing is too involved to be dealt with here, and I do not possess the necessary knowledge. It is hard to have to acknowledge that much of the beauty of simpler modes of life must be sacrificed to the utilitarian standards of a new generation. Perhaps better pay will lead to better standards of living, and in course of time beauty as well as utility be demanded. In most districts the landed gentry, who had the education to appreciate the finer values, are broken financially and their influence gone. The labourers are fumbling their way to fuller life. At present they appear to want only cinemas, darts, and beer in their leisure hours. No doubt better forms of recreation will attract them when pride and joy in their national heritage have been taught them again. My own great hope is in the splendid types of young men at present taking up farming. These may again build up a class comparable with the old English yeomanry, who will restore the countryside and give new life to the villages.

Beyond the Thurlows lie the Bradleys, and it was in the small, round-towered church at Little Bradley that I felt so near an understanding of the genius of England one day, on reading a quaint inscription beginning:

> Here lies the Daye that darknes could not blynd
> When popiſh fogges had overcaſt the sunne.

To find such tablets in remote villages is one of my greatest joys; comparable, I suppose, with the joy a botanist must feel when he stumbles upon a rare plant, or an ornithologist when an unexpected bird takes flight from a tree he had been watching with only half awakened vision. So I remember well the first time I saw this memorial, and as I had not the excellent Mr. Dutt at hand to tell me to expect this brass, as he does in his *Little Guide*, I gazed at it a moment waiting for a bell to ring in my mind before the identity of John Daye dawned on me. Then I realised that this was the Daye of the Psalms—the Daye who printed the first collection of psalm tunes in English, and, as I recollected later, the first Church music to be printed in English. For further information about him I had to refer to the *Dictionary of National Biography*, where I learned that he printed the works of many of the great divines of his age, including those of Parker, Latimer, and Foxe. This man was the expert typographer of his day, the first to abandon "black letter" type. His brass refers to his ardour as a Protestant, for which he suffered imprisonment in Mary's reign.

We may discover memorial tablets to such men in innumerable English churches, and be reminded again and again where the roots of England draw their nourishment. John Daye is no longer to me a half-forgotten worthy, but part of the living tradition of England, still written on the heart, as it were, of our ancient mother, the Church. Sometimes we are inclined to be irritated at the number of nonentities whose names figure on the walls of the churches they once supported. I do not know whether we are right or wrong in this, but I do know that it is a fine and commendable practice to set up a tablet to such a man as John Daye. "Let us now praise famous men, and our fathers that begat us." In addition to the brass at Little Bradley there is a memorial window, erected by the Stationers' Company, which, by the way, means Booksellers' Company, for a stationer used to be a man who had a station, or stall, for the sale of books.

It was fitting that I should find John Daye, and be reminded that the springs of English craftsmanship are in such remote places, when I was seeking one of the three sources of the Stour in the tiny rivulet that runs under Sipsey Bridge. Like the river he was one whom Essex and Suffolk share, for he was born at Dunwich, and died at Saffron Walden.

While reflecting on the past, and the Church's part in preserving tradition, we might glance here at the church at Kedington, only a few miles away, because Kedington's is to me the Suffolk church where the past comes most vividly to life. It did not suffer restoration at the end of last century, and consequently features common enough at one time, but hard to find now, are seen here exactly as they have always been. Not only is the old hour-glass still in position in its stand, but below it in the clerk's desk there is the wig-pole where the old man would hang his wig on a hot day, while waiting for the sand to trickle slowly through in the hour-glass above him. This is an extremely rare if not a unique feature to-day, and it is particularly appropriate that Kedington should preserve it, for John Tillotson, the first English divine to wear a wig, was vicar for a short time. His stay was not a happy one. He could hardly be an acceptable preacher at Kedington, for his predecessor, Samuel Fairclough, had been a fanatical Puritan, who had drawn great congregations to his village church every Sunday, some of them coming from as far away as Cambridge. Tillotson personified the reasonable element in the Anglican tradition, so the excesses of Puritan Kedington must have been extremely distasteful to him.

On the east end gable is an interesting Saxon cross, dug up inside the church in 1860. On it the head of Our Lord hangs over a little to the right; the body is naked to the waist, and below it the loin-cloth is draped in horizontal folds drawn up and tucked away over the right hip. The heavy, rounded folds are similar to those on the Saxon crosses at Ilkley in Yorkshire. Much could be written about this church, especially about its fine woodwork, and the imposing tombs of the Barnardistons, an ancient Suffolk family who flourished here in direct line for twenty-seven generations. Their power is shown in these magnificent memorials, and even to-day fear hangs about their name, for many villagers will not pass along the noble avenue of elms after nightfall, because tradition holds that ten knights lie buried under ten lofty elms. Whether this is fact or fable has not been confirmed, but when one of the elms was blown down in a gale some time ago human remains came to light.

It was one of this family who gave rise to the name Roundhead. During the seventeenth century it was a common practice for younger sons of noble families to be bound apprentices with London merchants. These were the men who built up England's wealth, and Samuel Barnardiston was a typical example. Later in life he made a fortune in the Levant, and it was while he was deputy-governor of the East India Company that he became implicated in the Rye House Plot to assassinate Charles II on his return journey from Newmarket races. For this he was fined ten thousand pounds, which he refused to pay; but after four years' imprisonment he paid six thousand pounds and was released. When Samuel Barnardiston was twenty-two—in 1641—he took part in a procession of London apprentices who were petitioning for peace. These apprentices wore their hair cut short, and when the queen, Henrietta Maria, saw him pass she exclaimed: "See what a handsome roundhead is there." Later in the month the word was used by Captain Hyde and introduced into the national vocabulary.

An interesting feature of the Barnardiston pew in Keding-

ton church is that it is fitted with pegs for the family to hang
their hats on. But of the many remarkable furnishings of
this church, the most noteworthy is the great three-decker
pulpit, believed to be the oldest in England. It symbolises
the importance of the pulpit to the Puritans, and here for
thirty-four years we can imagine Samuel Fairclough thunder-
ing out his messages to awe-struck congregations. It is a good
thing that this pulpit should be preserved and admired, but
I would far rather take anyone visiting Suffolk to the nearby
church at Stoke-by-Clare, and show him the pulpit there.
This is to me the most beautiful pulpit in the county. Indeed,
I think we would have to go far to find a better example of
what a pulpit should be. In contrast to the great pulpit at
Kedington, the pulpit at Stoke-by-Clare is only twenty-one
inches in diameter and about seventy-six inches in height.
Its lovely tracery and simple perfection of form must delight
anyone with an eye for beauty and propriety.

This pulpit is thought to have been the gift of Archbishop
Parker, the last dean of Stoke College, as memorial windows
in the church record. Of this college, where "well-bred"
choristers used to be taught plainsong and priksong, and the
boy who wrote a good hand would be allowed to try his skill
at illuminating manuscripts in crimson, blue, and gold, all
that now remains is the tower near the gate to the present
college, the residence of Lord Loch. Like so many places in
East Anglia, from which escape to the Continent could easily
be contrived, Stoke College was a place of sanctuary for
several notable men. Ridley, Cecil, and Latimer all took
refuge here. When we are inclined to forget the harsher
aspects of the past in contemplating such examples of its
craftsmanship as the pulpit at Stoke-by-Clare, it is well to be
reminded of the persecution that so often disfigured it.

So many places are being ruined to-day that my memory
dwells fondly on a scene at Stoke-by-Clare one warm July
afternoon. The village looked clean and well cared for. Cottages had been newly plastered in the best traditional style
without any self-conscious attempt at display. The thatch
was in good condition everywhere, and the cottages near the
church, built like so many in Suffolk, with two short rows at
right angles, caught and held the sunlight. It is the beauty

of this arrangement that when the light is on one face, cooling shadows fall across the other.

The "Celerer's Cottage" was there to remind me of the days of Archbishop Parker, and the great elms stood tall and dignified. In a field behind the church a cricket match was in progress. A few men were pottering about their gardens while their wives sat knitting or reading. Young boys were fishing in the slow river, which here is full of bulrushes and those common yellow water-lilies with cups that smell like brandy, so that country people often call them brandy-bottles. It was an idyllic scene.

The present Stoke College is a gracious old house, with beautifully wooded grounds sloping down to the river. The house itself is overhung with creepers; two bays on the south side are covered with roses. In the grounds stand great copper beeches, cedars, and other fine trees, with the shadowy, sensitive willow. The succeeding houses on this site have reflected many phases of English life and character, and the present one is the happiest. For a long time this was the home of the parsimonious Elwes family. Sir Gervase Elwes, who died in 1705, so encumbered the estate that when his grandson, Sir Hervey, inherited it, he found that he had only an income of a hundred pounds a year clear, and vowed that he would never leave the place until he had entirely relieved it of debt. This he did, and in addition amassed a fortune of more than a hundred thousand pounds. For about sixty years he lived here in gloomy solitude, rarely allowing himself the comforts of either fire or candlelight. The roof leaked and the wind blew through the broken windows, but Sir Hervey cared only for his money. When he was a very rich man he still spent only a hundred and ten pounds a year on his establishment, maintained by one man and two women, who fed principally on fish from the river and game shot on the estate. But for all his meanness the old man was not without friends. In the village inn he used to meet two neighbouring landowners, Sir Cordell Firebrace and Sir John Barnardiston. These two were not much better than himself, for when the reckoning came there was always an argument about how much each should pay. One day while they were wrangling, a local wag who was with them called out to a passer-by: "For heaven's sake step upstairs and assist the poor. Here are three baronets, worth a million of money, quarrelling about a farthing."

Sir Hervey Elwes died in 1763 and was succeeded by his nephew, John Meggot, who assumed the name of Elwes when he came into the fortune. His mother, Sir Hervey's sister, had been left a widow with a fortune in the neighbourhood of a hundred thousand pounds, but was reputed to have starved herself to death. Her son was a worthy inheritor. While his uncle lived, John Meggot visited him regularly, and in order to keep in the old man's good books always brought cheap and shabby clothes with him, changing into them before going up to the College so that his uncle should be impressed by his economy.

For nearly fourteen years John Meggot—now become John Elwes—lived comfortably at Stoke, spending as much as three hundred pounds a year on a pack of hounds and a few hunters. Then he became a Member of Parliament for Berkshire, and left Stoke to live in his constituency, which he served with scrupulous care. Gradually the habit of economy grew on him till he became as miserly as his uncle had been. His journeys to London were made on horseback. All turnpikes were avoided, and his meals were of hard-boiled eggs and bread carried in his pocket. His horse was allowed to crop the grass at the sides of the roads when he was hungry. When an election came round John Elwes retired to save the expense of a contest.

On retiring from Parliament he took up residence at Stoke again and the people, still ignorant of the change in their master's habits, looked forward to merry scenes, with fox-hounds baying and hunters champing and pacing in front of the College door. But Mr. Elwes explained to them that he had grown wiser with age, and had no intention of spending his money on foolish pastimes. The house had fallen into disrepair while he had been away. Many of the windows had been broken by village boys, so for some time Mr. Elwes was kept busy repairing them with brown paper and odd bits of glass. He seemed to the villagers even more miserly than his uncle had been. After harvest he would glean in the fields of his own tenant farmers, and at night would sit in the kitchen in order to save the expense of another fire. Yet, curiously enough, he would break out of this rigid economy at times and indulge in a bout of gambling, paying up like a gentleman if he lost, and being a most generous victor when he won. There were also instances of extraordinary generosity to friends in straitened circumstances. And it was common knowledge that he had a weakness for the ladies. Though he never married, he had two sons to whom he bequeathed half a million pounds. At his death the last rites were decently observed, and as one tenant who looked on said, it was a good thing the old man not could see the ceremony or he would begrudge the cost.

From Stoke the road leads quickly into Clare, the neatest, trimmest town in the Stour valley. The long street leading into it, with pleasant old houses set well back from the road, the market square, the church, the cottage overlooking the churchyard, and many other pictures of Clare frame themselves in the mind and are not easily forgotten. They were amongst the pictures that I used to recall during the terrible nights of the London blitz, when I would sometimes allow my mind to wander over all the scenes I had known and loved in peace time, that I might be refreshed by their fragrance and have a clearer vision of the England we were fighting for.

Some places are so jumbled in the mind that we can never see them in clear outline, just as there are human faces that elude the memory. Clare is not one of these; it has a face as clear as its name. I think that apart from the cleanness and preciseness of the houses themselves, the chief reason for this quality is the composure of the place. You will never see Clare in any kind of bustle. There is none of that confused traffic common to places on main roads, which so distracts attention from the buildings. In Clare a man can stand and gaze about him without endangering his life. His mind becomes like a still pool in which all the buildings are reflected. Many are painted, and with their smooth façades and crooked shapes they sometimes look more like houses seen in a pool or mirror than houses seen by the eye direct. There must be a fair amount of business done in Clare, but it seems to be done more quietly than in most places. I hope the more progressive of its townsfolk will not resent it if I say that the quietness of benign old age is on Clare, for so it seems to me. It is a town that dreams beside a slowly moving river. Most riverside towns have something peaceful about them, for slowly moving water has that effect, especially when the river banks are overhung with drooping trees as here, and where dignified old houses have smooth lawns and long flowei borders running down to the water's edge. In most of these towns the effect is soon spoilt when the river bank is left behind. In Clare this impression is retained even to the market square, where the noble church imparts such dignity to the wide streets that lead up to it.

Time goes slowly in Clare. Those who enjoy reflections of seventeenth- or eighteenth-century life must revel in it. To those who are more interested in earlier periods the town is less satisfactory. Its castle, once guarding the frontiers of East Anglia, is now only a conical mound, overgrown, and with great difficulty approached through nettles and saplings. I have climbed it once and have no desire to do so again. The railway station was built in the earthworks, and the whole scene is one that can only sadden the archaeologist. When the ground was cleared to make room for the railway, a small gold crucifix with a chain attached to it was discovered. Mr. Dutt, in his *Little Guide*, informs us that "the crucifix was so made that the plate which bore the figure of the Saviour could be removed, and in a small cavity two fragments of wood and one of granite were enclosed—probably relics." This Clare Cross was declared to be treasure trove, and is now at Windsor Castle. It is believed to have belonged to Edward III.

To appreciate the importance of Clare as a frontier defence, we must visualise East Anglia when it was isolated on the north-west by undrained fens and marshes from Ely to the Wash, and on the south by the dense forest of Essex. Only the chalk hills of the west gave access to an invading army on the landward side.

This kindly old town reached its greatest glory in the thirteenth century. Between 1230 and 1240, while Richard, seventh Earl of Gloucester, was a minor, Henry III was in residence at Clare more than once. My friend, Dr. Gladys Thornton, in her history of the town, tells us that in 1235 the king sent down his huntsman with orders to take ten bucks from the park in preparation for the arrival of the court. Edward I spent many long and merry days hawking by the Stour.

In 1248 the Austin Friars came to Clare, and Joan of Acre, the second daughter of Edward I and Queen Eleanor, who married Gilbert, Earl of Clare, when she was eighteen, and later Ralph de Mortimer, was buried in the church of Clare Priory at her death in 1307. Her funeral, we are told, was attended by representatives of most of the noble families of the day. Her daughter, Elizabeth de Burgh, founder of Clare College, Cambridge, lived at the Priory in considerable state after her mother's death.

Owing to the seclusion of the town to-day, the inns of Clare are not so busy as they used to be, though one, the "Bell," during the forty-five years Willie Bareham held the licence, was famed for the bounty of its fare. Willie Bareham was a licensed victualler in Clare from 1887, when he became host of the "Royal Oak," to 1946, when he retired from the "Bell." And throughout his long career it was his pride to maintain the best traditions of English hospitality, sitting at table with his guests, a genial and popular host, and carving the joint before them.

The "Half Moon" is the old posting inn, and has a picturesque yard; but the inn that attracts most attention is the "White Swan," with its remarkable sign. The building itself is not interesting. It is the sign that catches the eye, and well it might, for it is a fine piece of carving, dating from the fifteenth century, and is probably the oldest sign of its kind in England. In a solid piece of wood measuring nine feet eight inches by two feet four inches, originally supporting an oriel window, is carved a chained swan, between conventional trees to which are attached small objects said to represent the arms of many noble English families. The arms of France and England, quartered, are at one end of the sign, and those of Mortimer and de Burgh at the other end. A carving of similar character is to be seen at Monk's Barn, Newport, Essex.

The other building that attracts the attention of the casual visitor is the old cottage overlooking the churchyard. It is dated 1473, and there is no reason to question the accuracy of this. The cottage is built in fifteenth-century style. But the plaster-work, or parge-work, which is so notable, is much later. This pargeting, so attractive a feature of Essex and Suffolk cottages, was originally done by village craftsmen with a kind of comb. The designs were simple: the rope, the dot, and the bird's foot were the most common, and it is interesting in moving from one village to another to see the variations introduced by different craftsmen, each of whom had his own individual style. The craft was a pleasing example of the artistic impulse in the village workman who delighted in his job. The cottages themselves are usually timber-framed, and these are so morticed and tenoned that though to-day they lean at the craziest angles, they are still as secure as ever. Originally the timbers were exposed, but in course of time the drying-in of the wood and the settling of the earth caused cracks to appear, which made the rooms draughty. The richer occupiers sometimes overcame this with interior panelling. The poorer found it cheaper to plaster the outside. For some time now it has been the fashion for new owners to strip off the plaster and expose the old timbers again, sometimes bringing to light beautiful old carving that had been hidden for centuries.

Most of this pargeting belongs to the end of the sixteenth and the beginning of the seventeenth centuries, and was done with the spontaneous charm that often characterises amateur work. Later, professionalism crept in, especially after the Restoration, when elaborate styles were imported. The cottage at Clare is an example of this late pargeting, which was done with a trowel.

The great house at Clare is the Priory, but there are other notable examples of English domestic architecture, of which Nethergate House is the best. It is a pity that the more ornate buildings should commonly attract a disproportionate amount of attention. So often simple cottages and old farmhouses are far more beautiful. The old farmhouses of Suffolk and Essex are especially fine. Many of them were originally important halls and seats of noble families. They were built in good periods, and have never been spoilt by enlargements, as were many of those the wealthier families continued to occupy during the heyday of the English aristocracy. These mellow old houses have come down to us from days before professional architects planned buildings in London offices, or worked from designs copied from other architects. Instead, they were the work of local craftsmen, who themselves built what their brains had conceived and did it from local materials in the local style. Thus they belong to the country-side from which they appear to rise as naturally as the hills and trees about them. To-day when we glance at building trade journals, and see plans of houses which large contractors undertake to erect anywhere in England at a stated price, provided the order is for not fewer than five, six, or seven hundred of a type, these individually planned houses, or groups following the line of stream, or clustered round a well, built with a knowledge of local conditions of the most complex character, are the more precious.

The next village along the Stour is Cavendish, where again we see two rows of cottages built at right angles to capture the sunlight, beautifully placed on a swathe of green between the highroad and the church. They are now so old that they are no longer ideal as dwellings, but if they should have to be demolished, something would be lost to the generation follow-ing that we and our forefathers have been the richer for possessing. Cavendish, like its neighbour, has a restful air about it. On a market day you may see a shepherd drive his flock on to the village green while he spends an hour in the "George," his dog lying watchful on the grass while the sheep crop undisturbed.

Instead of going on to Long Melford, we may turn left and take the Glemsford road past Blacklands Hall. Sir John de Cavendish, Chief Justice of the King's Bench, who was murdered at Bury in 1381 by some of Wat Tyler's rebels, lived in a house on this site, though the original home of the Cavendish family stood in the village. Blacklands is a beauti-ful house, and I could well believe the lady in Cavendish who told me that the loveliest sight she ever saw was at Blacklands Hall on a spring morning. Wallflowers were in the pride of their bloom in the garden. They were bordered with forget-me-nots, and as she stood in the road quietly admiring the combination of colour, a peacock stepped slowly round the bed, to stand and preen his tail with the sunlight full upon it.

Through high banks and rolling country, the Glemsford road leads into the heart of the county, presenting the most delightful prospects when the grain is ripening, or when fields of mustard cover the gently rising slopes with their gleaming gold. This road is little used, yet between Cavendish and Hawkedon two excellent examples of Suffolk architecture are to be found. They exhibit brick-nogging at its best. Between the massive timbers of a house, bricks would be arranged diagonally, chequerwise, or in herring-bone formation, according to the space available, producing what is to me a most satisfying effect. Thurston Hall, close to this road, is an admirable example of this work. It is dated 1607. A large house, with diamond-paned lattices and a lovely, simple garden, Thurston Hall, as I remember it, had large lawns without flower-beds, a group of hollyhocks in one corner, and lavender bushes round one of the two great chimney-stacks at the back. These two colours brought out so well the colour of the brick and the warmth of the timber that I can never forget them. The dignity and restraint of the arrangement left the beauty of the house unhampered in its expression, serving also to suggest in the quietest manner its owner's awareness of the fine thing he had in his keeping.

The gable end of Swan's Hall in the same parish is another good piece of work. Though somewhat neglected, it makes a charming picture with the pond against it.

Over yet another low hill the road leads to Hawkedon, with its cluster of cottages and church on a green slope behind a screen of poplars, and its houses with tall Tudor chimneys.

Less than two miles away is Stansfield, where the Rev. S. Ogden, D.D., was rector. This divine was given to writing turgid verses on important national occasions. I mention him solely for the joy of quoting Gilbert Wakefield's description of him: "He exhibited a black, scowling figure, a lowering visage, embrowed by the honours of a sable periwig. His voice was growling and morose, and his sentences desultory, tart, and snappish. His sermons were interspersed with remarks eminently brilliant and acute, but too epigrammatic

32

in their close." What, I wonder, did the simple country folk of Stansfield make of their formidable rector?

In the straggling parish of Wickhambrook stands Bansfield Hall, a moated manor-house with a stone-paved, oak-panelled hall, and boasting a minstrels' gallery. Edna Lyall described it in a novel popular a generation ago. More recently Wickhambrook has been the home of Adrian Bell, whose studies of country life, set in this Suffolk countryside, are among the best written in our day.

Cavendish

CHAPTER III

SUDBURY AND LONG MELFORD

A PERFECT English town is far harder to find than a perfect English village. Nature is a merciful judge. Almost every old thing in farmyard or village becomes beautiful at last, while in towns the greed of commerce leaves ugly scars that are seldom hidden. So much has been written about the importance of preserving rural England that we may now at least be certain that every act of vandalism in the villages will be resented even if it is not resisted. Our cottages and manor-houses are regarded as treasured possessions. We can hardly pick up an illustrated newspaper on a bookstall without finding the beauty of some part of the countryside extolled. But at the next stage of social development vigilance lapses. Our smaller country towns are at the mercy of anyone who cares to exploit them, and some of the best parts of Sudbury were ruined to make way for new industries at the beginning of last century. Many of its cottages are far from ideal. The damage that was done by manufacturers who settled in the town because labour was cheap there cannot be repaired; but the people of Sudbury to-day are more alive than most townspeople to the dangers besetting the English market town.

My own reactions to Sudbury have been mixed during the twelve or more years I have known it. I remember that when I first ran into it from Clare, Cavendish, and Long Melford it seemed to be all that a country town should be. It was market day. The streets were busy with country folk buying and selling; and when I turned to look up Market Hill and saw the Gainsborough statue I felt that a statue to an artist in a market square was so rare and remarkable a sight that I must lose my heart to Sudbury at once. I noted also the fine street views from both sides of the foot of Market Hill, and after carrying those views in mind with me while wandering through every Suffolk town I still feel that they are the best street views in the county, not excepting Angel Hill at Bury St. Edmunds. The curve of the shops on the rising slope, the fretted line of the roofs against a clear East Anglian sky, with Gainsborough's statue and St. Peter's tower at the head, make this an altogether exceptional scene.

Later I visited Sudbury several times on Sundays, and found that Sudbury on a Sunday is one of the dullest places imaginable. Market Hill is deserted and the shops and houses are lifeless. Coming into the town from lovely country as you must whichever way you approach it, the lack of foliage, the greyness of the Suffolk "white" brick and the hardness of the buildings are nothing short of depressing. Often I have wondered how I could ever have thought Sudbury attractive. Later again I was able to visit it on Thursdays and frequently on Mondays, and each time it came to life with the people going about their business. To observe this difference is to realise how much our towns owe of their character to the small traders whose shops line their streets. Yet most of these traders in small country towns complain that the buses are taking their trade to the larger town that may be ten or twelve miles away. If you discuss the future with them, and they are frank, you will learn that most of them suffer from a measure of defeatism. They have made provision for their sons elsewhere, and are only hanging on to their shops in the hope that a multiple store will one day be seeking premises in the town and will make them a good offer. Many have already found a happy solution to their economic problems that way. One sign after another is taken down and a far too familiar one goes up in its place. Names that have been household words in the town and neighbourhood for generations, and that are as much part of local life as its place-names, pass out of hearing. Old Mr. Pretty, or Suckling, or Partridge, to recall three typical Suffolk names, is no longer there with his friendly enquiries about the family. In his place there is a smart young manager from another county. One after another the old shop fronts are removed, and standardised chromium frames to be found anywhere are fitted instead, until the street looks exactly like any other street in any other town. The commodities in the shop windows, the style of their arrangement, and even the faces behind the counters become equally standardised. So pervasive is this movement towards the impersonal that if a local girl has the courage to start a small business on her own account she rarely puts her name on the sign. Instead, she uses a pseudo-French abomination, or a fanciful first name that she has culled from a cheap novelette. These things are happening in every town in England, yet they are seldom mentioned. Is it not time we tried to enlighten people to what is seemly and proper in the treatment of property in our fine old English market towns?

Since the Industrial Revolution we have tended to regard our market towns as small industrial centres, struggling to compete with more prosperous neighbours. It may be difficult to decide which way a town that is both a market town and an industrial centre should develop, but it is surely reasonable to argue that the claims of the village people to their market town should be recognised, and that every effort to preserve and foster the amenities of the countryside should include in its purview the small country town of anything up to at least twenty thousand inhabitants. Only the sentimentalist thinks of country life without seeing it centred in its market town. Agriculture is an industry, and like every other industry it has its heart where its buying and selling are done. The countryman commonly knows the streets of his market town better than he knows the lanes of his own parish. Few country people have time for leisurely strolls across the fields for amusement. They are busiest and happiest on their weekly trips to market, and it is tragic to see towns that for centuries belonged to the villages surrounding them, where the farmer in his breeches and his wife with her baskets looked easy and at home, so transformed in character that slick young people who take their cue from the city or the cinema glance at them with ill-mannered amusement.

Sudbury, like so many similar towns, has sacrificed much during the last hundred years. In the course of its industrial development it has lost many of its fine old houses. A small number remain, of which Salter's Hall in Stour Street, built about the middle of the fifteenth century, is the best. It has the usual high-pitched gable, an oriel window with leaded lights and fine tracery on the upper storey, and grotesque heraldic figures decorating the bowing-lintel of the middle window. Near it is "The Chantry," with its stout timbers and carved corner-post. There are other interesting old houses in Cross Street, but they are fewer than the long history of the town might lead us to expect. Instead of the beautiful half-timbered houses and pretty pargeted cottages of the neighbouring villages, most of Sudbury is built of Suffolk "white" brick, a local product that in its first form may have been introduced by the Romans, whose funeral urns have been found in the neighbourhood, or may be even older. This so-called "white" brick is found all along the eastern side of the county from Stratford St. Mary to Lowestoft and also in Bury St. Edmunds. At one time it may have been the county's pride. It can never have been its glory, for of all the building materials used in East Anglia this is the least attractive. It is usually grey and grimy, and has a flat, dead appearance, though with bright paint on doors and casements, and evergreen foliage in the garden, I have seen many of the plainer houses look dignified and pleasing.

Sudbury's churches, too, are disappointing when compared with Long Melford's or Lavenham's, though St. Peter's has well-carved parclose screens and a narrow, carved oak canopy over the chancel arch, which is an unusual feature worth noting, and has other good carving inside the chancel. All Saints' has a beautiful fifteenth-century octagonal pulpit, delicately carved and worthy to be associated with the pulpit at Stoke-by-Clare. But the most interesting and beautiful church in Sudbury is St. Gregory's, which, though it is the mother church of the town, is some distance from the centre. St. Gregory's is well worth visiting. Suffolk churches are so magnificent and full of interest that it is impossible to deal with them adequately in this survey. I am so conscious of the inadequacy of any notes I might write on them that it has seemed to me better to mention only features that have specially delighted me, rather than repeat information readily available in Mr. H. Munro Cautley's fine book, *Suffolk Churches and their Treasures*, a book it would be impossible to over-praise. But St. Gregory's must be mentioned, and if the visitor can have the pleasure of the verger's company he

will indeed be fortunate, for he will learn from him what
cannot be found in any guide-book, and in particular he will
hear about Sudbury's bells. This grey old town has three
perfect octaves in its towers, and the verger of St. Gregory's
is one of the oldest ringers. Never have I heard bell-ringing
described as in a long conversation I had with him one
Wednesday afternoon. The intricate movements were made
to seem like the steps of an old-world dance, especially as they
were described with such briskness of movement, and such
knowledge and pride. As I listened I thought also of *Nine
Tailors*, a novel by Dorothy Sayers, and gave myself over to
the atmosphere of mystery that so often surrounds a belfry.
Nor was it only the bells that produced this atmosphere. St.
Gregory's has a gruesome relic locked away in the vestry.
This is the head of Simon of Sudbury, who was beheaded in
1381 by a London rabble during Wat Tyler's rebellion.
Simon was born in this parish, and rose to be made Bishop
of London in 1361 and Archbishop of Canterbury in 1375.
Like many of the eminent ecclesiastics of his day he dabbled
fatally in politics, and when the famous hundred thousand
assembled on Blackheath in 1381 they recalled that Simon
had referred to them as " barefooted rebels," and had coun-
selled Richard II, whom he had crowned, to subdue them.
Under Jack Straw's leadership this insurgent crowd gathered
on Tower Hill and demanded that Theobald, or Tybald,
which was Simon's surname, should be handed over to them.
The following morning, after he had celebrated mass before
the king, they captured him, and his head was struck off by
John Starling, an Essex man, and fixed by the rebels over
London Bridge. There it is said to have remained for six
days before being stolen by a priest and taken to Sudbury,
for which he had always kept a warm place in his heart. He
and his brother had rebuilt much of the church, and had
founded a college for five priests and a warden on land where
their father's house had stood. It is interesting to find also
that this same rising was finally put down in Sudbury, though
apart from the vicar of All Saints' few of the burgesses appear
to have had any part in the revolt.

Another curious feature of St. Gregory's is the Latin inscription to Thomas Carter, who died in 1706. In translation it

reads: "Traveller, I will relate a wondrous thing. On the day on which the aforesaid Thomas Carter breathed his last, a Sudbury camel passed through the eye of a needle. If thou hast wealth, go and do likewise." Another memorial worth noting is that to Sieve de St. Quintin, wife of Robert de St. Quintin, a Sudbury wool merchant who was living in the town in 1275, which is an indication of the great antiquity of Sudbury's weaving industry. It was in St. Gregory's church that the statue of Our Lady of Sudbury used to stand. On Lady Day, in harvest time, it was carried round the town in procession with sheaves of corn and barrels of wine. The ceremony has been restored by Father Gerard Moir, and a new statue of Our Lady is carried through the streets. The lovely old phrase, expressing the courtesy and devotion of country folk, "the homecoming of Our Lady at Sundown," is again real.

On leaving the church and returning to the centre of the town, the tall, red-brick weavers' cottages of the early nineteenth century should be noticed. These are in rows; but set at different angles, and thus escape the dull uniformity of the cottages built for Lancashire weavers during the handloom weaving days. These Sudbury cottages are threestoreyed, with larger windows on the first floor, fitted in order to get the maximum amount of light on the two looms engaged there.

Sudbury was the first manufacturing town in East Anglia to prosper. Edward III settled some of the Flemings there, and in Elizabeth's reign silk weaving was introduced by the Huguenots who found asylum in this part of the country. Early in the nineteenth century the industry was revived, and Sudbury velvets and jacquards attracted much attention at the Great Exhibition of 1851. A century later they still hold their own, for Gainsborough silk tapestry, designed and made in the town, is known everywhere. Sudbury fabrics have figured in more than one coronation. They were, in fact, used when our present king and queen were crowned.

Throughout its industrial history Sudbury has had a remarkably fine record for so small a town. Besides its fabrics it produces wrought-iron work that if you saw you would long to possess. The sad part of the story is that for most of the time Sudbury people have worked hard for little money. Poverty has frequently been rife.

One of the most interesting of its former industries was bell-founding. A famous master of the craft named Henry Pleasant lived in Sudbury, and this good man took advantage of his name to indulge in pleasantries upon his bells. On the sixth bell at St. Nicholas's Church, Ipswich, which he recast, he inscribed the legend:

> Henry Pleasant have at last
> Made me as good as can be cast.

His campanology was better than his metre, but the rhyme he inscribed on a bell at All Saints', Maldon, is worth quoting:

> When three this steeple long did hold,
> They were the emblems of a scold:
> No music then, but we shall see
> What *Pleasant* music six will be.

Reflecting on Simon and the Peasants' Rising, on Henry Pleasant the bell-founder, and on Sudbury's weavers while passing through the weaving quarter, we may return to Gainsborough Street and think again of Thomas Gainsborough, Sudbury's most distinguished son since the days of Simon himself.

The Gainsboroughs had been connected with Sudbury for two hundred years when Thomas was born in 1727 at what is now the Gainsborough House Hotel. His father was a prominent local Dissenter, a manufacturer by trade, who is said to have been much admired in the town, a good employer, a man of fine presence, careful of his personal appearance, and generally " of good reputation; but not rigid in the matter of smuggling." Mrs. Gainsborough was a cultivated lady, the sister of the Rev. Humphry Burroughs, vicar of St. Gregory's and master of Sudbury's ancient grammar school, founded in 1491, where Thomas Gainsborough himself was educated. The statue already noted on Market Hill was erected in 1913, and was unveiled by Princess Louise.

Gainsborough grew up in Sudbury to be an elegant young

man of vivacious manners and courtly bearing, who was enabled by personal charm as well as by genius to become a fashionable portrait painter. At nineteen he married a young lady named Margaret Burr, whose birth was the subject of romantic speculation. It was rumoured—and she herself believed it—that she was the daughter of an exiled prince. She is now known to have been the daughter of the Duke of Beaufort.[1] Clearly she was the one girl in this sleepy market town to capture the heart of the aspiring young painter. What more natural than that he should paint her portrait? And what more inevitable in a town where the daughter of a duke or an exiled prince was a creature of romance than that the two should become lovers? It was a most fortunate marriage. Gainsborough himself was not an easy man to live with. He was temperamental and often unreasonable, but Mrs. Gainsborough had an unusually sweet nature.

A pretty story relates that each had a pet dog. Gainsborough's was named Fox, his wife's Tristram. When Gainsborough had been irritable and desired forgiveness he would write a note to his wife, sign it with the name of his own dog, Fox, and address it to Tristram. Fox would then take the note in his mouth and deliver it to Tristram, who would pass it to his mistress. Mrs. Gainsborough would return the answer by the same bearers. This would be couched in the most endearing terms; for example: "My own dear Fox, you are always loving and good and I am a naughty little female ever to worry you as I often do, so we will kiss and say no more about it."

This distinguished association with a great artist seems remote from the everyday life of Sudbury to-day, but genius belongs to the wind that bloweth where it listeth, and Sudbury was just as likely to produce its man of genius as any other town.

Later it was to engage the attention of Charles Dickens, a genius of a different order, who made several excursions into Suffolk. Dickens knew Sudbury, which claims the distinction of being the Eatanswill of *Pickwick Papers*, where we read: "With these dissensions it is almost superfluous to say that

---

[1] Sydney Harrison: *Connoisseur*, January and February, 1922.

everything in Eatanswill was made a party-question. If the Buffs proposed to new sky-light the market-place, the Blues got up public meetings and denounced the proceeding; if the Blues proposed the erection of an additional pump in the High Street, the Buffs rose as one man and stood aghast at the enormity." The first of Mr. Pickwick's excursions into Suffolk was by Norwich coach to Sudbury in order to study a Parliamentary election. On arrival he dined at the "Town Arms," where the Blues had their headquarters. This, no doubt, was the "Rose and Crown," burnt down in 1922. The Buffs had their headquarters at the "Peacock," which was probably the "Swan."

And so in every age since it was first noticed in the *Saxon Chronicle* of A.D. 799, Sudbury has had something worthy to record. Money was coined in its mint as early as the reign of Ethelred the Unready. It received its first charter from Queen Mary, in reward for the loyalty of its inhabitants at the time of the Duke of Monmouth's rebellion. But always it has preserved the character it holds by natural right as the market town of the Stour valley, with traditions maintained through every age associated with its inns and churches. The farmers no longer resort to the rear of the "Black Boy" to watch the sport in the cock-pits, or to bull-baiting on the Croft; but the "Black Boy" still flourishes. The suggested origin of its name is interesting. In the eighteenth century it was fashionable for rich ladies to employ black boys in their boudoirs, and it is said that this particular inn was kept at one time by a negro who had formerly been in that kind of service. If true, this is yet another memorial to the fashions of a vanished age. That is part of the charm of such places as Sudbury. In every street there is a reminder of something curious or distinguished in its past.

The surrounding country is so attractive that well-to-do Sudbury merchants have long been in the habit of building their houses in one or other of the neighbouring villages. Of these, Long Melford is the most attractive. It is one of those roadside villages or small towns that seem monotonous as you travel along what seems a never-ending street, then suddenly surprise you by opening out into a spacious green or market square. Those who enter Long Melford from

Sudbury after hearing that it is one of the finest villages in the county are probably disappointed at first. From the station to the "Bull" Inn the long street has little to catch the eye except an old house, now a Guest House, and Melford Place, formerly an E-shaped mansion, that for four hundred years was the home of the Martyn family. Much of the south side of the original house remains, of which the most interesting part is the galleried chapel adjoining the entrance hall. This has a wagon roof, with "the monkey in the vine" design on the main beam and beautiful carving. The panel on the south wall came from the Martyn pew in Long Melford church and is carved with the family arms. In one of the panels of the window-pane there is a figure of Henry VIII. Anne Boleyn is said to have attended mass here while living in Suffolk for a short time. The chancel arch is now the window-frame facing the road, upon which, it is thought, the sanctuary of the chapel abutted. This fine old house was restored by Henry Westropp early last century.

After passing Melford Place the road runs between rows of small cottages, and you are puzzled to know why so much fuss should be made about this very ordinary village. Then suddenly you catch sight of the "Bull," the old house opposite and, a little ahead, the old mill by the stream from which the village takes its name, until finally the real Long Melford opens out before you.

Starting from almost a point where the street ends, the long green gradually broadens as it rolls across a gently rising hill to the summit crowned with one of Suffolk's noblest churches. At the point of this tapering green stand a group of elms, and half-way up it an octagonal conduit built of Tudor brick, which used to supply Melford Hall with water. Along one side of the green, pleasant cottages and substantial family houses climb the hill to the church gate. Along the other side runs the stout wall, also of Tudor brick, and the tall trees in front of Melford Hall. At the top of the hill stands— or reposes would be a better word—the Hospital of the Holy Trinity, Tudor almshouses founded in 1573 by Sir William Cordell of Melford Hall for twelve poor brethren, a warden, and two servants. The monotony of the first part of the journey is completely forgotten, and Long Melford is readily acknowledged to have every virtue that is claimed for it. With so much Tudor brick about, it is easy in surveying the long green to recall the villagers of Long Melford in Shakespeare's *Henry VI*, who went to the court to petition the king against the Duke of Suffolk for "enclosing the commons of Melford."

To the motorist the distance between Sudbury and the "Bull" at Long Melford is negligible. He has no time for idle thoughts by the way. The pedestrian, however, may be glad of company, even of imaginary company, and if so he could not do better than call up the shade of William Kempe, the Elizabethan buffoon who passed along this road when he danced his famous morris from London to Norwich. At Sudbury he met a "lusty tall fellow—a butcher," who offered to dance with him towards Melford. But the nimble buffoon was too sprightly for the butcher, who was obliged to drop out, whereupon a "lusty country lassie" took his place, strapped the bells round her legs, and "thus merrily garnished and with mirth in her eyes, she readily tucked up her russett petticoate," and danced with him a mile.

Defoe, another traveller along this road, always had an eye for the economics of a county, and in his *Tour of the Eastern Counties* we find him recording that Long Melford, though so much smaller, was richer that Sudbury. Since Defoe's day so much has been written about Long Melford's charm that by now it must have a considerable literature of its own. One in particular of the many tributes is worth recalling. When Robert Louis Stevenson was staying at Cockfield Rectory with his cousin, Mrs. Churchill Babington, and her husband, he walked into Long Melford and afterwards wrote to his mother: "I am too happy to be much of a correspondent. Yesterday we were away to Melford and to Lavenham, both exceptionally placid, beautiful old English towns. Melford scattered all round a big green, with an Elizabethan Hall and Park, great screens of trees that seem twice as high as trees should seem, and everything else like what it ought to be in a novel, and what one never expects to see in reality, made me cry out how good we were to live in Scotland, for the many hundredth time. I cannot get over my astonishment—indeed, it increases every day—at the hopeless gulf there is between England and Scotland."

In Long Melford churchyard there is another reminder of that lively teller of tales. If you walk along the main path to the church tower you will read on a gravestone the name of that most celebrated pirate, John Silver. You will see that Melford's John Silver did not die until 1899, and Stevenson, according to Graham Balfour's *Life*, was at Cockfield in 1870 and 1873 only, so he cannot have seen this stone, which was erected after the death of John Silver's wife, Sophia, in 1889. But if Stevenson did not take the name from the stone, did he, I wonder, get it from the man himself? Did Stevenson meet John Silver in Melford? And was he "long"? Or was Long John Silver a combination of John Silver and Long Melford? Perhaps these questions have been answered in some book that I ought to have read. If so, I confess my ignorance of what should be an interesting sidelight on this romantic subject. Certain it is that one John Silver lies in Melford churchyard now.

That last sentence is reminiscent of a line by Thomas Hardy. Perhaps it was prompted by his shade, for Hardy often seems close to me in Suffolk. If he had been a Suffolk man I believe he would have written a poem on John Silver's grave. Suffolk would be an admirable county for a man possessing Hardy's insight into rural life, for it has about it the ancient, crusty character that he could express so well. There is something of it in that fine study of Suffolk life, *Lord of the Harvest*, by M. Betham-Edwards, where lanes are described as "good tidily rough," where the dairy-maid "fleets" the milk, and where fooling is called "nannicking."

After Lavenham, and some would set it above Lavenham, the church at Long Melford is the finest in all Suffolk. The hospital obscures it until the churchyard gate is reached, so that its beauty is not disclosed until it can be fully appreciated. This imposing church, with its thirteen hundred and fifty sittings, is nearly two hundred feet long and has nearly a hundred windows. One of its entrancing features is the long row of clerestory windows. There are eighteen on each side, and from the churchyard gate the sky is seen through them. The glass takes on its colour, so that on a clear day the combination of the luminous azure of the sky with the grey flint of the church is something to delight and excite the imagination, for "Blue was Our Lady's colour."

Inside, the positions of six former altars are indicated by piscinae. In the north aisle, close to the screen, there is a fourteenth-century alabaster carving of the Adoration of the Magi, which was found under the floor, where it may have been hidden to save it from the Puritan zeal of William Dowsing, who played such havoc with the Suffolk churches.

At the east end of the north aisle is the Clopton chapel, with a scroll running round the cornice, carved and painted with verses by John Lydgate, the monk of Bury St. Edmunds, who claimed to be Chaucer's disciple. At the east end of the south aisle is the Jesus Chapel, where the priest of the Jesus Guild said the daily offices. Later it became the private chapel of the successive owners of Melford Place, the Martyn and Westropp families. The Lady Chapel, formerly a detached building, and slightly later in date than the church, with its aisles, or "cloister ther abowte," and timber roofs supported by carved spandrils and trussed principals of fine workmanship, is of great beauty.

For the distinctive beauty of the interior of Long Melford church we are chiefly indebted to John Clopton, a Lancastrian in politics who narrowly escaped death for treason in the fifteenth century, and in his enforced retirement made the rebuilding and adornment of the parish church his chief preoccupation. For the latter purpose he engaged two Flemings, Henry Phelypp, a sculptor, and Anthony Ammoson, an artist, who designed and executed windows full of contemporary portraits of people from every walk of life. These are now lost to us, but they represented judges, ecclesiastics, mayors and burgesses, all in the attire of their day and office. They are thought to have been portraits of Clopton's friends and acquaintances.

The list of rectors of Long Melford dates from 1309, and of one of these, Dr. Robert Warren, an amusing but sad story is told in Walker's *Sufferings of the Clergy*. Warren was ejected from his living in 1643, as well as robbed of his household furniture and of "five very good horses." One of the charges brought against him was that he used the sanctus bell, and when he was dragged from the pulpit one of his traducers walked in front of him beating a frying-pan in mockery. Dr. Warren was restored to his living in 1660, but was then ninety-six years of age, so it is not surprising to find that he resigned at the end of the same year, and died soon afterwards. No doubt the great hope of his last years had been to return to his rectory at Long Melford. That hope realised, he passed peacefully to his rest.

Long Melford has the unusual distinction for a village of its size of having two great houses, Melford Hall and Kentwell Hall, where the Clopton family was long seated. Melford Hall, built in Elizabethan style round three sides of a quadrangle, with its Tudor chimneys and leaded cupolas, has long been the home of the Parker family, whose baronetcy was created in 1681. It stands behind a broad, reedy moat, close enough to the road to be seen clearly by anyone of normal curiosity who happens to be passing that way. Sir William Cordell, who built the present mansion, seems to have acquired a large fortune by contriving to make himself equally acceptable to both Mary and Elizabeth, both of whom bestowed favours upon him. In 1578, with a great retinue in attendance, he met Queen Elizabeth as she entered the county and escorted her to Melford Hall, where he entertained her in the most lavish style. Others followed his example so nobly that Churchhouse recorded how Sir William " did light such a candle to the rest of the shire, that many were glad, bountifully and franckly, to follow the same example," and Richard Topclyffe, writing to the Earl of Shrewsbury in August 1578, said: "I did never see her Majestie better received by two counties in one jorney then Suffolke and Norfolke now: Suffolke of gentillmen, and Norfolke of the meaner sorte."

Life at Melford Hall in the seventeenth century has been preserved for us in a letter written by James Howell, Clerk of the Council and afterwards Historiographer Royal, who, while visiting Lord Savage there, wrote to his friend Daniel Caldwell: "Though considering my former condition in life I may now be called a countryman, yet you cannot call me a rustic (as you imply in your letter) so long as I live in so civill and noble a family, so long as I lodge in so vertuous and regular a house as any I beleeve in the land, both for economical government and for choice company; for I never saw such a dainty race of children in all my life together. I never saw such an orderly and punctuall attendance of servants, nor a great house so neatly kept. . . . The kitchin and gutters and other offices of noise and drudgery are at the fag end. There is a back gate for the beggars and meaner sort of swains to come in at. The stables butt upon the Park, which for a chearfull rising ground, for groves and browsing ground for the deer, and for rivulets of water may compare with any for its bigness, in the whole land. . . . Now, for the gardening and costly choice flowers, for ponds, for stately large walks, green and gravelly, for orchards, and choice fruits of all sorts, there are few the like in England. . . . Truly this house of Long Melford, tho' it be not so great, yet it is so well compacted and contrived with such dainty conveniences every way, that if you saw the landskip of it, you would be mightily taken with it, and it would serve for a choice pattern to build and contrive a house by."

Kentwell Hall, also Elizabethan, is built in the shape of the letter E, and is approached along an avenue of limes, planted in 1678. Julian Tennyson, in his delightful *Suffolk Scene*, tells us that he counted them and found a hundred and thirty on each side, so that even here the village characteristic of unusual length is maintained. Kentwell Hall is much the more beautiful of Melford's two great houses. It has suffered less alteration than its neighbour and is, indeed, generally admitted to be one of the finest old manor houses in a county that is so exceptionally rich in them. A moat still completely surrounds it. Its waters lap the timbers and brick-nogging of the old brewhouse when the wind disturbs them, and are spanned by two bridges, which cast their shadows in summer, while the water-lilies hold up their pale cups to catch the light.

Both these halls are rich in interest, but neither can compete historically with the "Bull" Inn, a house much older than either. The "Bull" was originally the home of a rich wool merchant, but there is evidence that it has been an inn since 1580. It was then about a hundred years old. So when

48

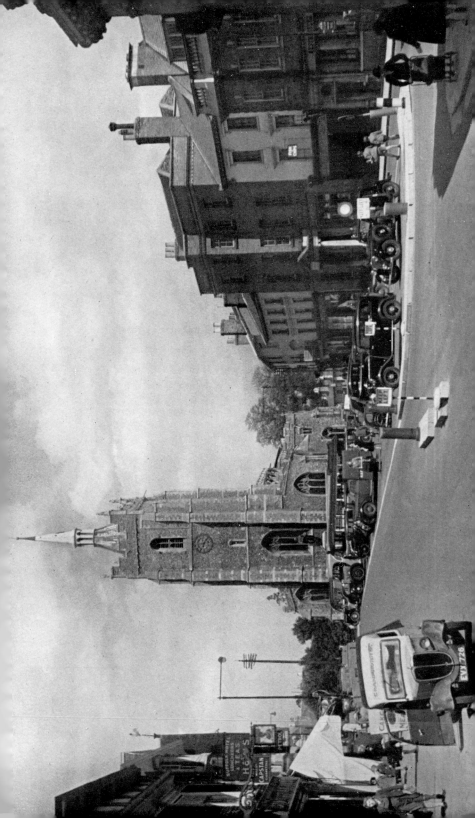

William Kempe danced through Long Melford in 1599, the "Bull" was already there to welcome thirsty travellers, and we are not surprised to learn that he enjoyed "unexpected entertainment." To-day, when the future of social life is so uncertain, it is well to reflect upon the part played throughout the centuries by these three ancient institutions, the church, the great house, and the inn. In Long Melford, all three may be seen at their best. There can be few villages in the kingdom able to show such splendid examples of each, and at present it must be agreed that the inn seems best fitted to weather the storms of transition. I do not think that is an unhappy reflection, for after all, Christianity began in the stable of an inn, and it may have its revival from one.

A curious feature of the "Bull" is that it looks so much older to-day than it did in 1935; but this does not imply that its appearance is faked in any way. About 1820 Suffolk folk were so enamoured of their "white" brick that they actually built a wall of it in front of the original timbers of the "Bull," a thing incredible to modern taste. When this was taken down several of the old studs were found to be decayed, and the restorers were obliged either to strengthen or replace them. But the process was a genuine restoration, so to-day, after suffering indignity for more than a century, the "Bull" as it challenges the street again receives the respect due to it. The back is even more interesting than the front, for it has a galleried courtyard, once open, now enclosed in glass. Indoors, moulded beams and wood-carving can be seen, as clean in outline as when they left the bench three or more hundred years ago. Near the door of the lounge, just below an enormous moulded beam, is a remarkable carving of a naked "wodewose," or wild man, the original of the "green man" who gave his name to so many of our inns. The wild man of Long Melford has a garland of foliage round his head and another about his loins. In one hand he clasps a rudely hacked club, in the other the long, outstretched neck of a bird, apparently flying down to its young, for a small head protrudes from a nest below.

This grand old inn, so much older than the two Eliza-bethan mansions above it, was probably built by a wool

Long Melford Church

merchant, or may have been built by the abbot of Bury himself as a rest house. But whatever its origin, no better sign could have been chosen. The bull was the badge of those who supported the arms of Edward IV, and it played a great part in the history of English sport. What could be more appropriate for the inn of so English a village as Long Melford?

CHAPTER IV

THE CONSTABLE COUNTRY

To those who love the byways of Suffolk the title of this chapter may read more like a warning than an invitation, for the places that Constable painted in his prime, and where he worked in white cap and apron as the handsome young miller, are now popular beauty spots visited by thousands. Yet the title is inescapable, for in spite of every change it is impossible to think of the Stour between Sudbury and the sea as other than Constable's. We might as reasonably try to withhold Bury from St. Edmund. And I do not think Constable himself would renounce it. There is much that he would regret. The sight of so many dead willows would grieve him, and while he would appreciate the honour paid to his memory by the careful restoration of the Valley Farm and Willy Lott's cottage, his feelings would be mixed, I fancy, if he could revisit the old mill. He would be grateful for its careful preservation, but he could not fail to regret that it no longer serves its original purpose. As he was by nature a sociable man I cannot believe he would regret the invasion of Flatford by laughing crowds at Easter and Whitsuntide. No doubt he would be puzzled to know where they all came from, but I think he would laugh with them for a few minutes before stealing away upstream to find a quiet corner.

The association of an artist with a district may be merely incidental to his development or it may be of first importance. Every artist must work through a medium of some kind, and if nature's language suits him best he must find the region most in keeping with his temperament. The perfect union of the mind of genius with a regional medium is rarely found. I do not think it would be exaggerating to say that only Wordsworth in poetry, Hardy in fiction, and Constable in painting, have achieved it completely in England, and all three had the advantage of being able to respond wholeheartedly to the beauty about them when they were young and most impressionable. The region between Kendal and Cockermouth served Wordsworth for most of his life, Wessex served Hardy, and the lower reaches of the Stour served Constable for more than forty years. Both the others might say, as Wordsworth said in his preface to *The Excursion*:

> How exquisitely . . .
> The external world is fitted to the mind.

There are many English rivers as beautiful as the Stour, and critics might argue as to how far this particular one was indispensable to Constable's genius. His own opinion is certain: "Those scenes made me a painter," he said, "and I am grateful." There can be no doubt that it had a unique appeal for him. In describing his old home he wrote: "The beauty of the surrounding scenery, its gentle declivities, its luxuriant meadow flats sprinkled with flocks and herds, its well-cultivated uplands, its woods and rivers, with numerous scattered villages and churches, farms and picturesque cottages, all impart to this particular spot an amenity and elegance hardly anywhere else to be found."

This honest English painter and this homely English valley were so perfectly matched that, to those who see personality in landscape, a brief summary of the lower Stour and a brief summary of Constable's own character might be expressed in identical terms. Neither was ever spectacular. Both were kindly and cultivated, and well disposed towards simple human aims and affections—towards "joy in widest commonalty spread." Constable was never happier than during the long days he spent in the fields painting, with only harvesters for company. He wished to be a "natural painter." To his friend John Dunthorne he wrote: "The great vice of the present day is *bravura*, an attempt to do something beyond the truth. Fashion always had, and will have, its day; but truth in all things only will last, and can only have just claims on posterity." In telling the truth about the Stour as he saw it, he succeeded, as the good artist will, in telling the truth about life as he understood it in terms of these trees and water meadows. Another man might paint other scenes from the same valley with no less fidelity and produce entirely different effects. Gainsborough did so when he painted woodland scenes at Cornard. It is interesting to discover which elements seemed most significant to each artist. In Constable's paintings we are particularly struck by the part played by his affections. He was aware of this characteristic: "Painting is with me," he said, "but another word for feeling." Much as he admired the amenity and elegance of his native vale, characteristics that were equally apparent to Gainsborough, he loved still more the work and pleasure of his neighbours, and even inanimate things their hands had touched. He loved to watch the light on "rotten planks, slimy posts, and brickwork," for he aimed to cast the glow of his sympathetic imagination over these things. Like Hardy, "He was one who had an eye for such mysteries."

Apart from his personal absorption in the scenes about Flatford Mill, it is interesting to see what use Constable made of features noted by more casual observers. We find that church towers were as important to him as the mill-dams that belonged to his happy boyhood, and we know how much he loved these—how he was fascinated by the movement of the great wheels at his father's mills, and revelled in the sound of rushing water. He used these strong, upstanding towers, pinnacled and battlemented, as points of rest in his pictures, and to emphasise by contrast the prevailing softness of the Suffolk scene. The great tower that crowns the hill at Stoke-by-Nayland and dominates the surrounding uplands was frequently the subject of his sketches. The tower of Dedham church was even more important to him, and must have contributed something to the moulding of his own character. In "The Cornfield" he went so far as to use it in a landscape where no cartographer could place it. Constable's cornfield is at the end of a lane—a much altered lane—branching off the main road between Flatford Mill and East Bergholt. If you visit it you will see the field, but you will not see Dedham church tower.

To appreciate the full effect of these Suffolk towers we cannot do better than study them in Constable's paintings, and, at the other end of the scale of sensitivity, no one can reveal better than he the essential quality of the wistful, grey-green willows that stand along the river banks. I spent some time in a caravan in a Constable water meadow, with a row of willows constantly in view. In dull weather their appearance was so melancholy that I was glad to leave them. From the same place I could look down the river to Nayland church tower, and I think I felt something of what Constable must have felt when he saw such towers, alert and serene through the mists of November, while the face of earth grew shabby and dull about them.

Midway between the strength of the tower and the wistfulness of the willow there was always the river itself, shifting and unstable, yet giving life to the valley, a highway for the barges and power for the mills. Water is the sympathetic element in landscape, and Constable's was a sympathetic genius. And so we might continue to study his interpretation of life in relation to the character of this quiet English valley. Its church towers, its trees, and its rivers are three of the many features he delighted in. Though he selected his material, as every artist must, from the confusion about him, he accepted the whole. This is particularly noticeable in his work. He was a forerunner of the Impressionists, but he did not over-simplify. On the contrary, he sought throughout his life to increase his command of her infinite gradations of light and shade, for above all was the sunlight, and sunlight he loved. To his friend Fisher he wrote: "That landscape painter who does not make his skies a very material part of his composition, neglects to avail himself of one of his greatest aids. . . . It will be difficult to name a class of landscape in which the sky is not the key note, the standard of scale, and the chief organ of sentiment. . . . The sky is the source of light in nature, and governs everything."

This, I suggest, was not the discovery of an artist so much as the understanding of an East Anglian. Nowhere else in England is the air so luminous as here. Those who look only at the configurations of landscape have dismissed Essex and Suffolk as plain—as indeed they are in dull weather. But, with their slight tilt towards the east, when the sun climbs the heavens, these low-lying counties receive the light with a grace unmatched elsewhere in England. Nowhere else is the air so free from veiling moisture, yet the earth so dewy and fresh. The slopes of the hills have just sufficient rise to take the light evenly. They are nowhere broken to produce glaring light and lowering shade. Constable saw this and took full advantage of it. He saw, too, that the clouds do not envelop these low hills, or hang like dark umbrellas over the valleys, but that they float high in the heavens, casting long shadows across the level fields, or lumber like harvest wagons across the raised slopes. He studied all their movements as they gathered like an army in the distance, or dispersed before a current of wind. As a miller's son he knew the ways of the clouds from boyhood, and painted them as a countryman would expect them to be. Not only did he know the weather; he knew the machinery of mills from practical experience of them. As his brother used to say: "When I look at a mill painted by John, I see that it will *go round,* which is not always the case with those by other artists."

These water mills could be found all along the Stour till long after Constable's day. They are now converted to other uses. Tea gardens are often found by an old mill-stream, with the great wheel a mossy, mildewed relic in the background. The mill on the Box at Thorington Street is still working, but there are few others on the Suffolk side of the river. Formerly there was one in every riverside village and town, and their prosperity is realised when we learn that as many as fourteen hundred sacks of flour, milled from wheat grown in the neighbourhood, would be sent from Nayland to London in a single week.

Constable painted these locks and willows, these bridges and lazy cattle, so often that we still see them through his eyes. Between Nayland and East Bergholt he must have known every stump and stile, yet he never tired of these places and never wearied of painting them. There was Willy Lott's cottage, for example, where the old man, whose gravestone may be seen in East Bergholt churchyard, lived for more than eighty years without being away from it for more than four whole days together. Willy and Constable must have been good friends, and much as the old man may have loved his home, he must have been puzzled to know what the fine folk in London could see in it when they had such grand buildings of their own to look at. There was "A Cottage in a

Cornfield," "The Valley Farm," and many others. To Constable, they were the homes of his people, and he loved them. When his work was exhibited in Paris he laughed at the thought of "the lovely valleys and peaceful farmhouses of Suffolk forming part of an exhibition to amuse the gay Parisians." In this affection for country sights he had much in common with William Cowper, who was, in fact, his favourite author.

The heart of Constable's country is Flatford Mill, but we have him in mind all the way from Sudbury, though in the Cornards we are nearer to Gainsborough. Great Cornard is almost part of Sudbury now, but Little Cornard is a small, secluded village, scattered about some of the narrowest and most circuitous lanes in this elaborate web of byways threaded across the entire region between Sudbury and Hadleigh. It is on high ground, and its farms have names that suggest a militant past. Such names as Dane's Hole, Killingdown Hill, and Sharp-fight Meadow, remind us of the time when this quiet countryside, now old and composed, had the vigour of youth. At this time invaders could come up the river as far as Sudbury. There was no other way, for the passage across Essex was barred by forest.

At Bures, "an ancient Royal town, the known bound between East Sexe and Suffolk," as the twelfth-century chronicler, Geoffrey of the Well, describes it, "situated upon the Stour, a river most rapid both in summer and winter," Edmund, King and Martyr, was crowned on Christmas Day, A.D. 855, when he was little more than a youth. The river, like the pulse of life generally in this part of the country, seems to have lost force since then. No one could call it rapid to-day.

The main road from Sudbury to Bures runs under an eminence called St. Edmund's Hill, but that was not the hill where St. Edmund was crowned. We approach this from Bures. Instead of taking the Sudbury road we continue to climb the steep main street of the town up the Boxford road, until, at the crest of the hill, a lane is found leading into the fields on the right, and from the end of this may be seen an old barn standing on the edge of a wheat field, a short distance to the left. The place is marked "Chapel" on the map, and this, according to established tradition, is the place where the ceremony was performed.

This ancient memorial is well worth visiting, even for those who,

> When Zephirus eek with his swete breeth
> Inspired hath in every holt and heeth
> The tendre croppes,

are not among those who long "to goon on pilgrimages." The scenery here is West Suffolk at its best. West and south is the valley of the Stour itself, which makes one of its sweeping bends at Bures. East and north is a feeder of that river. St. Stephen's chapel stands on a knoll overlooking these valleys. It was consecrated on St. Stephen's Day, 1218, by Archbishop Stephen Langton, and stands on the site of the Saxon place of worship where Edmund was crowned. After being used as a granary for many years it has now been restored, and additional glass from the demolished Colne Priory has been introduced, together with alabaster figures of the fifth, ninth, and eleventh Earls of Oxford.

When I visited this chapel in 1946, carefree English land girls in green woollen jerseys and fawn corduroy breeches, and German prisoners-of-war in overalls, were gathering the harvest in the fields all round it. No doubt their minds were occupied with the complications of present rather than of past events. Each age has so many problems of its own that it is not surprising to find places that must have been visited by pilgrims for centuries now neglected and almost forgotten. I must confess that the field workers claimed more of my own attention than the Chapel did. The Germans worked vigorously, but in silence. The girls were provocatively gay. Thoughts that had no connection with St. Edmund, but that were older than the Chapel itself, inevitably filled my mind as I stood for a few minutes watching the work. They were thoughts that may have exercised the farmer's mind also.

I did not find the people of Bures particularly interested in the history of their quiet little riverside town. They are probably sufficiently occupied with everyday tasks. Even the elaborately carved beam on the front of a cottage built into the maltings seemed of little interest. The first man I asked about it did not know what it was, but ventured the opinion that it had been there "a day or two." The second said he had heard that the building was fourteenth-century. The third shook his head and said, "Very old, very old. About ten years ago I remember people coming here to look at it. They were making a bit of a fuss about that kind of thing in this part of the country just then, but I haven't heard anything about it since." The fourth remembered something about it in the parish magazine once. He pushed his hat back and allowed the air to cool his forehead for a few seconds, then he remembered that this neglected old building had once been the Guildhall. Clearly, Bures does not make its living out of displaying its ancient treasures.

About a mile and a half east of Bures is Smallbridge Hall, another of the many old halls of Suffolk that have seen the rise and fall of famous families, and now await submissively and not very hopefully the verdict of a new age upon them. Such places are melancholy sights to-day. For more than three and a half centuries this was the seat of the Waldegrave family, to one of whom there is a fine monument in the church at Bures, where the south chapel, 1514, is the Waldegrave Chantry. As I left the hall I recalled the gay scenes its gardens must have witnessed when Elizabeth was entertained there in both 1561 and 1578. A Cottonian manuscript in the British Museum preserves a record of the expenses incurred by the Waldegraves during the two days she spent as their guest on the first of these two occasions.

As Wissington, or Wiston, as it is now called, for Suffolk people never waste their breath on redundant syllables, and are apt to be careless with the participle ending, there is a Norman church, a rare feature in this part of Suffolk. John Nash rented a bungalow on the Essex side of the river near Wissington in 1929. The valley had much charm for him, but he, too, was conscious of a melancholy hanging over it. His painting of Wormingford Mill Pool has on it the stillness of the Stour as we see it to-day. Something was lost to the life of this river when the mills were abandoned. Constable painted it in its bustling prime. John Nash has painted it as a forgotten valley, romantic but lifeless—a place where a ghost might walk.

When Constable's family first came to Suffolk they settled at Bures, and it is from there that we find Constable associations increasing as the river widens. Nayland has one of his two altar-pieces. The other is at Brantham, near the mouth of the river, and both have been much disparaged. They were painted, we are told, while he was under the influence of Sir Joshua Reynolds, whose paintings he was copying for Lord Dysart. As he painted no more subjects of the kind, we may conclude that he was perfectly well aware that he had no special gift for them. They were experiments only. He was not the kind of man to be carried away by conventional religious symbolism, and it seems foolish to be disappointed at finding them no more moving than they are. Yet while I cannot claim to be a worthy critic I am impelled to say that I think the Nayland study deserves more praise than it has had. I believe the critics agree that it is better than the Brantham painting. But if we forget the critics and look at this painting with open mind, I think we shall feel that while it has neither originality nor passion, there is warmth and humanity in the lamp-lit face of Christ, reminding us of Rembrandt rather than Reynolds. The broken browns, yellows, and purples, which are substituted for the conventional blues and reds, are to me entirely pleasing, though they suffer from having the light of the east window behind them. It is the painting of a reverent and modest man, for to say that the painting has no originality to speak of is also to say that the painter has not irreverently obtruded himself. In the simple homeliness of the treatment there is surely something of value. It was not painted for a cathedral, but for a village church, and its simplicity is therefore appropriate. As I knelt at the altar rails in front of it I felt that whatever Constable failed to do, he did reveal Christ as the Son of Man, and the altar as the table where the homely bread is broken and the cup shared. The people of Nayland are rightly proud of their painting, for it was actually painted in the village in 1809.

For Nayland I have special affection because I have spent so many happy days there. Its most interesting building,

Alston Court, a fifteenth-century house with good woodwork, was built by the Derham family, whose arms may be seen in some of the windows. Its great hall, with large leaded windows, is so reminiscent of a Dutch master that we expect to see a lady in a blue silk gown behind the casement, reading a letter, with the sunlight streaming through her hair, and perhaps lighting up a rug on the table behind her.

With its high walled garden and pleasant rooms, Alston Court is a kindly old house, standing without pretence or ceremony in the centre of the village. One of the best Nayland views is to be seen looking along its front, with the arched doorway, probably dating from William and Mary, or possibly from Queen Anne, past the leaded windows and long brick wall, towards the grey church porch at the far end of the lane. Across the main street from Alston Court stood the Guildhall, now a baker's shop.

Nayland is most pleasingly approached from the river. This way several of its houses incline towards you as you enter, as though turning to smile a welcome. Through open doors in tottering walls, sunny enclosed yards may be seen, with hollyhocks standing along the walls. Like the valley elms and poplars, or like a standard lamp in a friendly room, they provide the restoring perpendicular. This lovable but rather shabby old village is on low ground, and is liable to flood now the river is choked with weeds. Along the Colchester road it has two humped bridges that would have delighted Constable, and may have done so though I do not know that he ever painted them. They have yellow lichens growing on them, and are stained with so many dyes that on a summer's day I have seen each look like a painter's palette. When the flood waters are out, sand-martins may be seen here in great flocks, swooping and twinkling over the waste of water, ready to snap up the insects the floods have dislodged.

As we have been so close to the river while travelling along the valley road, we are still without sight of Stoke-by-Nayland tower, and shall be until we are almost under it, with Tendring Hall, where the poet Earl of Surrey is reputed to have been born, on our right. Yet Stoke-by-Nayland tower is visible from as far away as Harwich.

Stoke-by-Nayland is one of the most attractive, and cer-

60

tainly one of the most carefully kept villages along the whole
length of the Stour. Unlike most of its neighbours, which
are built in sheltered hollows, it is on the crest of a hill, a
position we with our greater desire for airy dwellings usually
prefer. It is a village much favoured by people of means who
wish to live in the country. Water was always the chief problem for villages built on high ground, and formerly the
supply at Stoke was provided by wells. There was one near
the church gate, which was worked in the old-fashioned two
bucket manner. Now the water for Stoke and Nayland is
pumped up from the Box and piped along the main roads,
though few, if any, of the cottages have piped water indoors.

Stoke-by-Nayland church, admired by Constable for its " continuous line of embattled parapet, and its finely proportioned
chancel," as well as for its commanding tower, has the distinction of having a Jesse tree carved on its doors. The cottages grouped round it are old and picturesque. The
almshouses in particular attract the attention of visitors.
They are built along a prominent ridge—somewhat incon-
siderately, we may think, for the elderly occupants must find
the climb trying, especially when carrying a heavy pail or
basket.

Giffords Hall here, built by Sir William Capel, who was
Lord Mayor of London in 1503, was empty when I visited it,
so I was able to wander at will through its beautiful, sheltered
gardens. The house is built round a quadrangular court,
entered through a stately red-brick gateway with octagonal
towers on either side. The doors have smooth linen-fold
panels. Peeping through the crevices, for the gate was locked,
I could see into a courtyard with an inner gatehouse with
timber and old brick on the upper storey, and grape design
carving above the leaded windows. Giffords Hall is a
rambling house of several periods, but the new part is at the
rear, so new and old are not seen from the same approach,
and it has a beautiful walled garden where peaches and
nectarines ripen in the sun.

There are several amusing stories told about the Sir
William Capel who built it. One relates that after entertaining Henry VII on a certain occasion he demonstrated his
loyalty by flinging into the fire a number of bonds for money

the king had borrowed from him. On another occasion he made public avowal of his affection for the king by dissolving a pearl worth hundreds of pounds, and drinking it to the king's health in a glass of wine. These gestures were wrongly interpreted by Henry, who seems to have thought them better proof of Sir William's wealth than of his loyalty, for he proceeded to relieve him of the possessions he squandered so lavishly. In spite of this, Sir William died a rich man.

Besides being beautiful in itself, Stoke-by-Nayland is the centre of an attractive group of villages. A short distance behind is Polstead, famous for its cherries, which are used to make the best cherry brandy, and another candidate for the honour of being Suffolk's prettiest village, though in Suffolk there is no undignified striving for such prizes. The most charming villages appear to be quite unaware of their own beauty, and in consequence carry themselves with the easy grace of the well-born.

In view of the gracious character of Polstead, with its stone church spire and its Gospel Oak, believed to be thirteen hundred years old, where early Christian missionaries must have preached to the heathen Saxons, it is a pity that it should only be known to most people as the scene of the *Murder in the Red Barn*, a crude melodrama formerly acted by strolling players all over England. To-day the play is something of a museum piece, and is probably hardly known to a generation younger than mine. To an older generation it was so familiar that little is left of poor Maria's gravestone in the churchyard, so many visitors have chipped off their souvenirs.

Briefly, the story relates that Maria Martin, the daughter of a Polstead mole-catcher, was in love with William Corder, the village scoundrel, who induced her to meet him secretly in the Red Barn on the pretext that his parents disapproved of the courtship. Maria stole out to this secret meeting-place one night in man's attire, ready to run away with her lover to Ipswich and there be married. She was never again seen alive. Some days later her stepmother asked Corder if he knew where she was. He replied that she was in Ipswich, and they were to be married shortly. Weeks went by, until when Corder found his story no longer believed he, too, disappeared, boldly declaring that he was going to his wedding, which would take place at Yarmouth, not Ipswich. The next news came from London, where the couple, now alleged to be married, were said to be living. Then Mrs. Martin had a dream, which, like all the best dreams, was repeated twice. She dreamt that Maria's body would be found buried in a certain spot in the Red Barn and could not be pacified until search had been made. Accordingly the floor of the barn was dug up, and the body was found exactly where Mrs. Martin had seen it in her dreams. Corder was traced, arrested, and tried at Bury St. Edmunds, where he confessed to the murder and was hanged. Many gruesome items connected with this sordid village tragedy may be seen at Moyses' Hall, Bury St. Edmunds.

This story of the murder of Maria Martin in the Red Barn, which, by the way, was burnt down some years ago, is to my mind one that requires a little comic relief, and this was provided one day when I was in conversation with my friend the village constable. He told me that one night a lorry broke down near the Red Barn, and the driver reported that it was blocking the road. The two went over to the scene to take measures for ensuring the safety of other cars travelling that way. Then the driver said he must inform his employer of the accident. "You can tell him," said the constable, "that you broke down opposite Maria Martin's Red Barn. That may tickle his fancy a bit."

The driver's mate pricked up his ears.

"Coo," he said, "is that the plice?"

"It is," replied the constable, "and I have heard people say that at certain times she can still be heard, crying for help."

Just then a vixen's yelp cut through the quiet air.

"It's 'er. I 'eard 'er," stammered the boy in terror. He had never heard a fox before.

This seems to be a district where the sensational and the beautiful are found together. I know of no other place than Boxford, one of my favourite West Suffolk villages, where a young man might be seen walking along the street with a lion at his side. This strange pet died a short time ago and is buried in front of the "White Hart" Inn, where a mound marks the grave. There was a stone over it at first, but this appears to have gone. Perhaps the souvenir hunters were again busy. This young man was "Tornado Smith," the "wall of death" rider, and the lion used to occupy the side-car in his spectacular performances.

Perhaps Boxford people have always had original ideas about life. In the church there is a mural tablet to "Elizabeth Hyam of this parish, for the fourth time widow, who by a fall that brought on a mortification, was at last hastened to her end on the 14th of May 1748, in her 113th year."

From Boxford, where bent old houses lean towards the sun, narrow lanes lead out in all directions. One goes over the hill to Kersey, which, if choice must be made, really is Suffolk's loveliest village. I remember hesitating at a cross-roads behind Boxford, where the sign-post offered the choice of Polstead, where the cherries grow, Lavenham, with its timbers like the fingers of tired old hands stretched towards the hearth for warmth, and Boxford, with its sunny cottages and winding lanes. With these three villages in mind I stood long before deciding which road to take. Here, I thought, was a choice that only Paris could have faced with equanimity. Could there, I wondered, be another place in England where the villages beckon more invitingly than here in the hollows of these low hills. On a sunny day it is impossible to pass through one of them without being surprised and delighted again by the patterns of light and shade on sharp gable and under wide eaves made by the overhanging thatch.

The Box, on which Boxford stands, joins the Brett in that romantic valley seen from the road that falls from Stoke-by-Nayland to Higham. At Higham Bridge we pass from West to East Suffolk, but not, I hope, before noticing the remarkably fine crops that grow each year in the low fields on the Stoke side of the bridge, and Thorington Hall, now National Trust property, a beautiful old house close to the road.

From Higham one road goes to Stratford St. Mary, another to the main Colchester to Ipswich road, and after crossing it runs through pleasant lanes to East Bergholt and the villages on the headland between the Stour and the Orwell.

Constable's birthplace has gone, but there are many places to be seen in the village that are interesting both in them-

Lavenham Church

selves and by association. There is the great wooden cage in the churchyard where the bells have been hung for the past four hundred years, the only belfry in England where the bells are reached at ground level and rung by handling the bell stock. The tenor weighs twenty-five hundredweight; the second bell, Gabriel, is five hundred years old.

The story of East Bergholt's church tower is rather curious. Wolsey himself started the building of it about 1520, but it had not reached more than half its projected height when he fell from power and the building was abandoned for lack of funds. A local legend maintains that the Devil took unusual interest in this tower. Each day he watched it rise, and each night he brought it down again, until the builders grew disheartened and the tower was abandoned.

But it was not the Devil who disturbed John Constable's life at East Bergholt. It was Dr. Rhudde, the rector, who disapproved of the young painter's attachment to his granddaughter, Maria Bicknell. The two lovers appear to have met in 1800 when Miss Bicknell was on a visit to the Rectory. Their friendship was deepened by correspondence and occasional meetings for ten years before they so much as intimated to their families that they wished to become engaged. Not until another five years had passed were they bold enough to marry, and the chief obstacle all these years was the stubborn old rector, who seems to have kept the entire family in awe of him. It would be interesting to know how many ill-matched couples he married in his village church without the slightest compunction during the fifteen years he kept these lovers apart.

Often the parson is the only educated man in a village, and it is to him we look for the discovery and encouragement of such boys as Constable must have been. But it was the village plumber instead of the village parson who quickened Constable's soul. So there is a second John to be honoured: John Dunthorne, plumber and glazier of East Bergholt, one of those men in humble life who by the grace of God, and apparently by no other advantage whatever, live with freedom and distinction intelligent and cultivated lives. Such are treasures among men, and happily we may still find them. They are like flowers that grow from seeds sown by the wind,

F

Kentwell Hall, Long Melford

and are the more refreshing for being to all appearances inexplicable.

John Dunthorne was himself a painter, and he and the miller's son discussed together ideas that were later to have such an effect on English and French landscape paintings. We know how much we owe to Constable for these. We shall never know how much we owe to his friend John Dunthorne. But we may be sure that if we were able to discuss this debt with the pair of them we should find them of one mind. Both would say that it was "dear old Bergholt," a Suffolk river, and Suffolk skies, that enabled Constable to bring pure and vivid colours into landscape painting.

CHAPTER V

THE WOOL TOWNS

AMONG English counties Suffolk has the rare distinction of owing most of its architectural beauty to the prosperity of a local industry. The decayed but beautiful wool towns along the valleys of the Stour and Brett are now acknowledged to be national treasures, though they are still unknown to many who claim to know their England reasonably well. Of these Lavenham, only four miles from Long Melford, is the richest in what Thomas Fuller called "observables." In all its winding streets memorials to the woolmen may be found. Their trade signs are on the fabric of the church itself. Trade is now so completely secularised that we are apt to forget how the craft guilds of the Middle Ages maintained altars in parish churches, each adorned with an image of the saint to whom the guild was dedicated. Sometimes in organising their guilds the richer merchants went so far as to maintain a separate priest to conduct services at the guild altar and visit the sick and poor they clothed and fed. In all these old wool towns the first building to search for is the guild-hall, and it must be added that in most it is in a dishonoured if not derelict condition. Lavenham is an exception. It has the finest guildhalls in Suffolk. Valuable work might be done if one of the societies engaged in preserving our national memorials were to give special attention to guildhalls. Trade guilds were exceptionally strong in Suffolk, and in addition there were various parish guilds, some of great antiquity. The "Fraternity of the Clerks of Glemsford," for example, associated with St. Mary's church, Bury St. Edmunds, claimed to date from the reign of Canute, and certainly received the recognition of a formal constitution from Abbot Baldwin in Edward the Confessor's reign. The principal obligations of this particular guild were to watch over the body and chant at the funerals of Bury monks. Like the later craft guilds, the

Clerks of Glemsford were also concerned with protecting the interests of the fraternity. No cleric who was not a brother was permitted to teach the psalter, and no layman was allowed to have his son instructed in letters except by someone approved by the guild.

When the Church had been so strong in Suffolk—as elsewhere—throughout the Middle Ages, it was inevitable that the trade organisations formed at the end of that period should be modelled on Church lines. There was nothing incongruous to the mind of the medieval villager in mixing what is now considered secular with what is now considered sacred. In the early days of industrial development the parish church was the only place large enough for public assemblies. Even courts were held there. Only the chancel was regarded as dedicated to religious uses exclusively. There was, in fact, an agreed appropriation of the various parts of the church to specific uses. Legal difficulties, for example, were straightened out—or further complicated—in the porch. A reminder of this custom may be found in an interesting inscription over a dole table standing in the porch at Eye. It reads:

> Seale not to soone lest thou repent to late,
> Yet helpe thy frend, but hinder not thy state.
> If ought thou lende or borrow, truly pay,
> Ne give, ne take advantage, though thou may,
> Let conscience be thy guide, so helpe thy frend,
> With loving peace and concord make thy end.

With the development of the industry, separate buildings became necessary for the orderly management of guild affairs, and the various halls were built. Lavenham had three, of which two remain; the third, dedicated to the Holy Trinity, was demolished as long ago as 1879.

We do not know when East Anglia's cloth trade began, but it became prominent in Edward III's reign. Emissaries were sent to the Continent to induce weavers to settle in England under promise that "if they would but come over into England, bringing their mystery with them . . . they should feed on fat beef and mutton [instead of herrings and mouldy cheese] till nothing but their fulness should stint their stomachs." That, at least, is Fuller's account of the matter, and we trust those who responded got their beef and mutton, as they probably did, for at that time Suffolk was largely pastoral. Above all, we trust that they were saved from the penalty of being obliged to eat Suffolk cheese, a product that has never been any credit to the county, though Fuller was so misguided as to describe it as "most excellent," and to quote a learned Dutch physician as saying that he counted the cheese of Suffolk equal to that of Parma in Italy.

In thinking of the Suffolk wool trade, it is natural to think first of Lavenham, because Lavenham has been so much more successful than its neighbours in preserving its typical character, though it was not, as it is sometimes said to have been, the most important of the old wool towns.

In every Lavenham street beautiful Tudor cottages are found, most of them plastered and pink-washed. Some have the fleur-de-lis design on them, often surmounted by a mitre, the emblem of Bishop Blaise, patron saint of the wool combers, whose flesh was combed from his bones in the horrible persecution of Diocletian. The 3rd of February, Bishop Blaise's day, was formerly observed as a public holiday in the town.

The glory of Lavenham is the church, built by those wealthy wool merchants, the Spring family, in conjunction with John de Vere, thirteenth Earl of Oxford, and lord of the manor. In looking at Lavenham church I often wonder how these two proud families came to agree on the displaying of their respective emblems. At the top of the tower, which is a hundred and forty-one feet high, are the arms of the Spring family, while under each of the windows is the mullet or five-pointed star, the cognizance of the de Veres. The porch is entirely de Vere, with the family badge, the boar (verre), on the spandrils of the arch, and the mullet at the base of each buttress and again in the vaulting. On the shields across the porch are the arms of the ninth, tenth, eleventh, twelfth, and thirteenth Earls of Oxford, and on the sixth shield the boar and the harpy appear as supporters. Above them is the beautiful fascia carved in foliage, with sculptured flowers in the pierced battlements, a design that is continued above the aisles on each side. Above the clerestory windows mullets

69

and shields are carved in alternate panels. The balance appears to have been lost to the de Veres until we reach the chapel south of the chancel, where buttresses and battlements are charged with the arms of the Spring family.

Like most Suffolk churches, Lavenham is Perpendicular in style—in this case late Perpendicular—except for the chancel, which is Decorated. The nave is considered by experts to be perfect in its proportions. The feature that strikes the visitor most forcibly on entering is the loftiness of the nave, with its six bays and tall pier shafts embellished with Tudor flowers. He is at a loss to account for this impression until he notices that the church floor is so much lower than the churchyard surrounding it, from which he first assessed the height. In the spandrils of the tall arches between the nave and the aisles are shields which were formerly blazoned with the arms of the de Veres.

The most conspicuous monument in Lavenham church is found against the north wall, inside the sanctuary. It is in memory of Dr. Copinger, rector of Lavenham for forty-five years, who died in 1622, and of his wife. This worthy couple are represented in black costume, with white ruffs about their necks. They kneel at a table, the rector with a book in his hands, his wife in the attitude of prayer. Fuller, that rare old worthy who delights me so much both as man and writer that perhaps I quote him too often, says of Dr. Copinger: "he lived forty and five years the painful parson of Lavenham; in which market town there were about nine hundred communicants, amongst whom, all his time, no difference did arise which he did not compound." Then he adds: "His father on his death-bed, asking him what course of life he would embrace, he answered he intended to be a divine. 'I like it well,' said the old gentleman; 'otherwise what shall I say to Martin Luther, when I shall see him in heaven, and he knows that God gave me eleven sons, and I made not one of them a minister.'"

After complaining in a previous chapter about the tendency of our present age to choose names that are impersonal and meaningless, we ought here to notice the delightful street names of Lavenham. If after visiting the church we descend the hill into this quaint old Tudor town, we find such names as Lady Street, Shilling Street, Prentice Street, and just outside that most delightful name of all, Bright's Drift—a drift being the Suffolk name for a cart-way between fields. At the end of this drift is the fifteenth-century half-timbered farmhouse of Bright's Farm.

Lavenham is so full of genuine Tudor architecture that we can easily imagine the scene in 1578 when Elizabeth visited the town after she had been entertained by Sir William Cordell at Long Melford. Sir William Spring, a grandson of the "Rich Clothier," who was High Sheriff of Suffolk that year, spared no expense to entertain his royal mistress. Two hundred young gentlemen in white velvet coats, three hundred "of the graver sort" in black velvet, with fifteen hundred retainers on horseback waited upon Sir William as he accompanied the queen round the county. We can imagine as easily the elaborate processions at Corpus Christi whenever we look at the old Guildhall, formerly the hall of the guild of Corpus Christi, which stands in the market square, and was built about 1520-6, or at the Wool Hall, formerly the hall of the guild of Our Lady, which stands at the foot of Lady Street. And Lady Street, it should be noted, is really *Our* Lady Street. To this day it possesses the grace becoming to its name. After varying fortunes the Wool Hall was actually taken down and removed from Lavenham in 1913, but a few enthusiasts under the leadership of the Rev. Henry Taylor succeeded in recovering it from the purchaser, and under the supervision of the Society for the Preservation of Ancient Buildings it was again erected on its original site. It is now a convalescent home. This is still the most perfectly restored house in Lavenham, and is a fine example of the excellent work of the society. On each side of the main hall, with its high windows, balcony, and outstretched timbers supported by a massive king post, are two-storeyed wings, entered through arched doorways with carved spandrils. The rooms on the south side have ribbon carved beams that are among the finest in the county.

One of the most interesting houses in Lavenham is Shilling Grange in Shilling Street, a fifteenth-century house with secret hiding-places, one in a chimney and another between a floor and a ceiling. This was the home of the Taylors of Ongar

71

from 1786 to 1793, before they removed to Arundel House,
which Mr. Taylor bought for two hundred and fifty pounds.
Either here or in Colchester Jane wrote *Twinkle, Twinkle,
Little Star*, and Ann, *Meddlesome Matty*. In the garden
behind, Mr. Taylor painted the study of his two daughters
now hanging in the National Portrait Gallery. A print of it
lies beside me while I write.

Though a Dissenter, Mr. Taylor published a book of
engravings of Lavenham church, for which he had special
affection because three of his children were buried in the
churchyard. In a bakehouse at the top of the street, now
replaced by another baker's shop, Jane used to recite her
verses to the women who waited for their bread to brown.
Public bakehouses were well patronised in Suffolk. Many
older people will remember the scene in Long Melford after
church on a Sunday morning, when the staid, respectably
dressed villagers used to be seen walking across the green
after matins to pick up their Sunday joints at the bakehouse.

On one occasion Mr. Taylor found himself the object of
violent attack from his "Church and King" acquaintances.
An alarm was given by a friendly neighbour who ran into the
Taylors' house with news that a furious mob had assembled
in the market-place, that flags were flying and drums beating,
and that this insurgent assembly had already vowed to burn
down Mr. Taylor's house. Deliverance came just in time. A
portly clergyman named Mr. Cooke stepped into the street
as the mob approached, held up his hand to command attention, and addressed the rioters so persuasively that they retired
without carrying out their avowed intentions. Mr. Taylor
was touched by this unexpected intervention of the Church
on his behalf, and the following morning presented himself
at the clergyman's door with suitable words of acknowledgment. To his embarrassment he was informed that his
reverend neighbour's eloquence had not been used to save
the Taylors from being rendered homeless, but because Mr.
Cooke's sister was ill, and he feared so much noise in the
street might distress her.

In the nineteen-twenties, Shilling Grange became so derelict that it was thought dangerous and marked for demolition,
but like the Wool Hall it was saved by timely intervention,

and part of it restored—again through the good offices of the Society for the Preservation of Ancient Buildings.

In a sheltered nook behind the church we find Lavenham Hall, a dignified, kindly old farmhouse, part of which is fifteenth-century, standing on the site of a Saxon grange. This was the home of the bailiff during the centuries in which Lavenham was ruled by the de Veres, and at one time was probably a religious house. Lavenham Hall is away from the town, but an interesting feature of Lavenham is that so many of its important old halls stand cheek by jowl with humble cottages along the narrow streets. The house we are most anxious to discover, the home of the de Veres, is lost to us. This great family, described by Macaulay as "the longest and most illustrious line of nobles that England has seen," held the manor of Lavenham for five hundred years. Their park is known to have covered half the parish, and Mr. F. L. Ranson informs me that there is strong reason for believing that their mansion stood between Bright's Farm and Park Farm. The road leading to this part of the parish is shown on old deeds as the Oxford Way. The moat that surrounded the house is still there. They must have lived in great splendour. Stow has a vivid description of how the sixteenth earl "rode to his house in London with 80 gentlemen in liveries of Reading tawney, and chains of gold about their neck; and with a hundred tall yeomen in like livery without chains, but having a blue boar embroidered on the left shoulder." But the seventeenth earl, believed by many to have had at least a considerable hand in the authorship of Shakespeare, is the one on whom the greatest interest centres to-day.

A Chinese proverb says that "the trouble with most of us is that we have not enough bees in our bonnet to pollinate the flowers of our mind." In Lavenham, however, may be found a mind well pollinated by this particular bee, if indeed it is a bee. Some would call it a star. This is the mind of Lavenham's worthy historian, Mr. F. Lingard Ranson. To sit in Mr. Ranson's shop in Lavenham market-place and hear him discourse on the history of the town is a delightful experience. To hear him holding forth on present-day neglect and lack of understanding of the ceremonial of the

73

Church is even more delightful. But best of all is to hear
Mr. Ranson on Edward de Vere, seventeenth Earl of Oxford:
"Our Lord of the Manor, sir! " I wish I had the skill—and
in these pages the space—to sketch a worthy portrait of Mr.
Ranson. I discovered him after spending an unusually dull
morning at Ipswich. It was one of those days when all the
colour seems to go out of life. Ipswich seemed full of
commonplace people doing commonplace things. Everyone
in the "Great White Horse " looked bored and tired. Even
the road through Hintlesham and Hadleigh seemed dull,
though in the former place I did reflect upon the interesting
fact that this little Suffolk village had recently been the retreat
in old age of two distinguished men, Havelock Ellis and
Hensley Henson. It was perhaps as well that they were not living there at the same time, for they had, I suppose, only two
things in common, the title of doctor and mastery of English
prose. I stopped my car to ask a countryman if he knew either
of these two gentlemen. He shook his head about Ellis; " a
strange sort of man." Of the bishop I received a glowing
account. Hintlesham folk, I learned, had felt it a great
honour to have him as one of themselves, and it was quite
clear that Dr. Henson had really entered into the life of the
village and known most of the cottagers by name. This information did something to cheer me, but it was one of those
days when greyness settles upon everything. Lavenham itself looked shabby and dejected. Then I met Mr. Ranson.
He scrutinised me over his glasses almost fiercely. His words
were sharp and clear. He had the shrewdness of a lawyer
in his eyes, and his head would sit worthily on the shoulders
of a Cambridge professor. What a character! I thought
Few things are more delightful than to find originality of
mind and bearing in unexpected places. I had looked for
relief from the day's gloom in a bustling town, in talk of great
men, and here where I never expected it was this bright little
fire of a man.

Mr. Ranson took out some of his beautiful photographs of
Lavenham church.

"The mullet," said I.

"The 'star that guides my moving,'" said Mr. Ranson,
quoting Sonnet XXVI.

74

"The blue boar," said I.

"'Fierce thing replete with too much rage,'" replied Mr. Ranson, quoting Sonnet XXIII. And then I learned that the backward look "Even of five hundred courses of the sun," in Sonnet LIX, is a reference to the five hundred years the de Veres had flourished since the first appearance of that "white Starre . . . which to every mannes sighte did light and arrest upon the standard of Albry" de Vere in 1098. And so we rattled on till the time came to part, whereupon we promised each other another merry meeting.

Such is the enthusiasm this illustrious family can still quicken, and I am happy to number among my friends another man who is not afraid to allow a few bees to buzz in his bonnet, to the delight of all who know him, who, be it whispered, cherishes the belief that he is descended from this illustrious line. But the de Veres are now without property in Lavenham. In Elizabeth's reign the last earl was obliged to sell the manor. Their name, however, continues to be associated with the town in the De Vere House in Water Street, though the last of the name to own it was Lady de Vere, who died as long ago as 1671. In 1926 this house was nearly lost to Lavenham. It was sold and dismantled like the Wool Hall already mentioned, but again was saved and erected on the original site at great cost to himself by the purchaser. It can easily be recognised. Figures of Tudor huntsmen are carved on its door-posts, and the mullet and the boar appear on the spandrils above. The brick-nogging, however, is much later than the timber framework.

The passing of the de Veres did not mean the end of all splendour and display in Lavenham. A merchant family rose to such wealth and power that a member of it actually married a de Vere when Margaret, daughter of the second Thomas Spring, married Aubrey de Vere, the second son of the fifteenth earl. From this marriage sprang the last two earls of the line, the nineteenth and twentieth. But it was Thomas Spring the third who became known as the Rich Clothier. He was born in 1456, and when he died in 1523 he owned land in no fewer than a hundred and thirty parishes in the four eastern counties of Essex, Suffolk, Norfolk, and Cambridgeshire. His methods of making money may not

always have been open to inspection, for in 1508 he was
granted by the king a general pardon, a thing not uncommon
in those days, " of all murders, felonies, accessory murders or
felonies, rebellions, contempt, etc., also of all usurious con-
tracts, usurious bargains, corrupt covenants, etc., of illicit
sales of cloth, wool, linen, and for non-payment of foreign
merchants, for all false deception and offences in making
cloth, in stretching out the length, or the breadth of it, and
all deception in the selling of Woollen Cloth."

The Tudors, after plundering the abbeys and distributing
the gains, had tremendous problems to face in finding
revenue and providing poor relief. Consequently the woolmen were of great importance to them as sources of revenue,
and those of the two or three generations following that of
Thomas Spring exercised great power. Even in his day the
demands of the Crown were steadily increasing, and much
of the burden was passed on to the weavers, who in 1525
organised a revolt. This disturbance was so skilfully handled
by the Dukes of Norfolk and Suffolk that little harm was
done, but four years later there was another rising, this time
accompanied by ugly scenes. In those early days of industrial development the interdependence of different classes in
the national economy was only very imperfectly understood.
It is easy to blame the woolmen for the sweated labour. Many
of them certainly provided for themselves handsomely, but
they also lived in fear of the consequences of international
quarrels, and they suffered severely from disputes between
England and Flanders.

The corrupt practices indicated in the general pardon
granted to Thomas Spring tended to increase. In seeking
information about the progress of the woollen industry we
look up the Alnage accounts. It is from these we learn the
production of each neighbourhood, or what purports to be
the production. It is generally agreed that these accounts are
far from reliable, especially those dealing with the later years.
Some of the earlier accounts may be perfectly accurate. The
later ones were certainly faked. These accounts were kept
by an official called the alnager, who collected customs. In
1347 a tax of fourteen pence was levied on each piece of broad
cloth exported by an Englishman, and twenty-one pence on

each exported by an alien cloth-worker. This was altered later, when cloth sold for home use also became taxable. The alnager sealed each cloth, charging an additional halfpenny for doing so. For this purpose every alnager had his measure of silk or thread, twelve yards twelve inches in length, with a seal at each end. He had his assistants in various parts of the county, and different seals for each town. The faking of the alnage accounts seems to have become flagrant when the collecting of the tax was farmed out by the alnager.

By the end of the fourteenth century Suffolk was ahead of both Norfolk and Essex in the production of woollen cloths. Some of these took their names from the villages where they were woven. Thus we get lindseys taking their name from a scattered village between Lavenham and Hadleigh, and kerseys from the lovely village of that name between Hadleigh and Boxford. Ipswich and Sudbury were important centres from very early times. Of the group of West Suffolk towns we normally think of as the wool towns, Hadleigh had the highest returns, though in making statements about the returns of the various towns and villages it is always necessary to bear in mind that we do not know for certain what area each place-name covered. Several villages might be included in one return. Hadleigh itself returned for several of the villages it served as a small market town as well as for itself. Nayland, Stoke-by-Nayland and a district extending to East Bergholt enjoyed considerable prosperity, as did Long Melford and the Waldingfields. Later the trade spread up the Stour valley as far as Haverhill, with Clare and Glemsford as important centres. By the sixteenth century many fortunes had been made and the Suffolk woolmen were among the richest merchants in the kingdom, not only employing the people in their weaving rooms, such as those reached from the yard of the "Bull" at Long Melford, but also putting out work at piece rates for the cottagers to do at home. From petitions of poor weavers still in existence these rates appear to have been pitiably inadequate. These poor people complained that "the Richmen the clothiers have their Loomes and weyvers and also their fullers dailie workyng within their owne howses" at rates so low that if they worked "nyght and day, holy day and worke day," they could not make a living.

77

The finished cloth was carried either to Ipswich or London for sale. At first it probably went to Ipswich or Sudbury, but West Suffolk early learned the advantages of dealing direct with London. It is interesting to speculate how far the present marked differences between East and West Suffolk are due to this division of markets. Few roads were constructed across the county, and even to this day there is surprisingly little communication between the two halves. Recent attempts to merge them for administrative purposes have proved abortive. Both the road from east to west through Hadleigh and the one through Nayland are still tortuous, and many loops can be seen by the way indicating how much longer they were three or four hundred years ago.

In that rare work, *Carriers' Cosmographie*, by John Taylor the Water Poet, published in 1637, we find the names of the London inns visited regularly by the West Suffolk carriers. The wagons from Bury St. Edmunds trundled into the yard of the "Four Swans" in Bishopsgate Street, and of the "Dolphin" nearby. The Sudbury carriers patronised the "Saracen's Head," while the Melford and Waldingfield carriers were to be found at the "Spread Eagle" in Gracechurch Street.

The decline of this interesting industry came in the seventeenth century when the Civil War played such havoc with the nation's trade. Many of the great Suffolk clothiers became bankrupt. Others retired from business with what they had left. The great days of Lavenham and Hadleigh were over, though many struggled on in a small way. Dr. Thornton (Mrs. Ward), in her admirable history of Clare, tells this story of the Suffolk woollen industry in considerable detail. She has an interesting sidelight on its last days in Clare, taken from an account left by Walford the antiquary, who wrote at the end of the eighteenth century. The story goes that an astute lawyer named Poulter lived in Clare at the beginning of the eighteenth century, and that this gentleman systematically stamped out the industry there by refusing to allow any of the saymakers to take apprentices. His reason for this high-handed procedure was that he foresaw the decline of the trade, and knew that if the young people went into it they would be thrown out of employment later and would become a liability to the town.

With the coming of steam power, industry passed from the south to the north and midlands, where coal was at hand and therefore cheaper. From that day to this the population of the Suffolk wool towns has declined until to-day they are villages, with only their magnificent churches to remind the visitor of their former prosperity. Many of them still seem to live in a bygone age, for the more enterprising young people have found their way to Ipswich, Colchester, or even London. When the Industrial Revolution passed Suffolk by, much was lost economically, but much was preserved of aesthetic and historical value, so we have this remarkable group of small towns and villages that are so dear to those who have a tender regard for the past. A price has to be paid for each advance we make in our social and economic life. What has been lost in many parts of England is preserved in Suffolk, and now that we are not quite so sure about the value of the gain as our more complacent parents were, we might study these places to see if something that a former generation threw away so airily might not with advantage be reinstated.

We must not, however, suppose that these historic villages have made no contribution to our national life since the decline of their principal trade. After the decline of its wool trade Lavenham, like its neighbours, continued to have small local industries, notably horse-hair weaving and the manufacture of coco-nut matting, industries long established in most of the old wool towns. In Lavenham itself the last of these factories closed down in 1930, and the population declined rapidly. In 1936 it was only fourteen hundred. Lavenham might well have felt that its long life was over. Now its spirit revives as the fame of its beauty is spread abroad, and with such an inn as the " Swan " it is sure to be visited increasingly. It has also attracted a small hand-loom weaving industry, and one utilising the agricultural products of the neighbourhood.

Hadleigh has maintained its reputation in a different way. This ancient royal town was the headquarters of Guthrum the Dane, who died here in 889 or 890, and is believed to be buried in the parish church. In 878, by the terms of the

Peace of Wedmore, East Anglia, Northumbria, and half of central England, was ceded to the Danes. In accordance with the same treaty, Guthrum became a Christian, was baptised Æthelstan, and held East Anglia as a vassal of Alfred, his godfather. But Hadleigh's greatest fame came through its connection with two eminent Churchmen, Rowland Taylor, the Protestant martyr, and Hugh James Rose, the Catholic revivalist. The one was honoured for resisting Rome, the other for emulating her. Thus do the Fates mock us when we aspire to be thought wise!

As persons both were delightful men. Taylor was described by Fuller as "a great scholar, painful preacher, charitable to the poor, of a comely countenance, proper person (but inclining to corpulency), and cheerful behaviour." "The same devotion," he observes, "had different looks in several martyrs, frowning in stern Hooper, weeping in meek Bradford, and smiling constantly in pleasant Taylor." Foxe has a vivid description of Rowland Taylor arriving at Hadleigh Bridge and of the welcome his old parishioners gave him: "The streets of Hadley were beset on both sides the way with the men and women of the town and country, who waited to see and bless him." All the money he had on his person he distributed to the poor in the almshouses as he was escorted past them. At Aldham Common, where a memorial still marks the spot, a great multitude had assembled. One of his faithful followers called out: "God save thee, good Dr. Taylor! Jesus Christ strengthen thee." He was not allowed to address his people, but seeing a man he knew named Soyce among them he sat down and said: "Soyce, I pray thee come and pull off my boots, and take them for thy labour; thou hast long looked for them, now take them."

When they had bound him and set up the faggots, a man named Warwick spitefully threw a faggot at his head, cutting his cheek. "O friend," said the good doctor, "I have harm enough, what needed that?"

The Hadleigh parish was what is called a peculiar, that is to say, a parish free from diocesan control, and subject only to the authority of the Archbishop, until all such were abolished in 1838. With this exceptional status went the title of Dean of Bocking, held by rectors of Bocking in Essex from

the thirteenth century to 1572, and then transferred to the rectors of Hadleigh until 1650, after which it was a co-title, held by the rectors of both parishes "conjointly and severally." The most marked feature of the church itself is its tall spire, rising seventy-one feet above the tower which probably belonged to an earlier and smaller church, and may have stood since the end of the twelfth century. Remains of a much earlier church have been found in the churchyard.

Hadleigh has several old houses with Tudor roses and royal arms embellishing the plaster work. One of the most noteworthy, Sun Court, which has a good moulded oak ceiling, was unoccupied for years, but fortunately was saved from demolition and has now been restored. There is another interesting old house in the High Street known as the Mayor's House. But the best of Hadleigh is in the church precinct. Overlooking the churchyard is the fifteenth-century guildhall, and south-west of the church a splendid brick gatehouse flanked by embattled hexagonal turrets that rise several feet higher than the rest of the building. This is known as the Deanery Tower, and was built in 1495 by Archdeacon Pykenham, the former rector of Hadleigh and dean of Stoke College, who also built the "Archdeacon's Gate" at Ipswich.

The rector of Hadleigh is responsible for services in the fifteenth-century chapel connected with the almshouses in George Street, where some fine woodwork, including a carved pulpit, may be seen. The church I will not attempt to describe in detail, but one feature should be noted. This is the bench end in the south chapel depicting a legend which relates how St. Edmund's head was found in the jaws of a wolf. The wolf is here represented as a monk, wearing ecclesiastical vestments and a collar of the time of Richard II. On his forefeet are an amusing pair of shoes of the same period.

The present deanery, standing at the back of the Deanery Tower, was built by Hugh James Rose, the most distinguished of Hadleigh's recent rectors. It was he who started the movement that is thought by many to have saved the Church of England. In February 1935 Archbishop Lang visited the old town for a service of thanksgiving and to dedicate a memorial to Dean Rose. He reminded his congregation of that historic

G   81

Boxford

conference convened at Hadleigh in 1833, when a small group
of friends met in the Deanery and agreed to issue the famous
"Tracts for the Times," which gave its name to the Trac-
tarian Movement.

In the list of distinguished men who for long or short
periods have held the Hadleigh living, one other must be
recalled: John Still, afterwards Bishop of Bath and Wells.
He was one of the most formidable theologians of his day.
Towards the end of Elizabeth's reign a movement was started
with a view to settling outstanding differences between the
various European churches. It came to nothing, but Dr. Still
was one of the two learned divines elected to champion and
defend the tenets of the Church of England. He was no less
astute in watching his own interests, for while Bishop of Bath
and Wells he was quick to gain an interest in lead mines
discovered in the Mendip Hills, and made a large fortune
from them. John Still was formerly reputed to be the author
of *Gammer Gurton's Needle,* but the evidence in support of
his authorship is now held to be inconclusive. It is a judgment that many besides myself must regret. I confess that
whatever conclusion my head must draw from the evidence
available, my heart will continue to credit this sturdy bishop
rather than an unknown Fellow of Christ's named William
Stevenson with the authorship of that rollicking drinking
song:

> I cannot eat but little meat,
> My stomach is not good;
> But sure I think that I can drink
> With him that wears a hood.
> Though I go bare, take ye no care,
> I nothing am a-cold;
> I stuff my skin so full within
> Of jolly good ale and old.
> Back and side go bare, go bare;
> Both foot and hand go cold;
> But, belly, God send thee good ale enough,
> Whether it be new or old.

In the valley of the Brett, between Lavenham and Had-

leigh, several of Suffolk's best villages are to be found along
the winding road that crosses and re-crosses the river in a way
that may remind the traveller of Chesterton's theory that the
rolling English drunkard made the rolling English road.
Chelsworth, with its beautiful vicarage and fine old oaks, was
Julian Tennyson's favourite among these villages, and it was
a good choice; Kersey is every man's love. So much has been
written of its beauty that I shrink from writing another page
on the charm of that one steep street, with cottages piled up
the banks on either side, dipping to the water splash in the
middle—a street like the crook of a strong arm, in which
the whole village is firmly but gently held. Above it towers
the grand old church. All these things are readily observed;
but one thing must be mentioned, because it could so easily be
missed. From the eaves of a house in Kersey hangs a stallion's
tail, the professional sign of a veterinary surgeon. It is the
only one I know of in Suffolk. Most of these old professional
and trade signs have gone now. A few years ago barbers'
poles were fairly common. We see few to-day. Even the
pawnbroker's three brass balls are hard to find in many towns.
But at Kersey you can still see this now almost obsolete sign,
the stallion's tail. The fact is worth recording. And writing
of signs, we must recall here that at Kettlebaston, near the
source of the river Brett, there is no inn, but the whole village
has a sign. On a hanging board are two crossed sceptres with
a dove on the head of each, recalling the grant by Henry VI
in 1445 of the manor of Kettlebaston to William de la Pole,
Marquis of Suffolk, to hold by the service of carrying a golden
sceptre with a golden dove upon the head of it at the coronation of all future kings of England, and an ivory sceptre with
a golden dove upon it at the coronation of all future queens.

CHAPTER VI

IPSWICH

IPSWICH, the capital of East Suffolk and by far the largest town in the county, though it claims to have been an inhabited place since Neolithic times, is as modern as this morning's newspaper. The nervous schoolboy who was asked if Ipswich was an ancient town and replied: "It used to be, sir," was not so foolish as might be supposed. Most of the evidence of its antiquity has been disguised if not obliterated. To-day it is the great power-house of Suffolk, a thriving modern port which is, in fact, the largest between the Humber and the Thames, a place of the present and the future rather than of the past. But in spite of its modern façade, evidence of its long history is still to be found. Archaeologists are able to point out traces of the Ipswich of a thousand years ago, whose inhabitants were called out to resist the marauding Danes. For centuries it was a fortified town, with ramparts maintained at considerable cost to the inhabitants from Saxon days to the Commonwealth.

The most devastating of these Viking attacks was launched in 993, when Anlaf sailed up the Orwell with ninety-three ships and sacked the town. In 1010 the Danes again landed in force, vanquishing the Saxons who fought under Earl Ulfketel on Rushmere and Kesgrave heaths, where numerous tumuli, particularly those near Orwell railway station known as the "Seven Hills," traditionally mark the burial-grounds of the slain. Reminders of this heroic past remain in such names as Tower Ramparts, where one fragment at least of the old defences can still be seen. These Saxon earthworks ran from the east end of Carr Street up Old Foundry Road, which was formerly called St. Margaret's Ditches, across Northgate Street and along Tower Ramparts and Crown Street to turn towards the river down Lady Lane; they continued in the same direction down Tanners Lane and behind

Friars Road, then turned to run eastward along College Street and Key Street, where they took a northward turn to reach Carr Street again by way of Lower and Upper Orwell Streets. Houses at the lower end of Lady Lane stand two or three feet above the street level, on an embankment that is part of the old ramparts.

Westgate Street and Northgate Street remind us of two of the gates leading into the old town, though the gates themselves have disappeared. The West Gate was demolished in 1780, the North Gate in 1794, and even the names of the south and east gates are no longer in use. Lady Lane preserves in its name the memory of the chapel of "Our Lady of Grace," which stood at the north-west corner. An image of the Virgin in this ancient chapel was reputed to have miraculous healing powers, and pilgrims from all over East Anglia might be seen making their way towards it throughout the Middle Ages. When Henry VIII stayed with Lord Curzon in Silent Street he attended mass in this chapel, but when Wolsey fell from power Henry ordered the shrine to be dismantled, knowing how much this action would humiliate the Cardinal in the minds of his fellow citizens. The image was despoiled of its jewels and carried to London, where it was cast into a public bonfire.

Such memories of its past as these can be indulged along many of the old streets of Ipswich, but the romantic antiquary will be wise to keep away from the main thoroughfares. The bustling Cornhill of the twentieth century is not the place for him to allow his imagination to recreate scenes from its history, interesting as these may be. But at home, when the lamp is lit and the fire burns brightly, he may think of the old market-cross that stood nearly opposite Lloyds Bank. It was a circular building, with a dome supported by Doric pillars and decorated with grotesque carved heads, one of which held a butcher's knife in his mouth. In the centre of the dome stood a figure of Justice. This curious old cross stood on Cornhill for nearly two hundred years, and before it another cross, erected by Edmund Daundy of Ipswich in 1510, occupied the same site. The butcher's knife in the carving was significant because the old Shambles stood where the post office stands now.

Bull-baiting was a common sight on the old Cornhill, for between the reign of Edward III and 1793—the year in which the Shambles were pulled down—it was an offence for an Ipswich butcher to sell the flesh of a bull that had not been baited for one hour on the Cornhill before it was killed. Unbaited meat was not considered fit for people to eat.

In the same place the people of Ipswich witnessed an exhibition of human cruelty much more serious than bull-baiting. Several martyrs were burnt at the stake there in Mary's reign. Of one of them, Nicholas Peke of Earl Stonham, we read that when the faggots were blazing at his feet Dr. Reading called out: "Peke, recant thy opinion, and I have thy pardon in my hand." To which Peke replied with vigour: "I defy it and thee."

In 1812 both the market-cross and the moot hall were demolished and the centre of Ipswich completely transformed. The old town was determined to be in the forefront of nineteenth-century progress. But if we make our way from the Cornhill of to-day down St. Nicholas Street we find an inscription on a chemist's shop recording that "near this fifteenth-century house on the opposite side of the way stood in 1472 the home of Robert and Joan Wolsey, where the great child of honour Thomas Wolsey . . . passed his boyhood." Opposite this house is the Hippodrome, and the site of Robert Wolsey's house is the open space in front of the building. This, however, is not the site of Wolsey's birthplace. He was born in St. Mary Elms parish, from which his father moved soon after the portentous birth.

No name is more commonly associated with Ipswich than Wolsey's. Shakespeare, we may recall, in generous mood wrote of him that:

> From his cradle
> He was a scholar, and a ripe and good one;
> And though he were unsatisfied in getting,
> (Which was a sin) yet, in bestowing, Madame,
> He was most princely.

But there is little evidence that Wolsey was ever princely in bestowing except to promote his own interests. He was at the height of his power and an extremely wealthy man when he founded his college in Ipswich, but he disestablished several Suffolk monasteries in order to raise funds for it, pleading in defence of his action that the monks were irreligious and immoral.

Robert Wolsey seems to have been as unscrupulous in his dealings as Thomas himself. He had many irons in the Ipswich fires. We know that he was a butcher because he was fined for selling bad meat. He was also an innkeeper to our knowledge, for he was frequently in trouble for allowing his house to be used for illegal purposes, or, to be precise, for " permitting friars and women of loose character to haunt his premises." He was also charged with selling bread at excessive prices, which does not mean that he was a baker. In his day it was the custom to buy bread in alehouses. He was also a farmer. Butchering, innkeeping, and farming go well together; but in addition to following these callings with more profit than integrity, Robert Wolsey is credited with having been a wool merchant. This industry was prosperous in Ipswich during his lifetime, so it is quite probable that this astute business man invested some of his savings in it, even if he did not participate actively in the management of the trade. But in spite of his offences, and they were not so serious in his day as they would be in ours, Robert Wolsey achieved the social status of being elected a churchwarden.

The streets in this low-lying part of Ipswich have lost their former elegance, but they still bear evidence of the prosperity of the fifteenth and sixteenth-century woolmen. Among the more interesting curiosities preserved from this exuberant period are several elaborately carved corner-posts. There is one in good preservation at the junction of Silent Street with St. Nicholas Street. It is carved out of a single piece of Suffolk oak—as most of them are—and is ornamented with lion heads and other designs that were in favour during the Renaissance.

Proceeding down St. Nicholas Street and St. Peter's Street we reach College Street, and there we find all that remains of Wolsey's College in the gateway of Tudor brick charged with the arms of Henry VIII. This was probably an unimportant riverside gateway. It was certainly not the main entrance. The building of this "College of Secular Canons," as he termed it, was begun by Wolsey in 1528, and the occasion celebrated in a procession to the shrine of the Virgin—to whom the college was dedicated—in the chapel of Our Lady of Grace in Lady Lane. He intended to establish here a school that would surpass both Winchester and Eton, and serve as a nursery for his own college at Oxford. If he had remained in power long enough his design might have succeeded, for after the suppression of so many monasteries in its favour Wolsey's College must have enjoyed enormous revenues. The building was never completed, but it reached a stage where it was able to accommodate boys from all over the kingdom.

When Wolsey fell from power in the autumn of 1529, those who had suffered from his rapacity were only too ready to take their revenge. He was extremely unpopular even in his native Suffolk. The woolmen were no less his enemies than the monks whose abbeys he had plundered. It was to him that Henry had looked when money was needed to finance the war with France, and Wolsey had found part of it by imposing a heavy capital levy on the woolmen. Later he became even more unpopular with them when his own policy involved the nation in a quarrel with Flanders, a valuable market for Suffolk cloth, and with Spain, from which the weavers got their oil. So when Wolsey fell from power the people of Suffolk were quick to raid the property he had controlled or owned. One of the college estates was at Hintlesham, four miles out of Ipswich, and there a tenant named Thomas Veysy led a number of his neighbours in cutting down trees and stealing cattle. Thomas Veysy also encouraged the tenants to withhold their rents, saying publicly: "My Lord Cardinal is not worthy to wipe his horse's feet."

In November 1529 the college was visited by Henry's agents, who said they were searching for £10,000 of Wolsey's treasure which they insisted was hidden there. At the same time they took an inventory of the property, and on leaving carried many of the more valuable things away with them. The dean, in reporting the matter, used a delightfully cryptic expression: "I entertained them as well as my wits served," he wrote. In October of the following year this ill-fated college was officially dissolved, and all its possessions passed to the Crown. On hearing of this, Wolsey wrote: "I am much indisposed and put from my sleep and meat in consequence of the news of the dissolution of my colleges. I cannot write for weeping and sorrow."

When Wolsey founded his college the revenues of the old grammar school were transferred to it, but when the college was dissolved, Henry VIII re-established the grammar school by a charter which was later confirmed and ratified by Elizabeth. The present Ipswich School, an independent public school with extensive premises in Henley Road, has developed from this ancient school, founded as long ago as the reign of Edward IV, and housed in its early days in the Convent of Black Friars in Foundation Street.

Foundation Street branches off Lower Brook Street, nearly opposite the point where College Street joins it. At the junction of Lower Brook Street with Foundation Street the most amusing of the Ipswich corner-posts is found on what was formerly the "Half Moon" Inn. This represents the fable of the fox and the geese. On one side the sly fox is depicted in friar's habit preaching to a congregation of geese. On the other side he has discarded his cunning disguise and is in the act of carrying off one of the foolish birds, or, as another version of the fable has it, on one side the young fox preaches to the geese, while on the other the old fox carries off the gander. This was undoubtedly intended to be a satire on the friars, whose convent ran along the whole of one side of Foundation Street. There was much opposition to these preaching friars. They were ridiculed even by religious people, and were always unpopular with the beneficed clergy, though in Ipswich at all events these do not appear to have been much better than the friars they criticised. When a certain Gilbert Debenham was returning home after a visit to the Ipswich cheese-market in 1475, he was suddenly attacked at three o'clock in the afternoon by five men, three of whom were clergy holding livings in the neighbourhood.

At the present No. 34 Foundation Street, or in a house that stood on the same site, Gainsborough lived soon after his marriage. Ipswich at the time would have a population of not more than ten thousand. It had much less enterprise than to-day, but not less gaiety. Gainsborough loved good company. He was a talented fiddler and a member of a musicial society that met at the "Waggon and Horses" Inn. Constable said he was usually the butt of the company, and that his wig in particular amused his friends. It was rather too dandified for the plain East Anglians, and was often snatched from his head and tossed about the room. Brook Street, which existed as "Broc Street" as early as Henry III's reign, was formerly the fashionable quarter of the town. In Upper Brook Street, which runs up to Tavern Street, on the site of Messrs. E. L. Hunt's shop, not of the "Coach and Horses" as used to be said, stood the mansion of the gallant Charles Brandon, Duke of Suffolk and grandfather of Lady Jane Grey. To this house he brought his young bride, Mary Tudor, the daughter of Henry VII who had been married as a girl to the elderly Louis XII of France, and by his death a few months later had become free to marry a more suitable husband. She and the Duke must have provided much excitement for the people of Ipswich whenever they drove along its cobbled streets. Near them lived Wolsey, who succeeded in re-establishing them in the favour of Henry VIII, whom they had offended by not asking him to sanction their marriage.

Every street in this part of Ipswich is rich in history, and retains at least a few specimens of the kind of architecture now more familiar in the smaller Suffolk towns. In Fore Street, for example, there are several sixteenth-century houses. One with high gables and neat plaster panelling will probably catch the eye, though shop windows have been fitted on the ground floor, and on the first floor only one has the original arched transom. It is to the gables we must look for the genuine sixteenth-century windows, which are good examples and remind us of similar windows at Hadleigh. The "Neptune" in the same street, a seventeenth-century building with elaborately carved timbers in good preservation, began as the home of a rich merchant. Then, like the "Bull" at Long Melford, it was converted into an inn, which in course of time became a famous rendezvous, known to sailors in half the world's ports. It was also reputed to be a favourite haunt of smugglers. Now it has settled down into a mellow and inoffensive old age as a private house. Another house in Fore Street is believed to have been the home of George Cavendish, Wolsey's biographer. And it is from Fore Street that we turn down Angel Lane to find at the bottom the passage where Sam Weller saw Job Trotter emerge from a green gate.

But all this time we are wandering round Ipswich in this rather inconsequent manner before coming to the three buildings that every visitor must sooner or later seek out. These, surely, are "Sparrowe's House," the "Great White Horse," and Christchurch Mansion. As "Sparrowe's House" is nearest we must visit it first. Every visitor to Ipswich who finds his way into the Butter Market gazes in wonder at this almost incredible building, now Messrs. Harrison's excellent bookshop. On the first floor it has five oriel windows with round-topped leaded lights. Four of these face the Butter Market, the fifth faces St. Stephen's Lane. They are lovely windows, with their arched transoms and curved glazing shadowed by the wide eaves above them. Nothing about the house delights my own eye so much as these. But the most remarkable feature is, of course, the elaborate emblematic pargeting. Below the Butter Market windows Europe, Asia, Africa and America are represented. The fifth window might be expected to bear the symbol of another continent, but when the house was built Australia was still unknown to England. Instead of having an emblematic representation of this fifth continent, the window in St. Stephen's Lane has a kneeling figure of Atlas, bearded and carrying the world on his shoulders. In the corner is a pretty pastoral scene illustrating the first eclogue of Virgil. The shepherd Tityrus, who reposes under a tree, represents, no doubt, the wool trade for which Ipswich was the port as well as being itself an important manufacturing centre.

The whole of the upper storey is covered with parge work of the most ornate design. Fruit and flowers intertwined with human and animal heads are figured in the moulding, while along the seventy feet of frontage on the ground floor there are eleven windows and two doorways framed in moulded oak.

The pargeting on "Sparrowe's House" is believed to date from a few years after the Restoration, and is similar in character to the work we get at the end of all periods of artistic development, just before the inevitable return to simplicity. Elaboration has gone to fantastic lengths here, and though "Sparrowe's House"—or the Ancient House, as it is often called—is an extremely interesting example of the last stages of pargeting in the late seventeenth century, the student of the history of art will realise in looking at it how inevitable was the severe classicism that followed it, and what a relief this must have been. To those of us who feel acutely the pressure of the over-elaboration of social life in our own day the question might well arise, whether in the social sphere a return to severely disciplined simplicity is not inevitable as a reaction from the chaotic hithering and thithering of this first half of the twentieth century.

The Sparrowe family, who occupied the house for about two hundred years, were ardent royalists and there is a tradition that Charles II was concealed here after the Battle of Worcester. How he contrived to reach Ipswich we are not told, and the only conceivable reason that could persuade any-one to believe the story is that advanced by Mr. Redstone, who suggested that it might be true because this would be about the least likely place in the kingdom for his enemies to search for him! A secret attic chamber was discovered at the beginning of last century when a workman fell through the roof into it, and this, it is said, was the king's hiding-place. The story, of course, is entirely without foundation.

And now it may be thought time to visit that famous Ipswich establishment, the "Great White Horse," mentioned as early as 1528, from which Tavern Street takes its name. It was here that Mr. Pickwick had his famous adventure with the middle-aged lady in yellow curl-papers, so vivaciously related by Dickens in Chapter XXII of *Pickwick Papers*. Anyone who has stayed at the "Great White Horse," no matter how sober his habits, will not be surprised that Mr. Pickwick lost his way along that web of passages and reached the wrong bedroom. It is a mistake I have nearly made myself, and I can assure you that it is one that Dickens was wise to discourage. Mr. Pickwick's room, No. 36, is still indicated to visitors.

Dickens himself stayed at the "Great White Horse" for two or three weeks in 1835, and on at least three subsequent occasions, so the house cannot have been so uninviting as the description in *Pickwick Papers* would lead us to suppose. Certainly we cannot compare the "large, badly furnished" room described there, "with a dirty grate, in which a small fire was making a wretched attempt to be cheerful, but was fast sinking beneath the dispiriting influence of the place," with any room in the "Great White Horse" of to-day.

Christchurch Mansion, our third place of special interest, is found opposite the end of Northgate Street that is farthest from the "Great White Horse," and all who wish to get a clear picture of the social history of Ipswich should visit it. The mansion was built between 1548 and 1550 by Sir Edmund Withypoll, a stubborn old gentleman who was frequently at loggerheads with the local authorities, and the estate was bought and presented to Ipswich in 1894 by Mr. Felix T. Cobbold, M.P. In crossing the park in order to reach the mansion we may be amused to recall one of the few disparaging references to Ipswich that has been placed on record. While Lord Rochester, a typical Restoration buck, was staying at Christchurch Mansion he saw the park-keeper rolling the lawn and noticed that the donkeys drawing the roller had leather pads over their hoofs to protect the turf. This caused him to write of Ipswich that it was "a town without inhabitants, a river without water, streets without names, and where the asses wore boots." Ipswich, a town exceptionally well provided with open spaces, is fortunate in having this fine park so near its busy thoroughfares.

In the great rooms of Christchurch Mansion we are back in the spacious days of Tudor and Restoration England. In the kitchen, with its wide, arched fireplace and roasting spit worked by a draught mill in the chimney, we can imagine the excitement there must have been when Charles II was expected. The servants' hall has Jacobean panelling and an elaborately carved overmantel. Panelling of the same period is found in the study, with the arms of Charles I on the back plate of the fireplace. In addition to the fitted examples of

Suffolk woodwork there are many interesting specimens which have been brought to the museum from old houses that have been dismantled, including several corner-posts, and there is some delightful modern needlework.

In the Tudor wing we see linen-fold panels and moulded beams that date from the end of Henry VII's reign, together with an Elizabethan mantelpiece, a Jacobean mantelpiece, and seventeenth-century murals. Wolsey is remembered not in the earliest but in the latest part of the building, for a picture gallery, added on the four hundredth anniversary of his death in 1533, is a memorial to him. Other distinguished Ipswich men and women have memorials in various parts of the mansion. There is a Wingfield room with oak panelling and a sixteenth-century overmantel brought from the Wingfield house in Tacket Street, the street where, incidentally, David Garrick is recalled, for he made his first public appearance at the old Theatre Royal there. In Room 13 there are memorials of Nelson, who bought a house in Ipswich with the intention of retiring there, and of Captain Broke, commander of the *Shannon*, which captured the American frigate *Chesapeake* in 1813, while in the FitzGerald Room we find portraits of Edward FitzGerald himself, Thomas Woolner, Thomas Clarkson the abolitionist, with other Suffolk worthies, and Margaret Catchpole, the heroine of Richard Cobbold's popular Suffolk story, a courageous young woman with whom we must renew our acquaintance presently.

Nowhere else in the county is the history and character of Suffolk so worthily represented. It is here that we discover what a very distinguished part she has always played in the nation's life. After spending a few hours among its treasures we are better able to appreciate the buildings we have already inspected in the town itself, and will be all the more ready to notice others. The old house in St. Margaret's Plain will catch our eye on leaving if it had not already done so, and as we return down Northgate Street, past the Public Library, with its reference room well stocked with borough and county records, we cannot fail to stop to examine the Archdeacon's Gate, built in 1471 by William Pykenham, Archdeacon of Suffolk and dean of Stoke College, and the half-timbered house below it. This substantial old house has another inter-

esting corner-post at the junction of Oak Lane with Northgate Street. This one represents a blacksmith working at
his forge, an elaborate piece of work probably commissioned
by John Bemit, a bladesmith who lived here at one time.
The bases, caps, and angle-shafts are Gothic in treatment,
while the scroll ornaments on the sides seem to suggest a
foreign influence.

Christchurch Mansion is a museum of general interest, but
with a special appeal to the student of social history. The
Corporation Museum in High Street, with its departments of
general and local natural history, archaeology and ethnology,
is of more interest to the scientist. Marine shells and fossils
from the coastal crags and sand-banks are displayed in one
room, and in the archaeological and ethnological galleries
on the first floor Palaeolithic implements and flaked flints
that attract specialists from all over the world. This remarkable collection was made by the late J. Reid Moir, F.R.S.,
for many years president of the museum, who interpreted the
prehistory of Suffolk with so much learning and insight.
Here may be seen evidence which carries the history of
Ipswich back to the Beaker period, 2000 years B.C.

One of the most interesting exhibits in Ipswich Museum
is the letter written by Margaret Catchpole to her mistress
just before going into exile. The story of Margaret Catchpole is to Suffolk what the story of Lorna Doone is to Devon,
though not so well known outside the county. Cobbold was
not the master of romantic narrative that Blackmore was, but
in this one book he mingled fact and fancy so convincingly
that the characters seem as real to us as the members of our
own household. The story is substantially true, and no one
knew the facts in it better than the author. He was a member
of the family with whom Margaret Catchpole lived as a
trusted and respected domestic servant, and he made her so
real to others that the Cobbolds' house, at the junction of
St. Margaret's Street with St. Margaret's Green, now the headquarters of the Ipswich branch of the British Legion, is still
called Margaret Catchpole's House.

John Cobbold, head of the household and husband of the
lady to whom Margaret wrote letters frequently, was an
Ipswich brewer whose family and firm still flourish in the

town. This is hardly surprising perhaps, for John Cobbold had sixteen children by his first wife, fourteen of whom were living when he married his second wife, by whom he had six more. As for his business, the number of inn signs on which the Cobbold name appears to-day is sufficient testimony to its prosperity. The second Mrs. Cobbold used to say that when she married, the only books in the house were Bibles and account books. With so many births recorded in its pages the Family Bible itself must have been something of an account book. Perhaps the two were equally indispensable. Many of the largest businesses of the period were built up on Scriptural precept securely linked with sound finance. Whatever the secret of his success may have been, John Cobbold prospered so continuously that after bringing up that large family he was able to provide a university education for each of his two youngest sons—his twenty-first and twenty-second children—and afterwards to buy for each of them a benefice worth approximately a thousand pounds a year.

The story of the ploughman's daughter who was so devoted to the Cobbold family, until she made her one fatal mistake, seems all the more tragic when her lot is contrasted with theirs. Margaret was born in 1773 not far from the "Seven Hills" already mentioned as the site of the battle between Earl Ulfketel and the Danes. It was still a tract of waste land during her wild and carefree girlhood. She learnt to ride while still a child, and in course of time became a fearless and tireless horsewoman. Her lover, Will Laud, was the son of the ferryman who plied between Harwich and Landguard Fort. He was a clever and likeable youth, and he and Margaret were a promising young couple until Will was enticed into joining a band of smugglers, attracted, no doubt, by love of adventure no less than by hope of gain. The requisites of a capital story can easily be discerned in these circumstances, but the end was tragic. One night Margaret stole a horse from her master's stable and rode it to London in order to join her lover there. The following morning she was detected in the act of selling it. She was brought to Bury St. Edmunds, where, in accordance with the law, she was tried and sentenced to death. John Cobbold intervened on her behalf and succeeded in getting the sentence commuted

Bell cage, East Bergholt

to seven years' imprisonment. Margaret, however, made the foolish mistake of breaking out of gaol, and was thereupon sentenced to transportation for life.

Richard Cobbold rounds off the story with a happy ending, but for this he had no evidence. When a Catchpole Research Committee was set up to investigate the circumstances of Margaret's exile it only succeeded in discovering the entry recording her death in the register of St. Peter's, Richmond, New South Wales.

The people of Suffolk are not usually credited with being either romantic or sentimental, but their minds continue to dwell fondly on the story of Margaret Catchpole. It probably means more to most of them than the associations of the many eminent men and women who have lived in the county. They remember, too, their royal visitors, and being practical people they keep careful records of the money spent in entertaining their Sovereigns. These accounts are, in fact, rather interesting. We find, for example, that when Queen Elizabeth visited Ipswich in 1561 the Corporation spent what was then the large sum of £134 9s. 4d. Of this, £34 19s. 2d. was spent in cooking, and 4s. in "benevolence," which I take to mean tipping—evidently still an undeveloped art! William III, who visited the town in 1693, cost the Corporation only £30 19s. 5d., and Charles II, curiously enough, who was there in 1668, only reduced the exchequer balances by £39 12s. 8d. When George II reached the town from Lowestoft, where he had just landed in 1736, he was received at the North Gate by the Corporation and accompanied to the "Great White Horse," but after an address of welcome from Mr. Bailiff Sparrowe, "His Majesty being much fatigued, they soon after retired."

Perhaps the most successful visitor from the point of view of the progress and publicity that Ipswich early set its heart on was Cobbett. He wrote of it as "a fine, populous, and beautiful place," and found it "substantially built, well paved, everything good and solid, and no wretched buildings to be seen on its outskirts." Everything about Ipswich filled him with enthusiasm. From a hill outside he counted seventeen windmills, all whitewashed and with black sails. Of all the great men who have praised Ipswich, Cobbett is the one

Boxford Church

we recall with the greatest satisfaction because Ipswich is still Cobbett's sort of town.

We cannot feel quite so confident of Evelyn's enthusiasm if he could return after the passage of nearly three hundred years. On the 8th July, 1656, he wrote that it was "doubtless one of the sweetest, most pleasant, well-built townes in England." Twenty-one years later he was still of the same opinion, as we may see from his diary entry of 10th September, 1677. Every industrial town has its black spots, and it is no use pretending that Ipswich is free from them. It has a good deal of cleaning-up to do. Docks inevitably produce grime, and there are nearly thirty acres of docks in Ipswich. It has rows of drab, monotonous houses, as every town that developed rapidly during the nineteenth century has, but it has pleasant residential suburbs, particularly those on the upland by-pass leading to Woodbridge. Some are situated in breezy pine woods, and it is evident that these bright, modern houses have drawn many of the younger people from the less progressive towns and villages.

This modernising movement began in Ipswich about a century and a half ago, when the local merchants were so much alive to the prospects of expanding trade that they began to discuss the development of their port. In 1805 seventy-two gentlemen of the town formed themselves into a body of River Commissioners and secured from Parliament the right of "deepening, widening, cleansing, altering and otherwise improving" the stretch of river between Stoke Bridge and Levington Creek. They were also granted the right to levy duties on shipping and goods entering the port. Their enterprise prospered continuously, and in 1839 the construction of a new dock was begun, which when completed four years later made the harbour of Ipswich the largest wet dock in Great Britain. For this purpose the Orwell was diverted into a new channel, leaving a deep reach of the river at this point for use as the dock. The new cut which was made is now the popular pleasure resort of the town. From here steamboats sail to Harwich, Dovercourt and Felixstowe, and every summer there is a regatta.

The progress of Ipswich during the present century has been no less remarkable than during the last. In 1904 eight hundred feet of quay was added, with a further thousand between 1923 and 1925, and six hundred more completed in 1929. More than half a million tons of cargo was handled in the port in 1945, and this figure is expected to be doubled with the resumption of normal trading conditions. During the war years a great part of the dock was taken over by the Admiralty.

The town itself is just as enterprising. It is a hive of thriving industries, particularly of the engineering type. Every kind of agricultural machinery is manufactured here. The first lawn-mower was made in Ipswich. The famous Stoney sluice-gate, used for irrigation work in many parts of the world, is an Ipswich invention, and the town has a great variety of smaller, specialised industries. It has a modern airport, officially opened in 1938, and is in every way fitted for the leading part it plays in the life of East Anglia. It might appear that the whole of this otherwise quiet and apparently unprogressive county had been storing up energy for hundreds of years to produce this thriving borough, or, to put the idea in another way, as though a good old Suffolk couple had been putting away their savings all their lives in order to set up this fine healthy son of theirs in business. No doubt many an Ipswich tradesman is just such a son, for besides enterprise and efficiency Ipswich has about it an air of the country-bred.

On market day Ipswich is a grand sight. Ruddy-faced countrymen in riding-breeches and well-polished leggings shout hearty greetings across Tavern Street or the Butter Market. However slowly a man may saunter along the streets of his own sleepy little town he comes to life in Ipswich and bustles good-humouredly about his business. The town is only twelve miles from the sea, so the air is fresh and keen. The small groups of people come together and break up quickly after a friendly joke or brief exchange of news. No one ever seems to hesitate for a reply here. Wits are sharp. The shops are well stocked and efficiently run, and everything about the business side of the town is in good trim.

A little over a hundred years ago—in 1841 to be exact—the population of Ipswich was about twenty-five thousand. Fifty years later it was double that figure, and to-day it is

believed to be about a hundred thousand. Its future will
be worth watching, for the town is fighting fit. Perhaps its
long history of defence and the attack has contributed to that
character, for we have to remember all along the Suffolk coast
that these are the people who have guarded our shores for
more than a thousand years. Anyone who requires to be
reassured about the resources of the English character should
spend a few days in Ipswich. It is a town with a future
worthy of its past.

Chapter VII

THE GIPPING AND THE ORWELL

THREE of Suffolk's long, meandering rivers, the Stour, the Orwell, and the Deben, flow into the North Sea in the south-east corner of the county. Each has a wide, navigable estuary more than ten miles in length, and as they enter the sea almost together they are like three arms of a giant octopus. The Orwell is the middle arm, and with Ipswich at the head of its tidal waters it has enjoyed or suffered, according to the way such progress is viewed, greater industrial development than the other two. The twelve miles between Ipswich and the sea are navigable to large vessels, while beyond Ipswich, where the same river is called the Gipping, the further sixteen miles to Stowmarket were navigable to barges practically throughout the nineteenth century. Its locks are now in decay, in one place providing a picturesque waterfall, while in another the river has changed its course and left the lock entirely. Both the lower and upper reaches of the river are rich in history.

The Gipping rises from several springs north-west of Stow-market, and near each of the rivulets stands a manor-house that was formerly the home of a distinguished family. At Gipping, the village with the same name as the river, lived the Tyrrells, a family long settled in Suffolk, and previously at Langham in Essex. Over an arch leading into the vestry of its small church an inscription bids those who kneel before the altar "Pray for S. James Tyrell and Dame Anne his wyf." Sir James, it is believed, was responsible for carrying out Richard III's order that the Princes in the Tower should be put to death, and is said to have built the church at Gipping in expiation of his share in the crime. A tradition in the neighbourhood would have us believe that immediately afterwards he abandoned the court and spent the rest of his life as a country gentleman; but this cannot be true, for we find that he held appointments under both Richard III and Henry VII.

Authorities are not agreed as to how far Sir James Tyrrell was involved in the plan to murder the princes. Some would even acquit him, in spite of his alleged confession. The most reliable evidence appears to be that of Sir Thomas More. According to him, Richard III ordered the constable of the Tower to put the princes to death, and when he refused commanded him to hand the keys to Sir James Tyrrell, who entered with his two servants, Miles Forrest and John Dighton, and these two henchmen smothered the princes with the pillows of their bed while Sir James stood at the foot of the stairs directing them.

In 1502 Sir James was himself put to death for his part in assisting his friend Edmund de la Pole, Earl of Suffolk, to escape from the country, a judgment that appears ironic when we learn that the earl himself was pardoned and restored to favour.

A later member of the same family, Sir John Tyrrell, was an ardent Roman Catholic and a friend of Sir John Sulyard of Wetherden, another small village in the neighbourhood. In the parish of Harleston, on the road from Haughley to Harleston, there is a common called Rush Green. On the left, near a fork in the road, lies a block of stone which is said to be the place where Sir John Sulyard and Sir John Tyrrell burnt their victims at the stake during the Marian persecutions. This green is on high ground, and is thus comparable with the place on Aldham Common where Rowland Taylor gave his life as a Protestant martyr.

Sir John Sulyard was one of the first to take up arms in support of Mary against those who had enlisted in the service of Lady Jane Grey. The Sulyards had made a pretence of conforming with the reformed religion, but had continued to attend mass celebrated by Roman Catholic priests in a cottage at Wetherden, a village that was evidently divided in its allegiance, for besides the records we possess of the support that Sir John Sulyard gave Mary, we are assured that on the other side Lady Jane's followers met in the dining-room of a house here.

On her accession, Mary rewarded Sir John by making him

a present of the manor and park of Haughley, another village in this historic cluster at the head of the Gipping. Haughley had previously been held by Charles Brandon, Duke of Suffolk, who had lived with his wife, Mary Tudor, at Westhorpe nearby in a hall that has since been pulled down. That Lady Jane Grey had supporters in the neighbourhood is not surprising when we remember that she was the granddaughter of Charles Brandon and Mary Tudor.

We have already mentioned this romantic couple while walking along the crowded pavements of Brook Street, Ipswich. Here in these quiet villages we may allow ourselves more leisure to reflect upon their story. Charles Brandon was acknowledged to be one of the most handsome and accomplished young noblemen of his day when Mary fell in love with him. Marriage, however, was out of the question when her imperious brother, Henry VIII, announced that he had other designs for her. But when she was married to the elderly and ailing Louis XII of France, Brandon was allowed to accompany her as one of her attendants, a convenient arrangement that was nearly frustrated soon after the wedding when the jealous Louis dismissed all his wife's friends from his court. Brandon, however, now created Duke of Suffolk, was sent back to France at once as ambassador, and the two lovers appear to have conducted themselves with admirable discretion while the king lived, but when he died on the following New Year's Day their patience deserted them. They were married before the end of February, to the great displeasure of Henry and without his consent. Naturally this indelicate haste alienated their friends at the French court, and on returning to England they were obliged to live in retirement while Wolsey interceded on their behalf. Afterwards the Duke enjoyed the King's regard, attending him to the Field of the Cloth of Gold and proving a useful supporter in the plans to divorce Catherine, in which both he and the princess were specially interested, because Anne Boleyn had been one of Mary's attendants when she left England for France.

Haughley, a pleasant old village with thatched and plastered cottages along grass banks bordering the road, is one of the many in East Anglia that were once flourishing market towns.

There is a tradition that sometime during the eighteenth century it was destroyed by fire, and that subscriptions came in from all over the country to enable the inhabitants to rebuild. This, however, was never done to any considerable extent, and it is said that the destruction of Haughley led to the rise of Stowmarket. Scattered ruins, now hardly discernible, spread across seven acres in this parish are all that remain of a castle, probably originally built by Hugh de Montfort soon after the Norman Conquest. This is thought to have been a timber structure that was probably burnt to the ground when attacked by the forces of the Earl of Leicester and Earl Bigod in 1173. The moat remains, and surrounded by a tangle of trees and nettles stands a modern farmhouse.

Up to the eleventh year of Elizabeth's reign the lord of this manor exercised jurisdiction of Oyer and Terminer, which gave him the right to try all cases in his own court, and also the right of exacting certain duties. Thus the Abbot of Hales, who was impropriator of Haughley, was required to set up a gallows on what is still called Gallow's Field, and it is recorded that a man named Buxton held lands by the sinister service of providing a ladder for the lord's gallows. It is not surprising, therefore, to find that a barn that stood near this field was said to be haunted.

All round this area the place-names indicate stirring events in the history of these remote and inoffensive parishes. The ancient Battle of Stone Cross was fought near Newton Hall, and fragments of Roman and other early pottery found in the district bear witness of its long record as an inhabited region.

Old Newton, between Haughley and Gipping, was the birthplace of John Mole, a farm labourer who became a well-known mathematician and the author of at least two books on algebra. This was one of the estates of another prominent Roman Catholic, Margaret Pole, Countess of Salisbury, who was governess to Princess Mary, afterwards queen, until Henry VIII dismissed her for refusing to give up her mistress's jewels to Anne Boleyn. When Anne was beheaded the Countess returned to the court, but was always under suspicion because she was known to have Roman Catholic sympathies. In 1541, when in her seventieth year, she was beheaded without trial soon after news reached London that the Roman Catholics in the North were again in revolt.

There may be many more important things to record about Mendlesham, a village north-east of Haughley, but there is one record that specially endears it to me. In glancing through the list of local charities I found that a building for use partly as an almshouse and partly as a school was given by Peter Duck, and that twelve tenements to be occupied rent-free were given by Robert Cake. Two closes called Birds and land called Salmons are also listed among the charities, but their donors are not named. There is something pleasant in the thought of the priest and people of Mendlesham praying for the souls of Peter Duck and Robert Cake.

For most of the records of these ancient villages we must rummage through dusty old libraries or county archives. But this is by no means a tedious undertaking, for many of our English chroniclers have been witty and companionable men who have written not as dry-as-dust know-alls, but as men with a pint of good ale at their side. Such research, however, is not the only means of reviving our knowledge of the past. Spread across this little known district in the heart of Suffolk, all within a few miles of Stowmarket, there are no fewer than a score of moated manor-houses now used as farmhouses, and these have the story of the rise and fall of as many families written in their mellow brick and crumbling timbers. But as I glance at the map in order to refresh my memory with their names, my eye catches another name that I must mention first. It is Mickfield, a place between Stowmarket and Debenham on the map, though no road connects them. I have never been to Mickfield, and the name must have caught my eye in order to reproach me for neglect, for I have a special reason for desiring to visit it. In reading White's *Gazetteer of Suffolk* I remember how that painstaking worthy suddenly brightened its workaday page with a recollection of two fields in this parish that were covered with snake's-head lily when he was there. Ever since I read of this, I have promised myself a visit to Mickfield, so I here make a vow that next spring I will go in search of those two fields, and at the same time I will seek out two other places, delightfully

named—Four Elms and Three Pies. Both are near the
beckoning village of Mickfield.

Another name on the map catches my eye. It is the name
that did, in fact, first set me on the trail of those moated
manor-houses near Stowmarket. It is Columbyne Hall in the
parish of Stowupland, which I found to be an old house with
Tudor chimneys and foundations lapped by the waters of its
ancient moat. Other old manor-houses worth recalling are
Wetherden Hall, the home of the Sulyards, Rockyll's Hall at
the top of Shelland Green, and Broughton Hall at Stonham
Aspall, also with massive Tudor chimneys, once a seat of
the Wingfield family. Each of these fine old manors has its
story. In the moat at Cotton Hall, north of Gipping, a gold
cup was found towards the end of the eighteenth century.
Fasbourne or Copinger Hall at Buxhall, a little to the west
of Stowmarket, was the seat of the Copingers for centuries.
This family was so famous for its wealth and hospitality that
"to live like the Copingers" was a proverb in the county.
The forty-fifth lord of the manor was the eminent antiquary,
Dr. W. A. Copinger, who was also lord of the manor of
Cockerells, where he resided and housed part of his library of
thirty thousand volumes. We have already become acquainted
with the Copinger name at Lavenham, but perhaps the most
engaging of the older Copinger references is to Walter Copinger, whom Henry VIII granted permission to "use and
wear his bonnet upon his said head as well in our presence
as elsewhere at his liberty." He suffered, we learn, from
some kind of illness that made it desirable that his head
should be protected.

Fasbourne Hall was the family's original homestead, and
was mentioned as early as 1441 in a Copinger will. For two
hundred years it was another of the moated manor-houses
near Stowmarket in use as farmhouses, until Dr. Copinger
bought and restored it. One of the fields on this estate is
less pleasantly named than those we have been surveying. It
is called Bloody Meadow, and the story goes that it was the
scene of a furious fight between two harvesters who quarrelled
while mowing it. They had scythes in their hands and lashed
at each other with such fury that each cut off the other's
head.

Any number of remarkable stories are told in this district. There is the story of the farmer from Stowupland who in 1787 sold his wife to a neighbour for five guineas, and was so glad to be rid of her that he gave her a guinea for a new gown and then ordered the bells of Stowmarket to be rung in celebration.

But we must now leave these villages and make our way into Stowmarket itself, the first town of any size on the Gipping, and built at the confluence of its two principal rivulets. In history and natural beauty Stowmarket is, perhaps, poorer than some of its smaller neighbours. It certainly has less beauty, but in history it may be richer than at first appears. It is probable that some of the tiles in the church are of Roman origin, and in the Finborough Road, where Danecroft stands, numerous flint implements believed to date back to the Early Stone Age have been found. Relics of battles fought by the Saxons in defending their homes against the Danes are to be seen in the neighbourhood, and it is obvious that like every other settlement in this part of Suffolk, Stowmarket has been an inhabited place for a very long time.

What truth there is in the story that the rise of Stowmarket followed the destruction by fire of Haughley I cannot say. Its situation would guarantee it some measure of importance as a market town from an early period. We know that it had a market cross up to about 1685, and two of its inns, the " White Hart" and the " Rose," are fifteenth-century buildings. Like most Suffolk towns it had its wool trade, with a guildhall in the south corner of the churchyard, and from 1486 to 1685 it was a borough.

At one time the monks of St. Osyth's Abbey in Essex had a rest-house here. "Abbot's Hall" occupies the site, and some of the original fish-ponds are still to be seen behind the present house, while in the church there is what is called " The Abbot's Tomb." Such it was long thought to be, but I am now informed that this is doubtful. There are some who believe it belongs to the Tyrrell family, who have a chapel in the church.

The Stowmarket we see to-day is about the same size as Sudbury, but it has made even greater sacrifices to the demands of industrial progress. It has no house that can be compared with Salter's Hall. The last of the succession of Thorney Halls, each in its day the most important house in the town, and from the Norman Conquest to the reign of Henry I the residence of the king's bailiff, was built into the maltings near the station about 1850. It is this kind of depradation that makes Stowmarket one of the least attractive of Suffolk's market towns, though it was probably a pleasant little place when Milton visited it as the guest of its vicar, Dr. Young, who had been his tutor. He marked the occasion by planting in the vicarage garden a mulberry tree, which was blown down as recently as 1939.

After the decline of its wool trade, malting was Stowmarket's principal industry. An ironworks followed in 1816, and after the opening of the railway about the middle of the century its development was rapid and merciless. Now it has a chemical works, an iron foundry, and a Nylon spinning mill, in addition to smaller industries connected with the agricultural needs of the neighbourhood.

The most curious thing about this plain, commercialised, and—I regret to say—in my own experience inhospitable country town is that it is a centre of Suffolk lore. Some of the best fairy tales in the county are told here. The Rev. A. G. H. Hollingworth in his *History of Stowmarket* says that the whole of this hundred is remarkable for its folk-lore. That the hundred is remarkable does not surprise us. Any one of the moated manor-houses just mentioned would be an admirable setting for a ghost story. Now that the haunting of Borley Rectory, just over the Essex border from Sudbury, has been fully investigated, we may be introduced to a haunted house in the heart of Suffolk! Several of the families here could provide suitable subjects. Sir James Tyrrell himself, with the princes on his conscience, may still be restless. The centre of Suffolk should be one of the happiest hunting-grounds for those who have a flare for starting spirits. But that Stowmarket itself should be the haunt of fairies seems incredible. Yet we learn that these little people used to be seen in several houses in Tavern Street, and that the tenants used to hide in order to catch a glimpse of them. Mr. Hollingworth's parish clerk had many tales of the Stowmarket fairies. They were seen on one occasion by a wood-stack near the brick-yard. There was a whole crowd of them, dancing, singing, and playing fairy music, but as soon as they knew they had been seen they vanished. Here is the statement, taken from Hollingworth, of a man who saw them near the Bury road: "Their dresses sparkled as if with spangles like the girls at shows at Stow Fair; they were moving round hand in hand in a ring; no noise came from them. They seemed light and shadowy, not like solid bodies. I passed on, saying: 'The Lord have mercy on me, but them must be fairies,' and being alone there on the path over the field I could see them as plain as I do you. I looked after them when I got over the stile, and they were there just the same, moving round and round. . . . I might be forty yards from them, and I did not like to stop and stare at them. I was quite sober at the time."

One cottage where an old man lived alone was used by the fairies for their meetings. In return for his hospitality they kept the good man's cottage clean and tidy, supplied him with faggots for his fire, and even filled his oven with wood each night so that it would be dry for him to light his fire with the following morning. Having done all this they slipped a shilling under the leg of a chair for him to discover when he drew up to his table for breakfast. The fairy who was his special friend often warned him that he must never tell his neighbours about his fairy visitors, nor of the firewood they brought him. And, of course, he must keep the shillings a secret or he might not be able to buy his bread with them. One word to anyone, and the fairies would leave him for ever. But it is a hard thing for a man to have so much good fortune and never be able to speak of it. The old man got so nervous keeping everything to himself that at last he could hold it no longer. He told everything, and the fairies never came to his house again.

The fairies met in other cottages, but they always fled when the people came home from work. A strange thing about their disappearance was that the people of the house always knew they had been there, because "sparks of fire as bright as stars" would appear under the feet of the one who disturbed them.

At Woolpit, between Stowmarket and Bury, where people

with failing vision used to bathe their eyes in the Well of Our Lady, another Suffolk fairy tale is told by William of Newburgh. One autumn day, when the reapers were busy with the harvest, two children, boy and girl, came across the fields from some ancient trenches known as Wolf Pits. These children were different from those who ran about the field with their parents. They were green from head to foot. Not only were their garments green; their hair was green, and so were their hands and faces. Everything about them was as green as the moss that grew on Our Lady's Well.

When the reaping was done for the day the children went home with the villagers, who made them as welcome as they could, though they were unable to talk with them because neither could understand the other's language. When food was set before the children they looked at it shyly and then turned away. For months they would eat nothing but beans. Then gradually their shyness left them and they began to eat like other children. When they did so the green went out of their skin and they were as rosy and brown as the Woolpit children. But all this time the villagers were anxious to know where they came from, so as soon as they could speak English they were asked a great number of questions. In reply they said they had come from the land of St. Martin, a place where the sun never shone as it did in Suffolk, but where everyone lived in perpetual twilight, which was very strange, because on the other side of a broad river that flowed across the land of St. Martin there was a land of light where darkness never fell. They were then asked how they came to wander from the land of St. Martin into the Wolf Pits, and if they were Christian children. They said that they were indeed Christians, but that they could not explain how they reached Woolpit. All they knew was that one day while they were tending their father's flock they heard bells ringing—bells that sounded like the bells of St. Edmund. Whether they were in fact St. Edmund's bells or not they could not say, but while they listened they fell asleep, and when they woke they were in the field with the reapers. That was all they knew; but they were very happy at Woolpit, and would like to stay there.

These mysterious children continued to live contentedly

at Woolpit until the boy suddenly became sick and died. The girl was so sad to lose him that she, too, was expected to die, but she recovered her spirits after a time, and when last heard of was married and living at King's Lynn.

Most of the old rural superstitions have died out now, but a few still linger in remote hamlets. The cross on the donkey's back is still believed in some parts to be connected with our Lord's ride into Jerusalem on Palm Sunday, and there are several superstitious beliefs connected with birds. It is thought lucky, for example, if martins build against your house, for it is said that they never choose unhappy homes. The robin's nest is never disturbed in some parts of Suffolk, because the village boys still believe that if they take the eggs from a robin's nest their legs will be broken. A robin singing under a fence betokens bad weather. If he sings on the top branches the sun will shine.

Another popular Suffolk saying is related to the next town on the Gipping after Stowmarket. If a man plays fast and loose with his money shrewd old neighbours shake their heads and say that he will soon be on the highway to Needham, the highway to Needham being the highway to poverty. Another thrifty Suffolk saying is that hunger will break through stone walls, or anything in fact except a Suffolk cheese. But perhaps it is time for us to take the road again.

There is little to record about Needham Market. It is a pleasant little town which long ago displaced in importance Barking, an older place in the neighbourhood, owing to the advantage it enjoys of standing on the river bank. It appears to have prospered as a wool town until attacked by the plague in 1685. This scourge seems to have practically destroyed its trade, which, coupled with the aptitude of its name, was probably the origin of the proverb. Prosperity returned to Needham when the river was made navigable, and during the nineteenth century it developed a considerable trade in both malting and milling. Its one outstanding building is the church, which is justly famed for its fine double-hammer roof.

A remarkable Suffolk man named John Steggall was born at Needham Market in 1789. His autobiography, edited by Richard Cobbold, was at one time widely read. Steggall was the son and grandson of Suffolk parsons who himself became a curate after many and varied experiences. As a boy he was sent to a school at Walsham-le-Willows, where the headmaster was so cruel that the frightened boy ran away and joined a band of gipsies. In turn he became sailor, soldier, surgeon, fellow-commoner of Corpus Christi, Cambridge, and finally a clergyman. His first charge was an assistant curacy at Badingham, near Framlingham. Later he assisted with his father's cure at Wyverstone, until Lord Thurlow gave him the perpetual curacy of Great Ashfield. His income was sixty pounds a year as curate, but he increased it by attending to the bodies of his parishioners as well as their souls. He was doctor as well as curate. Lord Thurlow continued to take an interest in him, and paid for him to take a course in midwifery, which enabled him to get a medical certificate. His parishioners appreciated the convenience of having a curate who could bring their babies into the world for them—and they usually came far too soon after the wedding—but he was much less popular with the neighbouring doctors, who constantly accused him of incompetence, and would almost certainly have ruined him if he had not enjoyed the protection of his patron.

Great Ashfield, the village of his ministrations, is eight miles north-west of Stowmarket, and is chiefly remarkable as the birthplace of the first Lord Thurlow, the Tory Chancellor who presided at Warren Hastings' trial. It was of him that Dr. Johnson said: "I would prepare myself for no man in England but Lord Thurlow; when I am about to meet him, I should ask to know a day before."

Four miles south-east of Needham Market, on high ground overlooking the river, stands Shrubland Hall in its three hundred acres of beautiful park, where some of the finest chestnut trees in the county are found. In the church of the neighbouring village of Coddenham there was formerly an imposing Shrubland pew, which was fitted with a small private fireplace and adorned with panels carved to depict the Annunciation, the Nativity, the Visit of the Shepherds and similar subjects. And as we have given so much attention to names in this chapter, we cannot fail to note that in Claydon, the next village, and the last before Ipswich is reached, there

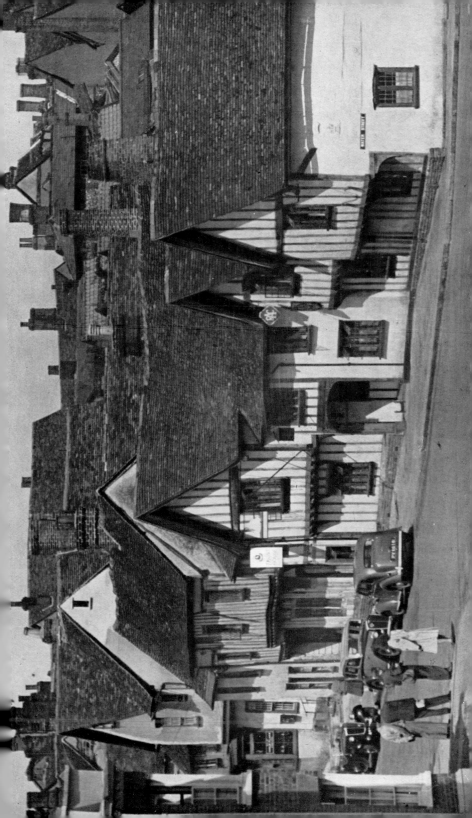

is an old house called Mockbeggar's Hall. The derivation
of this curious name is the subject of speculation. One
man explained it to me by saying that he believed the
hall had been paid for in farthings. He was probably
thinking of Farlingay Hall at Woodbridge, a house we
shall recall in connection with Edward FitzGerald in a
later chapter. A more credible story informs us that it
was unoccupied at one time, and therefore mocked the beggars who left the highroad to trudge up the drive in search
of alms.

Skirting Ipswich we pass from the Gipping to the Orwell,
where the river changes not only its name but every aspect
of its character. The quiet villages of the Gipping are
quickly forgotten as the eye sweeps the broad estuary of the
Orwell, its waters busy with vessels bearing their merchandise
to Ipswich or away to distant ports. Yachts and rowing boats
enliven the scene throughout the summer months, and when
the tide is out the gulls glide down to stalk about the mud
banks, where they chatter in the wind and search the ooze
for worms. The pull of the restless tide is felt as it runs out
of the spacious estuary, and we feel, too, that we are on the
brink of hazard and adventure.

If our way lies along the steep and romantically wooded
banks of the Orwell, we are in lanes that Gainsborough knew
as a young man when each day he would leave his home in
Foundation Street, Ipswich, to wander through these woods,
revelling in the bright light and seizing enthusiastically such
subjects as the one he used for *The Market Cart*. Along the
southern bank we pass the popular "Ostrich" Inn and are soon
in sight of Freston Tower, a landmark known to all who visit
the Vale of Orwell. It is a six-storeyed, quadrangular tower,
built of red brick, with one room twelve feet square on each
storey. An arcaded parapet with a polygonal finial at each
corner runs round the top, surmounted by a turret. No one
seems to know with certainty who built this tower or what
purpose it served. Richard Cobbold used it as the setting
of one of his stories, and explained its origin to the satisfaction, no doubt, of many of his readers. It must be remembered, however, that he was writing fiction, not history, and
therefore his statement that Freston Tower was built in the

The Deanery Tower, Hadleigh
Saddler's shop, Hadleigh

fifteenth century by Lord de Freston to the design of his kins-
man, William Latimer, and was intended to be a place of
study and recreation for the builder's only daughter, Helen
de Freston, should not be taken seriously. This ingeniously
invented origin suited the purposes of his story and that was
all that mattered. It also suited his story to explain how
each room of the tower was used for a different purpose. The
ground-floor room, he tells us, was for the reception and relief
of the poor; the second for tapestry working; the third for
music; the fourth for painting; the fifth for literature; the
sixth for astronomy, with the necessary instruments fixed in
the turret. It was a clever fancy, but on examination the
story seems to be even taller than the tower itself. Judging
by the brick and the architectural style of the building it
was probably erected about the middle of the sixteenth century, and the most likely explanation of its origin is that
Edmund Latymer, who appears to have built it, set it up
in order to have a place of retreat for himself, and built it
high so that he could see the whole of the beautiful Vale it
stands in. It is unlikely that he had anything else in mind,
except perhaps the not uncommon desire to provide himself
with a memorial.

It was long the custom for all young couples of the Gipping
parishes who married in May to make a pilgrimage to Freston
Tower in accordance with the rhyme:

> No burgess on his wedding day,
> Which falls in white-thorn merry May,
> Shall happy be in house or bower,
> Who does not visit Freston Tower.

Another building on the banks of the Orwell that Cobbold
invested with an even greater degree of romance is the moated
Priory Farm, situated in a wooded vale on the opposite side
of the river. At one time this old farmhouse was a priory.
Later it entered a more exciting phase of life as a favourite haunt of smugglers, and many engagements between
smugglers and preventive men are said to have been fought
here; but its chief title to fame is as a house where Margaret
Catchpole was employed in domestic service. It was from this

lonely spot that Will Laud, her dare-devil lover, planned to carry her away to sea.

On the evening before Harvest Home in 1793 a sailor came to the back door of Priory Farm and asked for a glass of water. He pretended that he came from Amsterdam, and that the captain of his ship was William Laud, who desired to meet Miss Margaret Catchpole. It was arranged that Margaret should be on the shore at nine o'clock that night and look out for a small sail-boat, which would come up the river and run ashore at the Creek. The watchword was to be " Margaret." That night the moon shone so brightly that as Margaret stood waiting she could see Freston Tower two miles away, and the dark shade of the woods at Woolverstone. Then she descried a sail on the river and a boat coming towards her. When it got nearer she saw that the man at the helm was not her lover but a strange and apparently genuine local character named Thomas Colson, commonly known in the district as Robinson Crusoe. This man had originally been a wool-comber; later he worked as a weaver until lack of employment drove him to join the East Suffolk Militia. After a period of service he returned to the Orwell as a fisherman, using a boat made with his own hands. This man was known to everyone in the district as a harmless but eccentric character who suffered from some malady which he believed to be caused by supernatural tormentors. To ward off these malevolent agencies he had covered his clothes with the bones of horses, rings, amulets, verses and charms of every conceivable kind. Cobbold had known this man as a boy, and had often been in the boat with him, so it was natural that he should wish to introduce him into one of his books. In due course Colson was followed by the expected Laud, who made his attempt to carry Margaret away with him, but was suitably thwarted.

Nacton, on the north bank of the Orwell, where Margaret Catchpole was born, is associated with two eminent British seamen, Admiral Vernon and Sir Philip Broke. It had long been the fashion to disparage Vernon until Sir Geoffrey Callender, in *Sea Kings of Britain*, went a long way towards reconciling the official with the popular estimate of his character. Vernon could hardly expect to enjoy the respect of

Admiralty officials, for he consistently attacked them throughout his career both on public platform and by scurrilous
pamphlet until his name was struck off the list of flag officers.
With the nation at large he was a popular figure from first
to last, and to his men he was affectionately known as "Old
Grog," from his habit of pacing the quarter-deck dressed in
a cloak of grogram, a serviceable material made of silk and
mohair. Vernon was the first captain to issue diluted rum to
his crew, and his own nickname was at once given to it. By
this means he gave a new word to the English language. There
is an old tradition, apparently insecurely anchored to fact,
though sufficiently characteristic to gain credence, which holds
that the National Anthem itself was first sung in present form
at a concert held to celebrate Vernon's victory at Porto Bello.
A rousing chorus he did inspire is that which goes:

> To our good King now loudly sing; may Providence
>   attend him!
> To Admiral Vernon toss a glass; may Heaven aye
>   defend him!
> To Commodore Brown toss another down, and to
>   each gallant fellow
> Who did so bravely play his part at the taking of
>   Porto Bello.

In 1739 Vernon boasted that he could capture Porto Bello
with a squadron of six ships. He was at once ordered to do
so. The Government probably thought that if he succeeded
the display of British force would enhance the national
prestige, and that if he failed there might be an opportunity
of getting rid of this pestering critic. To everyone's amazement Vernon succeeded in carrying out his design with the
loss of only seven British lives. On returning to England
he was received with tremendous acclamation. He was at
once accepted as a national hero, a role in which he excelled
so far as public expectations went, but to the great embarrassment of his opponents and of anyone else who might be
entitled to a share of national honour. Even the following
year his birthday was celebrated with public illuminations in
London. In May 1741, Admiral Vernon became Member

of Parliament for Ipswich, and continued to represent the
borough until he died sixteen years later. We can imagine
the pride Ipswich must have felt in him, especially as he
resided at Orwell Park just outside the town.

The failure at Carthagena in 1741 shook the confidence of
Parliament in Vernon, and later this failure was pilloried by
Tobias Smollett, who happened to have been present at the
action as surgeon's mate in one of the warships. Smollett
incorporated his account of what happened at Carthagena in
Roderick Random, repeating the substance of this account
later in his *History of England*. He was hardly qualified to
sit in judgment on Vernon's seamanship, but his report was
accepted because those qualified to judge were only too
pleased to see Vernon disparaged. The man who is in-
judicious in writing of others can hardly expect them to
be judicious in writing of him. Happily, better justice than
Smollett's was accorded Vernon on the monument to his
memory in Westminster Abbey, which simply, and according to Sir Geoffrey Callender truthfully, states that "At
Carthagena he conquered as far as naval force could carry
victory." The failure of that engagement appears to have
been the responsibility of another. Whatever mistakes
Vernon may have made he certainly lived up to his two cardinal principles, "that everything depends on our superiority
at sea, and this we stand in danger of losing when we fail to
retain the affection of our seamen." He died suddenly at
Nacton in the autumn of 1751, and was buried in the village
church.

Sir Philip Broke, who was born twenty-five years after
Admiral Vernon's death, lived at Broke Hall, the home of the
Broke family for centuries, which overlooks the river near
Orwell Park. Sir Philip was as different in character from
the admiral as it was possible for him to be. Where Vernon
relied on audacity and daring, Broke relied on careful training. His famous fight was with the American frigate
Chesapeake during the war between the United States and
Great Britain. Broke commanded the *Shannon*. When the
two ships met outside Boston harbour in 1813, the *Chesapeake* carrying forty-nine guns to the *Shannon's* thirty-eight,
and four hundred and forty men to the *Shannon's* three

hundred and thirty, Broke ordered his men to take up action stations with the words: "Don't cheer. Go quietly to your quarters. I feel sure you will all do your duty." He relied entirely on quiet efficiency and cool courage. The *Chesapeake* closed in on the *Shannon*, but it was not till she was within fifty yards that the British ship received her with a broadside which struck down a hundred of her crew. After a second broadside had been equally effective, Broke sprang on board the American vessel with fifty of his men behind him, and within fifteen minutes the engagement had resulted in a British victory. For his service in this action Broke was awarded a baronetcy, but he was severely wounded and suffered acutely for the rest of his life.

Nacton has figured bravely in English history ever since the battle with the Danes in 1010. It is said that it was from here that Edward III set sail when about to invade France in 1338.

To turn from gallant actions like Broke's to smuggling exploits might seem incongruous, but Adam Smith in the *Wealth of Nations* defends smugglers by arguing that they would have been excellent citizens if the laws of the land had not made that a crime which nature did not intend should be one. If nature were to be the sole authority in morals a great part of our ethical code would have to be revised, but it will be safe to claim that many a criminal smuggler would have made a gallant sailor in time of war. This, however, is not the place to discuss such questions, and we have only space left to point out that opposite Orwell Park, in the grounds of Woolverstone Hall, is the building called the Cat House, a lodge which is said to have been used to signal the smugglers who used the river. When the coast was clear, according to tradition, a stuffed white cat was placed in the window during the day and a lighted lamp at night. When the preventive men were about, these reassuring signals were removed.

Below Chelmondiston is the quaint little riverside village called Pin Mill, which was once a notorious haunt of smugglers. To-day it is a favourite resort of artists and pleasure seekers who enjoy its quaint charm. Its name is said to have been given to it because the daughter of a previous owner received the proceeds of the windmills in the district

as pin money. On the opposite bank is Levington Creek,
another favourite resort of smugglers, where in 1904 the
remains of a Viking ship were found embedded in the mud.
Beyond these are the lonely marshes that fringe the lower
reach as far as Orwell Haven, where the harbour opens out
like pincers, or like the jaws of a shark, between the sharp
defences of Blackman's Head and Landguard Point.

CHAPTER VIII

SUFFOLK AND THE SEA

IN shape, Suffolk has been likened to a galleon. It is an apt simile, for half the county's business has been with the sea. Its anchorage to the mainland has often seemed insecure in times of storm when the sandy cliffs have rocked and broken. All through the centuries land and sea along this coast have coaxed, cajoled, and fought each other by turns, and the sea has usually been victor. There are lifeboat stations at several points, and every winter brave men are called out to save vessels stranded on a beach of shingle or a sandbank off shore. In the December of 1770, when one of the worst storms on record spent its fury on the east coast, eighteen ships were sighted on a sankbank off Lowestoft. Nine of them had broken before nine o'clock in the morning. Other ships had already sunk near by, and it was estimated that two hundred men had been drowned.

All the way from the Orwell to the Yare these treacherous banks are still found. In the south are Cork Ledge and Cork Knoll; out from Bawdsey is the Culter Sand; seaward again are Kettle Bottom, Bawdsey Bank and the Shipwash. The Ridge and the Gabbard lie between Orford Ness and Thorpe Ness, with Sizewell Bank higher again, and beyond that the Barnard off Kessingland, the Newcome and the Holm off Lowestoft, and Corton Sand between Corton and Gorleston. In addition to the sixty-two buoys between Harwich and Yarmouth, there are the lightships about which Mr. George Carter wrote his vigorous book, *Looming Lights,* and when a mist hangs over the sea the dreary sound—heartening enough to the sailor—of the fog-horn may be heard all along the shore.

It is little wonder that weird, unearthly stories are told here. Sailors are naturally superstitious, and in every place on the Suffolk coast we hear of the ghostly visitor, Black

Shuck, sometimes called Moddey Dhoe, the shaggy black dog, the Hell Hound or Churchyard Beast. Children are frightened home with tales of him. When a storm was raging upon the dark waters, fishermen and their wives used to cower over the ashes and believe they could hear the howling of the dog, foreboding disaster. If they peered through the window and saw moving lights they believed them to be the blazing eyes of Black Shuck.

A popular Black Shuck story relates that a swarthy foreigner —probably an Italian—appeared in a Suffolk village and became the friend of a young fisherboy. The two would sit all day on one of the upturned boats on the quay, and the stranger would tell stories about other lands till the fisherboy became restless and dissatisfied with his dull life at home. One day the stranger said the time had now come for him to return to his own country, and he begged the fisherboy to go with him. But the fisherboy became nervous and afraid to leave his parents. Then the stranger gave him a huge black dog, which everyone in the village knew belonged to the stranger, though no one had ever seen the two together.

When the stranger had gone the boy and the dog became inseparable. They spent most of their time together on the beach looking out to sea, and the dog would run in and out of the water barking and wagging his tail till the fisherboy threw off his clothes and plunged through the waves after him. Because the dog was so fond of the water the fisherboy soon became an excellent swimmer, and the two were often seen farther from land than the village people thought safe. One day, when the fisherboy felt he had gone far enough and turned to regain the shore, the dog reared up in front of him and barred his passage. It growled and snapped at him whichever way he turned, except when he swam towards the open sea. On and on he was forced to swim with the dog at his side or close to his heels. Then a terrible thought came into his mind. The dog he had loved so much was not the friendly animal he had believed it to be, but Black Shuck, the dreaded hound. He was now afraid to turn round; but he knew the dog was there because he could hear it panting and growling behind him. Then it came alongside and he could see it through the corner of his eye. There was no longer any doubt about it. It was Black Shuck and nothing could save him. But when it came so close to him that he could not see it clearly he was horrified to find, not the head of the dog, but the head of the swarthy stranger grinning triumphantly at him from the water. Then again it became the head of a dog, and with a frightful howl it sprang at his neck and would have drawn him down into the sea if a ship had not been passing. The sailors on board had heard his cry of distress and had come to his rescue. They hauled him out of the water, and when he was safely on deck it was found that his throat had been torn by teeth, but whether by teeth of man or dog it was impossible to say.

Many of these Black Shuck stories and other tales of spectral apparitions were probably invented by smugglers who did not want too many people wandering down the lanes when they had business on hand.

Some of the true stories told along the Suffolk coast are no less exciting than its legends, and of these none is more amazing than the story of the lost city of Dunwich. If you leave the main road from Ipswich to Lowestoft at Yoxford and cross a wide heath covered with a great carpet of ling, which shines the brighter for the patches of white chalk breaking through the turf at intervals, you will reach a long grey wall, and through an archway look across the cliff to all that remains of this ancient city. Behind you are fields of barley through which the wind whispers its secrets, and below them the church, the inn, and the few cottages that make up the Dunwich of to-day. Northward lies the estuary of the Blyth, and whichever way you look you have a strange feeling of unseen presences. A friend tells me that this feeling is accentuated after dark, for voices can then be heard that seem to come from the ruins. The superstitious might believe they were, but the truth is no less strange, for these voices come across the marsh from Southwold, four miles or more away. This local characteristic of audibility has given rise to the popular saying: "He is a Walberswick whisperer; you may hear him over to Southwold." There are certainly strange sounds here. Old people will still tell you that on quiet nights they can hear the bells of the ruined churches of Dunwich ringing beneath the waves.

If ever Suffolk people are charged with lack of imagination the story of Dunwich should be told. Here, according to its chronicler, stood a walled city with gates of brass. Within it stood fifty-two churches along with other religious foundations, a bishop's seat and a king's palace. South of the city there was a great forest called the King's Forest, stretching for seven miles, and there was a harbour from which sailed stately ships with rich merchandise.

Whatever else may be said about this lost city it certainly makes a romantic story. Much is known about it, and a great deal more is sheer fancy. It can never have had fifty-two churches. That is quite certain. The original authority for this statement appears to have been Stow, and it is not improbable that the number of churches in the town has been confused with the number in a larger region to which Dunwich gave its name as the administrative capital. There were never more than ten churches in Dunwich itself.

The Dunwich historian was Thomas Gardner, a Suffolk worthy who lived at Southwold and was buried there between his two wives, Rachel and Mary. The headstones above their graves were formerly well known to visitors. The first was to Rachel, his first wife, and also to Rachel, their daughter. On it was inscribed the couplet:

> Virtue crowned, during life,
> Both the daughter and the wife.

The third stone was to Mary, his second wife, and was inscribed:

> Honour ever did attend
> Her just dealings to the end.

Between them was the stone to Thomas himself:

> In memory of Thomas Gardner, Salt Officer, who died
> March 30th, 1769, aged 79 years.
> Between Honour and Virtue here doth lie
> The remains of old Antiquity.

This one is now to be seen in a glass case inside the church.

The old man was evidently something of a character. He tells us how he came to write the story of Dunwich. Many tales were current in the neighbourhood about the bygone splendour of this ruined city, and these so excited Thomas's curiosity that one day he decided to cross the marsh and see it. On arrival he found " the Remains of the Rampart; some tokens of *Middlegate*; the foundations of downfallen *Edifices* and tottering Fragments of Noble *Structures*, Remains of the *Dead* exposed, and naked wells divested of the Ground about them, by the Waves of the Sea! divers *Coins*, several Mill-Hills, and part of the *old key*."

Thomas Gardner is not our only authority on Dunwich. Radulph (or Ralph) Agas, a Suffolk surveyor who became eminent as a cartographer towards the end of the sixteenth century, preparing a map of London in 1591, sent a report of the town's condition to Queen Elizabeth in 1589. He wrote: "Touchinge the State of the Toune in times past, it appeareth as well by their Charter, as otherwise, that it hath been one of the ancient Tounes of this Yland; that there hath benn a Bishoppes Sea, also a Minte, and a Market everie Daie in the Week, And hath also (for their sondrie faithfull and espetial Services, as makinge out at some one Time eleven strong and well furnished Shyppes for the defence of the Realme at their owne Costes and Charges, by the space of thirteen weakes and more, with Loss of 500 Men and 1000l in Goodes, &c.), from Time to Time stood in high Favour with the Kinges of this Land, of whome they have received most large and liberal Graunts of Priviledges, Liberties, Customs, &c., besides sundrie Letters from sutch Kinges, written to the Burgesses there."

From the more reliable sources we are able to construct a picture of this fascinating and important city. The cliff it stood on would be about forty feet high, and it appears to have been protected by ramparts of earth on the landward sides and by a fosse along the foot of the cliff. It became a royal demesne at the beginning of Henry II's reign, and received its first charter from King John in recognition of its services in fitting out several ships to assist in war against the French. As an episcopal see its history goes back to Felix, who was consecrated first Bishop of East Anglia in 630 or

631. Its principal streets were St. James's Street, which ran east to west, King Street, and Duck Street—all three busy thoroughfares. The entrance to the haven was on the north side and was protected by a pier. Besides the daily market there were two important fairs annually, one in St. James's Street on the festival of the saint, and the following day, the other, the great event of the Dunwich year, was held in St. Leonard's parish on the fifth, sixth, and seventh of November each year, and was known as St. Leonard's Fair. On these occasions the city would present a lively appearance with farmers from all over East Anglia, their wives and families, sailors who happened to be on land, and the ubiquitous strolling minstrels and mendicant friars holding out their hands for gifts. In the south of the city, near Middlegate Street, stood the Temple, a wealthy foundation of the Knights Templars.

On the festival of All Saints each year the Temple Court was held by the Knights Templars for the purpose of collecting revenues and granting pardons. But this part of Dunwich history was ended early and abruptly when Edward II ordered the arrest of all the Templars in his kingdom on the Feast of the Epiphany, 1308. He did not, however, follow the example of Philip the Fair, King of France, to the extent of seizing all the property for himself. Instead, he handed it over to a new order of Knights Hospitallers, which continued to flourish in Dunwich till the reign of Henry VIII, who took possession of its property at the time of the Reformation. Mary restored the order, but it was finally abolished by Elizabeth.

Dunwich had two priories, one belonging to the Grey, the other to the Black Friars. And from the reign of Edward I to the passing of the Reform Bill in 1832 it returned two Members to Parliament. One of them was Sir George Downing, from whom Downing Street takes its name.

The people of Dunwich received repeated warnings of the disaster that finally overwhelmed them. At the end of a great storm in January 1328 the harbour was found to be choked. A new harbour was made, but this was destroyed at the beginning of Henry IV's reign. A third harbour was washed away in 1464. Yet still the Dunwich merchants refused to be intimidated by the threatening sea, and a fourth harbour was constructed, which proved to be a danger rather than an advantage to shipping, and in consequence fell into disuse. In 1589 Dunwich resolved to build an entirely new port, but by this time Southwold was growing and had ambitions of its own. In the Wars of the Roses Dunwich made the fatal mistake of taking the wrong side, so that when Henry VII became king a charter of incorporation was granted to the younger town. But Dunwich was already doomed. The enmity of the sea could not be withstood for ever. The war of the waves was fiercer than the War of the Roses. As early as 1349 upwards of four hundred houses had been destroyed at once. By 1540 not a quarter of the old city was standing. In 1677 the sea reached the market-place. A few years later the town hall had gone. The final catastrophe came at the end of 1739 when a furious gale blowing hard for several days drove the sea with such force against the cliffs that they broke and crumbled and the sea roared in triumph as it surged like a victorious army across the town. The last church to remain was All Saints', which stood until recently, a lonely relic on the cliffs, described by Swinburne, who knew the Suffolk coast well:

> . . . one hollow tower and hoary,
> Naked in the sea-wind stands and moans,
> Filled and thrilled with its perpetual story;
> Here where earth is dense with dead men's bones.

This hollow tower has gone now. The last portion of its wall was taken down and re-erected near the modern church. The only fragment now remaining from the lost city is of a ruined monastery, and it is to this that Roman Catholic pilgrims go in procession on a certain Sunday in August each year in honour of the day when Sigebert, King of the East Angles, brought the Burgundian Bishop Felix to England to try to recover East Anglia for Christianity. Surpliced choristers and red-robed priests, attended by men and women carrying banners, assemble on these storm-washed cliffs and hold their Service of the Waves.

But strange things continued to happen at Dunwich, and

always will, it seems. Early one morning in the spring of
1808 the village folk of the small fishing village that had
sprung up among the ruins of the vanished city heard the
sound of guns being fired off shore. Cannon balls were then
heard whistling through the air. One fell near enough to
bring all the people to their doors. Quickly the alarm went
round that the French had reached the coast and were about
to land. Then the firing ceased as suddenly as it had begun,
and the people of Dunwich might have thought they had
been dreaming if a cannon ball had not been there as
evidence. The astonishing thing about it was that it came
from the stores of King George himself. Enquiries were made
at the Admiralty, but so far as I know the mystery was never
cleared up.

I said a moment ago that the war of the waves was fiercer
than the War of the Roses. That is true; but it must not be
thought that the waves were more powerful than the roses.
One of the loveliest things to be found in this place of so
many legends and proud memories is a simple white flower,
apparently growing wild, called the Dunwich rose. Tradition
says that this is the last survivor from a monastery garden.

> . . . the Dunwich rose, with snow-like blossom,
> Soft, pure, and white, as is the cygnet's bosom;
> This decks the stern and sterile cliff; and throws
> O'er its rough brow new beauty where it grows.

Suffolk has a coast unlike that of any other maritime English county. Its long estuaries and lonely marshes make it
one of the best for wild-fowling. Each river has its yacht
clubs; and the fashionable resorts, though each has its
luxurious hotels, have a quaint, old-world character that the
county prides itself on maintaining in defiance of every
attempt to standardise and sophisticate. Most of them belong
to a particular river no less than to the sea they have in
common, and it is this feature that gives them such individual-
ity. But it would be wrong to give the impression that the
Suffolk resorts lack those amenities that the majority of
townsfolk like to find in the place they select for a fortnight
of relaxation each year. Felixstowe, with its tall cliffs of red

crag, and trees growing down to the beach, is as charming a modern resort as you will find anywhere on the east coast. The coastline curves pleasantly round its cliffs, which have been laid out with gardens and winding paths to afford either shade or sunshine.

The Felixstowe of the twentieth century has almost entirely concealed the ancient town where Edward III had a residence, remains of which may be seen in a corner of the cricket ground, and where he spent several weeks before embarking in Orwell Haven on his expedition to France. The strategic importance of the tongue of land on which Felixstowe stands will be seen at a glance. This sunny resort was, in fact, a fortified promontory from early times, with the castle of the warring Bigods at Walton, and later, Landguard Fort protecting the entrance to the estuaries of the Stour and the Orwell. Walton Castle was destroyed by Henry II in his great attempt to break the power of the barons; but Landguard Fort, built in the reign of James I, is still one of our important coastal defences. Its most exciting occasion was on the 3rd July, 1667, when twenty-five Dutch ships lay off the Whiting and Bawdsey Sands. Eight of them sent out smoke screens to cover the landing of two thousand men at Felixstowe. Four hundred of these, with hand grenades and drawn cutlasses, and carrying twenty-feet scaling ladders on their backs, made their way to Landguard Fort. They were successfully repulsed twice by the garrison, and after their second attack were driven away in such confusion that they were obliged to leave their ladders and arms behind them and regain their boats as best they could.

What has been said about the cliffs at Dunwich must not lead anyone to suppose that the Suffolk coast is remarkable for cliffs. They are prominent at several of its best resorts from Gorleston at the northern tip to Southwold, and between Dunwich and Sizewell. There is no rock on the Suffolk coast. South of Aldeburgh, the cliffs are of red crag—closely compacted marine sands, dark red in colour, and often strikingly beautiful with the sea below them and the vivid green of the gorse and the purple of the heather along the slopes above. To the north they are of Norwich crag. At Easton Bavents, Kessingland and Pakefield, the cliffs have fallen away and

128

Sparrowe's House, Ipswich
Holbrook

exposed strata down to the forest-bed. Here rich deposits of Elephantine and Cervine remains have been discovered. At Tattingstone, Orford, Sutton, and Aldeburgh, isolated patches of Coralline crag are to be found. Even in the northern half of the coastline the cliffs are broken by streams. Behind the cottages in the sheltered hollow of the cliffs at Dunwich lies the Dingle, three miles of shingle between the lost city and Walberswick, and the southern half of the coastline is broken by the estuaries and marshes of the broad, slow-moving rivers. It is, in fact, the lack of continuous cliff that has saved the Suffolk coast from the exploitation that has disfigured so much of our English coast. No continuous coastal road could either be constructed or maintained for more than a few miles. The resorts on the Suffolk coast are not like beads on a single thread, all of the same kind and varying only in size. They are almost disconcertingly isolated and original, the delight of the artist, the despair of the conventional. Even Felix-stowe, which conducts itself with more propriety than most, is cut off from communication with its neighbours by Orwell Haven on the south and the Deben on the north. Not one of the Suffolk coastal towns except Lowestoft at the northern end is worried with the through traffic that makes most resorts so congested throughout the summer months, and almost frenzied during August. Instead, even in this twentieth century, much of the Suffolk coast is still as Swinburne described it, though many of us take a rather less gloomy view of this remoteness from civilisation.

> A land that is lonelier than ruin;
>   A sea that is stranger than death;
> Far fields that a rose never blew in,
>   Wan waste where the winds lack breath;
> Waste endless and boundless and flowerless
>   But of marsh-blossoms fruitless as free,
> Where earth lies exhausted, as powerless
>   To strive with the sea.

We must concede that the marshes that have saved the Suffolk coast are not to everybody's taste. I would not argue for one moment with the man who said he found them dull.

The Docks, Ipswich
Wolsey's Gate, Ipswich

Nor will I make any attempt here to define their charm to those of us upon whom they have cast a spell. I do not think their beauty can be defined or their appeal explained. It is, I think, a poetic appeal, like the appeal of the moors that stirred the soul of Emily Brontë, or the appeal of the desert that stirred some of our troops in the Second Great War, and which they found so difficult to analyse—like the appeal of the sea itself, for that matter. All these solitary places have one thing in common—they test a man's private resources. They bring also a sense of freedom, and this is particularly true of the marshes. It comes in part from the keen, exhilarating air that blows across the lonely stretches of land intersected with flashing, sword-like rivers, and makes the blood tingle and the limbs feel uncommonly light. The sea is a silvery waste in the distance with a single sail on the horizon, or if the eye turns inland there is green instead of grey, and instead of the sail there is the one church tower that has been a blessing to mariners on this particular bit of coast for five centuries or more. And there are the sunsets, which are singularly beautiful in East Suffolk.

The marshes appeal most strongly to the sporting man, and I cannot claim to be one of their company. But I am a countryman, and when I see two or three men go out across the marshes with their collars buttoned up, their hats pulled low over their ears, and a gun across their shoulders, I can feel a responsive tingle, though I have never had the good fortune to make one of such a party. Many of us who live happy and crowded lives sometimes regret that the absorbing interest of our own pursuits cuts us off from others, and long for more lives in which to explore the abounding pleasures of mere existence. If I could have half a dozen lives I think I would spend one of them with these men who go out to bag the coot that grow fat with feeding on the *zostera* grass that grows on the mud flats. In former days the flat-bottomed boat used for wild-fowling in these waterways was called a Peter Boat, after the Apostle Peter.

In reflecting on these pleasures I am reminded of an autumn afternoon when I sat by the fire in a lonely inn, unable to resume the road because the rain was blowing so mercilessly from the sea. A man and a boy came in, threw off their oilskins, propped a gun against the fireplace and rubbed their hair and faces with a towel till they glowed, then grinned across at me with eyes glistening with delight and faces expressing all the satisfaction you will see in a dog's eyes when it splashes out of the water and shakes itself. It is a memory that has stayed with me because at that moment I felt something of the keen life there is in the sportsman, enabling him to endure and enjoy hardships that would have reduced another man to misery. The rain was nothing to this particular sportsman. He recounted with glee the number of widgeon, teal and geese he had shot one night in a snowstorm.

It is not, of course, necessary to carry a gun to appreciate the wild life of the marshes, though I am inclined to think that the hunter is closer to nature than the mere watcher. He not only sees the owl that flies across the river in the twilight to search for voles, but also feels something of the same excited emotion of desire. On the other hand the watcher might be more likely to write such a sweet old song as that of the Suffolk owl. Perhaps you remember it:

Sweet Suffolk owl, so trimly dight
With feathers like a lady bright,
Thou singest alone, sitting by night,
    Te whit, te whoo!

Thy note, that forth so freely rolls,
With shrill command the mouse controls,
And sings a dirge for dying souls,
    Te whit, te whoo!

The Suffolk coast is a paradise for the bird-watcher. By night you will hear not only the owls but also the whirring notes of the nightjars on their moth-hunting excursions. By day you may see the golden plover above the saltings, or that beautiful bird, the sheldrake, which nests in rabbit burrows near the cliffs. On the marshes at Kessingland you will find white-fronted geese, and in hard weather, when the sea pounds upon the shingle, all along the coast the grey gulls may be heard, squealing and squawking as they fly inland to escape from the fury of the tempest, and see the terns that nest in the Lantern Marshes. Anywhere along this coast you may, if you have exceptional luck, see a golden eagle. At least one has been seen within living memory.

This solitary coast is a favourite haunt of the bird-watcher during periods of migration. Throughout March and much of April such winter visitors as larks, rooks, and starlings are seen departing, while in March pied wagtails, meadow-pipits, and buntings fly in, followed in April by swallows, willow-warblers and the rest of the summer visitors. In August and September the estuaries fill with waders, gulls, and terns, either arriving to take up winter quarters or coasting south-wards. Later, during the last ten days of October, when this autumn migration reaches its climax, Mr. Claud Tycehurst, the authority on this enthralling subject, says he has estimated that on favourable mornings as many as four thousand birds have flown across the coast in a single hour.

For one man who revels in the marshes, a hundred revel in the heaths, and these are continuous along at least three-fifths of the Suffolk coast. There are patches between Lowe-stoft and Gorleston, and between the Deben and the Blyth there is one vast heath, broken only by modern plantations and a few small efforts at cultivation. It is a remarkable tract of wild country to find in one of the highly cultivated counties of England. As I think of the Suffolk heath I am a little surprised to find that it is the scent of it that comes first to mind. The sense of smell I have always thought the most intimate of the senses. We all know the joy of seeing a loved village again, the joy of hearing the old, familiar sounds and the joy of touching a loved one's hand, but most moving of all is the peculiar scent of each particular place or person. The scent of the heath is peculiar to itself and at the same time variable. In spring the shoots of bracken are young and sharp-scented; in autumn a warm breath rises from the dry, purple heather and the sun-baked earth. The heath is one kind of place in rain and another in sun. But if the scent comes first to mind and touches the heart most closely, the scenes and sounds are no less clear and are, perhaps, more lasting. There is the skylark with his " silver chain of sound," the plaintive notes of the willow-warbler and the jingle of the corn-bunting. But these sensations are meaningless until you have experienced them. Perhaps they only amount to saying that the Suffolk coast has a strange, indefinable atmosphere, wild and restless and at times foreboding; at other times strong and exhilarating, with a voice that laughs defiance at the sea that threatens it when the wind whistles through the marram grass that mantles the bentlings or sand-dunes; at other times intimate and soothing as a lullaby.

The worst enemy of the heath itself is fire. Walberswick Common, Hollesley and Bromeswell Heaths, have all suffered severely during the present century, and in the dry sandy soil recovery is slow. The other enemy from the naturalist's point of view has been the Forestry Commission. This is controversial ground and I do not propose to venture on it. In a utilitarian age it was inevitable that these huge plantations should be made. No other productive use could have been made of these barren but beautiful commons.

Of the ancient and remorseless enemy of Suffolk, the sea, many writers have left their records. In our own day we have had Major Cooper, a worthy chronicler and true-hearted lover of the Suffolk coast. I have recently been glancing again at his record of the Suffolk lifeboats and their brave crews in *Storm Warriors of the Suffolk Coast*. Many of the most daring exploits were concerned with rescues off the Holm, the Newcome, and the Corton Sands. The first two lifeboats on the Suffolk coast were built, Major Cooper tells us, in the first year or so of the nineteenth century, one at Woodbridge and one at Lowestoft, where Mr. Robert Sparrow of Worlingham Hall founded a Lifeboat Society in September 1800. These first lifeboats do not appear to have inspired much confidence, but after the wreck of H.M. gun-brig *Snipe* on the 18th February, 1807, the Suffolk Humane Society was formed at Lowestoft, and Lionel Lukin, the life-boat inventor, was commissioned to design a boat which was built by Bareham of Lowestoft in 1807 at the cost of two hundred pounds. This boat was in use till 1850 and was the means of saving three hundred lives. Her name was *Frances Ann*, the name of the daughter of the president of the society.

The most curiously named of Suffolk's lifeboats was the

John Keble. The connection of the author of the *Christian Year* with Suffolk seems remote until we learn that this Dunwich boat was paid for by members of Keble's family and dedicated at Dunwich church. But there is no lifeboat at Dunwich now and the lifeboat-house has been washed away.

The lonely stretch of coast round Dunwich, with its great stretches of shingle where yellow poppy, thrift, and sea-pea provide what little colour there is, was a favourite place for landing smuggled goods. The cliffs provided a useful look-out station for the smugglers, who were so well organised that on the 4th February, 1734, it was stated in Parliament "that all the young, clever fellows in Suffolk were employed by the smugglers, and have 2s. 6d. a day while waiting and, when on horseback going about the country to dispose of the goods, they have a guinea a day and are well entertained. The gangs were forty to fifty strong, and so well mounted the dragoons could not catch them."

To the gallantry of the lifeboat crews and the hazards of the smugglers there is another aspect of seafaring life to be added. The county is justly proud of the fine naval establishments at Holbrook and Shotley, known as H.M.S. *Ganges*. The original H.M.S. *Ganges*, Captain Bush, R.N., the commanding officer at Shotley, informs me, was a sailing vessel built entirely of teak and completed in Bombay in 1821. She saw service in Indian, South American, Mediterranean and finally Pacific waters, where she carried the flag of Rear Admiral Sir R. L. Baynes, K.C.B., and thereby earned the distinction of being the last sailing vessel to become a flag-ship. When she returned to England in 1861 she was refitted as a boys' training ship, beginning her new career at Falmouth in 1866. Thirty-three years later she was towed round to Harwich, and it is from this old training ship that present-day Shotley developed. The first building of the shore establishment was completed in 1902.

The War Department owned the land on which the first hospital was built, for at that time military forces were still in occupation of the Martello towers, which were mounted with guns in readiness for any new Napoleonic ventures. The land, however, was at once transferred to the Admiralty, and by late 1905 recruitment began. At first there was accom-

modation for only five hundred boys, but with further building and the arrival at Harwich of another sailing vessel, the
Minotaur, renamed *Ganges II*, twelve hundred boys could be
trained. This second sailing ship was removed in the summer
of 1922, and H.M.S. *Ganges* then became a dry land ship.
To-day there is accommodation for over two thousand boys,
and the number of officers, ship's company, and W.R.N.S.
is about four hundred. Since 1922 the number of boys has
never fallen below twelve hundred. Up to the present time
over a hundred thousand boys have been trained here.

H.M.S. *Ganges* has had a proud record during both Great
Wars. During the 1914-18 war the boys spent much of their
spare time splicing the wire nets used in submarine defence
and carrying them to lighters alongside the pier. With the
outbreak of the second war in 1939, the *Ganges* bade a tem-
porary farewell to her boys. In common with similar establishments she was turned over in April 1940 to the training
of "hostilities ratings," and a new home for the boys was
found in the Isle of Man. In January 1946 she resumed her
normal life, and with her fine buildings, including a splendid
swimming-bath, gymnasium, drill-shed, naval museum, her
spacious playing-fields, and enthusiastic officers she flies a
challenging flag.

CHAPTER IX

THE DEBEN

THE Deben is one of Suffolk's kindlier streams. It has neither the fame of the Stour nor the pride of the Orwell, but in place of glory it has charm and a simple pastoral beauty that endear it to those who have an eye for the milder aspects of valley scenery. In Debenham, Wickham Market, and Woodbridge it has three of the friendliest old towns in Suffolk. Its poet is Edward FitzGerald—dear old Fitz! On its banks we may sit as he did, to

> Glance at the wheeling Orb of change,
> And greet it with a kindly smile.

Debenham itself, with its broad streets of pleasant, colour-washed and homely old cottages, is built on the slopes of a low hill that gives airiness and dignity to the town, which is now little more than a village in aspect and character. It has a clean, inviting appearance, though it lacks any particular distinction either of architecture or lay-out. The discovery of an anchor in the neighbourhood some time ago was further evidence that the river was formerly navigable as far as Debenham, though now it is navigable only as far as Woodbridge, twenty miles away.

The Deben rises at Brice's Farm, less than a mile north of the town, and runs through the streets of Debenham along a deep bed with neatly clipped hedges along the banks. There is some confusion about its course as it leaves. If you take the Framlingham road you walk along the side of what appears to be the river bed, but is in fact the old road, several feet below the level of the present road, and the water has drained into it.

I remember clearly every detail of my last visit to the Deben. From Debenham I made my way downstream past low-lying fields and old farmhouses to Cretingham, a small cluster of red roofs round a grey church tower. The whole village as I see it in mind, from the point where my eye first glimpsed it as I looked across the fields through a gap between two elm trees, might be painted on a small canvas. It is a painting any man would be happy to possess. Continuing along the winding road through this well-wooded, sheltered, and fertile countryside I came to Brandeston and sat for a few minutes in the church to reflect upon John Lowes, vicar of the parish for fifty years until he lost his life in 1646 when he was convicted of witchcraft and hanged at Bury St. Edmunds.

Belief in witchcraft was so strong in Suffolk during the seventeenth century that when persecution was at its height no fewer than sixty of the one hundred and nine convicted in England were hanged in Suffolk. John Lowes was in his eightieth year when that old witch-hound, Matthew Hopkins of Manningtree, sniffed him out, and after reducing him to a state of delirium gained a confession of familiarity with the devil. One of the Revetts of Brandeston Hall wrote of this case: "I have it from them who watched with him, that they kept him awake several nights together, and ran him backwards and forwards about the room until he was out of breath; then they rested him a little, and then they ran him again; and this they did for several days and nights together till he was quite weary of his life, and scarce sensible of what he said or did. They swam him at Framlingham, but that was no true rule to try him by, for they put in honest people at the same time, and they swam as well as he." Throughout the trial the poor old man maintained that he was innocent, but no mercy was shown him. He was even denied the consolations of Christian burial, but we are told that as he walked to the place of execution he calmly read the burial service through to himself, as though reading it over his own body.

Brandeston Hall, formerly the home of the Revett family and now a preparatory school for Framlingham College, is within sight from the church, and also from the road. The present house, which is of imposing appearance as it stands among stately lime and chestnut trees, is built in gabled Tudor style of warm red brick, but is in fact modern. Only the east wing of the original house is left; the rest was burnt down about a hundred years ago.

The most interesting member of this old Suffolk family was Nicholas Revett, who lived from 1720 to 1804, and who, in collaboration with James Stuart, wrote the first volume of the *Antiquities of Athens*, the book that may be said to have introduced Greek architecture to the English public. Later he prepared the *Antiquities of Ionia* for the society of Dilettanti.

After leaving Brandeston I followed the road through Kettleburgh to Easton, formerly a seat of the Dukes of Hamilton, and then turned off the main road along a secondary road close to the willowy Deben till I reached a few scattered cottages. This, I was assured, was Letheringham, but I saw no sign of the church, the abbey, or the Tudor gatehouse I wished to see. The church, I was informed, was straight ahead. Of the gatehouse I had been advised to visit, no one, apparently, had ever heard. But at least there was the church, so I continued along the road, which soon deteriorated into a rough track, and I was convinced that it led to nothing more public than a farm. I was almost right in this, for Letheringham Abbey is a farm now, and one that is obviously well conducted. After lingering a few minutes to admire its fine herd of cattle, I discovered that behind it was the church, a small, grey building, apparently lost and forgotten in its churchyard close to this modern and bustling farmstead. Yet here I found memorials to Wingfields and Nauntons, proud names in Tudor and Stuart England. Inside the church my fancy played with the figure of Sir Robert Naunton, secretary of state to James I and master of the court of wards, who wrote that valuable account of Queen Elizabeth's courtiers under the title *Fragmenta Regalia, or Observations on the late Queen Elizabeth her Times and Favourites.*

Sir Robert's book is interesting as the first of those collections of short character-studies that became so popular during the seventeenth century. Its subjects belonged to the previous century. Sir Robert wrote as an old man recollecting the scenes of his early life, and doubtless part if not all the *Fragmenta Regalia* was written at Letheringham, perhaps at the end of days spent in pacing those secluded water meadows, so conducive still to quiet reflection. The work was kept in manuscript during his lifetime, but was frequently reprinted after his death in 1635.

Sir Robert converted part of what had been a small priory here into a mansion for himself, to which he removed from the less sheltered village of Alderton. Much of this mansion was pulled down about 1770, and all that now remains of the Augustinian priory is the gatehouse, roofed and in good preservation, which I found at last in the field beyond the churchyard.

Not far from here, I am told, there is a green lane with a gibbet and chains standing close by it, and connected with the gibbet is a grim story of a murderer who was lynched by his own neighbours.

This had been a very pleasurable ramble through the Deben villages in company with several of their illustrious shades. But it was now time to take a brisker step forward to Wickham Market, and I was the better able to do so by finding that the river itself had been cleaned beyond Easton, for it seemed as though the Deben had resolved to come out of its slow and oozy bed and prepare itself for the gay life of the Woodbridge river-boats.

When Napoleon's armies were expected to invade England and Martello towers were built along the Suffolk coast from Felixstowe to Aldeburgh, the King's Dragoons were stationed at Wickham Market, ready to defend the Yarmouth road or any part of the Suffolk coast where the enemy might attempt to land. This sleepy little market town has had its moments of excitement in all England's wars, but it has always slipped back peacefully to fulfil its proper function as a centre of quiet country life. John Kirby, author of the *Suffolk Traveller*, lived here for twenty-one years. His son, Joshua Kirby, F.R.S., became Gainsborough's great friend when the two lived near each other at Ipswich. They met while Gainsborough was sketching on the banks of the Orwell and remained friends for life. When Gainsborough was dying he expressed the wish to be buried at Kew near his old friend, and the wish was respected. It was a strange companionship in some ways. The two appear to have been widely separated in temperament and the major interests of their lives, but there can be no doubt about the strength of their mutual regard. The Kirbys were a remarkable family. Joshua Kirby's daughter, Mrs. Sarah Trimmer, became a well-known writer for children and a pioneer of modern education.

The church at Wickham Market, detected at a distance by its tall spire, should be visited if only to see the beautiful wood-carving of the reredos and the Grinling Gibbons panel in the handsome pulpit, representing St. John writing the Fourth Gospel. This panel was formerly in the Savoy Chapel, London.

From Wickham Market the broadening river flows through rich parks and pastures with Loudham Hall on one side and Rendlesham Hall on the other, as it makes its way between Ufford and Eyke to Woodbridge. At Rendlesham, according to Camden, Redwald, the most famous of the East Anglian kings, held his court. He was the first East Anglian king to embrace Christianity, and the interesting thing about his story is that his wife remained pagan, with the result that two altars, one pagan and one Christian, were maintained together in the one church. For this Fuller called Redwald a " mongrel Christian." That such a thing was possible is an enlightening fact for those who study the early history of Christianity in England. But Redwald's faith can never have been firm. In the end his strong-minded wife drew him back into paganism.

While leaning across the fence of Rendlesham Park to watch the deer grazing under the oaks or running through the bracken, we may recall the Thelluson case, which gave the Rendlesham family so much notoriety a hundred and fifty years ago.

Peter Isaac Thelluson died in possession of what was then regarded as a large fortune, and the terms of his will caused widespread alarm. He bequeathed a hundred thousand pounds to his wife and family. The residue of his property, amounting to something like six hundred thousand pounds, he committed to the charge of trustees who were instructed to keep it invested in land, and allow the rents and profits to accumulate and again be used for the purchase of additional estates throughout the lives of his sons and grandsons. After the death of the last surviving son or grandson the entire property was to be handed over to the eldest great-grandson. By this means the old man hoped to establish his heirs as one of the wealthiest families in the kingdom. Various calculations were made as to the value of the property likely to be inherited by this prospective great-grandson, and many economists were of the opinion that if several other rich merchants followed his example the whole of the country's wealth would quickly fall into very few hands. The Thelluson family resolved to test the legality of the will in the court of Chancery, arguing that though Mr. Thelluson might leave his property to whomsoever he wished, he could not dispose of rents and profits that might accrue from the skilful management of these estates after his death, and that to allow such accumulation as the will enjoined was not in the public interest. They pointed out that the ultimate inheritor might become a danger to national liberty and too powerful for a subject. But in 1799 Lord Chancellor Loughborough pronounced the will valid, and on appeal his judgment was upheld. The will was within the letter of the law, but it was admitted to be against its spirit, so in 1800 Parliament passed an Act forbidding such accumulations to be made in the future for a period longer than twenty-one years.

The sequel is amusing. The last grandson died in 1856, fifty-nine years after Peter Isaac Thelluson, and a dispute then arose as to whether the eldest Thelluson great-grandson should inherit, or the grandson of the eldest son, Lord Rendlesham. The House of Lords decided on appeal that the present head of the family, the grandson of the eldest son, was the legal heir. But when this property that had been viewed with so much alarm was handed over it was found to be worth very little more than the original six hundred thousand pounds. The court of Chancery had safeguarded the national interest by eating up most of the annual profits which would otherwise have gone into the pockets of the old man's sons and grandsons, so he had, in fact, impoverished and not enriched his heirs.

The fifth Lord Rendlesham was a friend of Edward VII, who shot with him regularly over his Suffolk estates. He died in 1911, after being Member of Parliament for East Suffolk for many years and an extremely popular figure in the county.

In *What I Remember,* Dame Millicent Garrett Fawcett tells the story of a Suffolk vicar who was in the habit of pausing at intervals while reading the lessons in church, in order to explain them to his rural congregations. On one occasion he came to the passage, "King of Kings, Lord of Lords," and looked up to comment: "There's many a sort of lords. Lord Rendlesham, what is he? Nothing but a poorr earrthy worrum. That's not the Lord we have here."

After the First Great War a large part of the Rendlesham estates were sold to meet taxation, though the tenant-farmers and cottagers begged their popular landlord to try to carry on.

I am always obliged to hold myself in check on the subject of parsons, but as we are now so near Eyke church, with its fine Norman arches, perhaps I may be allowed to recall Ralph Garthe, who held the living in plurality with others towards the end of the sixteenth century, and so neglected his duties that the people of Eyke threatened to plough their fields on Sundays unless he gave them more attention. To-day this might not seem so shocking, though while I have been spending most of my Sundays touring Suffolk in search of material for this book, I could not fail to observe during the very wet summer of 1946, when a great part of the harvest was ruined, that though Sunday was frequently the sunniest day of the week, few farmers could be seen working in their fields.

Ufford, on the opposite bank of the Deben, named after Uffa, or Wuffa, grandfather of Redwald, after whom the royal house of East Anglia were called the Wuffingas, should be visited in order to see the remarkable font cover in its church. It is in the form of a papal triple-crown, surmounted with the Pelican in Piety symbol. And as parsons are in mind we must recall that Ufford had a parson in the seventeenth century, Richard Luskin, of whom his parishioners complained that he was "a very cold preacher and a common swearer." A petition for his removal was drawn up in 1641, but it was unsuccessful. Parson Luskin remained at Ufford till 1678. He is said to have taken the services up to the last Sunday of his life, and to have died at the great age of a hundred and ten years. Whether there is confirmation of this or not I cannot say. As we shall see in the next chapter, Orford had a parson who was credited with a much longer life than the records prove. As the Rev. Richard Luskin was so unpopular he may have seemed to his parishioners to be an unconscionable while a-dying. Perhaps in 1641 he pleaded with them to bear with him a little longer, adding something to his years in an attempt to persuade them that it would not be for long at the worst. I know of one parson who practised such a deception in asking a patron for the gift of a living. He pleaded to be old and needy and unfit for harder work, though he was in the middle of life and lived to enjoy the emoluments of his easy cure to a great age.

But however pleasant these leisurely strolls along the banks of the Deben may be, the one town that all men seek sooner or later is Woodbridge. I am reminded of this while writing of Ufford, because Ufford has an amusing anecdote about Edward FitzGerald, the *genius loci* of Woodbridge and one of the most beloved of English authors. FitzGerald called one day on Captain Brooke of Ufford, one of the greatest book collectors of his day. The drawing-room of Captain Brooke's house had been newly furnished, and it may have been its splendour that made FitzGerald more than usually nervous and ill at ease. He sat down on an amber satin couch, and presently a black stream was seen trickling down the front of it and forming a little pool at the poet's feet. Poor FitzGerald in sitting down had forgotten a penny bottle of ink he had tucked away in his tail pocket.

I am almost afraid of writing about Woodbridge with its narrow streets and wide river, so many have extolled its charms. It is one of the most lovable old towns in England, a place one never forgets and always thinks of with a feeling of friendly warmth. Alas, it is in grave danger of becoming too popular. Everyone knows the old mill by the river. It has been sketched by many artists, though it could hardly be called beautiful. Historically it is of great interest, for it is said to be the oldest tide-mill in England. There has, of course, been more than one building on the site, but for more than seven hundred and fifty years a tide-mill has stood on the Deben at this point.

Looking along the quay towards the old "Boat" Inn, to

which the ferry rights used to be attached, we can fancy we
see FitzGerald himself slouching along with his old Inverness
cape thrown loosely about his shoulders to display a double-
breasted flowered waistcoat underneath. He will probably
appear to the imagination in slippers and with a handkerchief
tied over his hat. FitzGerald's hat was one of the jokes of
Woodbridge. He used it as a pocket, and would frequently
remove it to make use of his pocket handkerchief or something else deposited there. On one occasion he was seen to
wrap a large piece of apple pie very carefully in his handkerchief and bear it away in his hat.

FitzGerald's dress was a curious mixture of the ceremonial
and the seafaring. His hat he wore indoors as well as out,
but while he kept that important extremity, the head, so well
protected, the other was usually neglected. In summer, in
fact, he often went bare-footed, with his shoes slung over his
shoulder at the end of a stick. He was a man much given to
losing things and was once heard muttering: "That is just
about the way I shall get to heaven, I suppose, searching for
what I cannot find."

This lazy and eccentric man, whose listlessness was probably due to his being the child of first cousins, and his mother
herself the child of first cousins, had a peculiar hold on the
affections of many of the best minds of his generation. When
at the end of his life Tennyson was asked which of his friends
he had loved most, he replied: "Why, old Fitz, to be sure! "
And Thackeray, before leaving England in 1852 to lecture in
America, wrote to FitzGerald that if anything should happen
to him on the journey he wished his daughters to know that
FitzGerald was the best and oldest friend their father ever
had. Yet he could be rude to people for whom he had no
use. When the rector of Woodbridge called on him and took
the liberty of saying that he regretted that he never saw him
at church, FitzGerald replied: "Sir, you might have conceived that a man has not come to my years of life without
thinking much of these things. I believe I may say that I
have reflected on them fully as much as yourself. You need
not repeat this visit." It was true that he never attended service in church, but he would often sit in the porch while the
service was in progress and slip away quietly before the con-

The Shire Hall, Woodbridge
River Deben at Woodbridge

gregation came out. It was his quiet sense of humour and
lack of egotism that made him so admirable a writer of letters
—after Cowper and Lamb the best we have had. He was also
a very quotable man. His chance remarks were often repeated
and laughed over by his friends. He had the Irish gift of
saying the unexpected thing. When, for example, he learnt
that he suffered from heart disease, he said he was glad of it
because "when he came to die he didn't want to have a lot
of women messing about him."

The church FitzGerald did not attend is a noble pile, built
by well-to-do merchants close to Woodbridge Abbey on the
site of a Saxon church. When alterations were made to the
present church the remains of a boar were found buried
under the western foundations, an instance of a pagan custom
believed to ward off evil spirits. The font is one of the three
in East Anglia with eight rayed panels depicting the seven
sacraments and the crucifixion. There are only thirty-eight
Seven Sacrament Fonts of any kind in England, and all except
two are in Norfolk and Suffolk.

A few steps across the market-place from the church is the
small shop marked with a tablet inscribed "E.F.G. 1860-
1873," where FitzGerald had rooms, and looking up towards
the Dutch style Shire Hall is the "Bull" Inn, which used to
be so busy on the occasion of the Woodbridge Horse Show
that not only would the yard be full of gigs, but they would
be lined up to the bottom of New Street, which, incidentally,
is probably the oldest street in the town. Another interesting
feature to children was that a man was buried in the "Bull"
yard, which was a matter of great wonder. But the most
interesting tale of the "Bull" yard is again a FitzGerald
anecdote. After Tennyson had stayed there with his son,
Hallam, FitzGerald had a word with the landlord, a genial
host who took great pride in his horses and had shown them
to the Tennysons.

"You ought to consider your house honoured by such a
guest," said FitzGerald, "he is Poet Laureate."

"Dissay," replied the landlord, "but 'e didn't fare to know
much about hosses."

FitzGerald's was a good sort of life; reading the same old
books over and over again, walking with his great black dog

L　　　145

Pinmill
The Tide-mill, Woodbridge

in the afternoon, and smoking his pipe by the open window at the close of day while the blackbirds and thrushes sang their last songs and finally left the garden to the nightingales, still as melodious as ever at Woodbridge. He was one of those rare souls who are able to live their poetry, and we frequently find in his letters a prose equivalent—as far as such a thing is possible—of a stanza from his verse. The familiar verse from Omar, for instance:

> A Book of Verses underneath the Bough,
> A Jug of Wine, a Loaf of Bread—and Thou
> Beside me singing in the Wilderness—
> Oh, wilderness were Paradise enow,

has its counterpart in the sentence: "I am happiest going in my little boat round the coast to Aldborough, with some bottled porter, some bread and cheese, and some good rough soul who works the boat and chews his tobacco in peace." The difference between these two passages is perhaps as interesting as their similarity. It amounts to the difference between wine and bottled porter, which in turn may be held to symbolise the difference between Persia and East Anglia.

There is much in the personality of FitzGerald that expresses the spirit of Suffolk. Neither he nor the county have ever been inclined to show off in the way some persons and places do. Men from mountainous regions are nearly always troubled with "an unco guid conceit o' themselves," or the Welsh or English equivalent of that expression. Fitz-Gerald was an individualist to the marrow of his bones, and Suffolk is the county for men who have the courage to live their own lives in their own way. I know a Suffolk naturalist who lives so defiantly his own natural life that he still refuses to alter his clock when Parliament decrees that the sun shall be deemed inaccurate in recording the time.

"I live by the sun," declared the naturalist, when I expressed surprise at the time registered on the face of his clock.

"It is rather awkward when we are two hours different from everybody else," his wife interjected.

"Not at all," said the naturalist. "Why should I pay attention to what other people are doing when I am eating my breakfast?"

No doubt he cared as little as he said he did, but when the country returns to normal time I cannot help feeling that he chuckles to see everybody else get back into step with himself—and the sun!

I know also of a Suffolk sportsman who was in the fields— or some other place that it is no part of my business to make public—when a bomb fell near his house. Instantly he ran home, but before going indoors to enquire about his wife and family he went to the rear of the house to speak reassuring words to his dog and see that his gun was undamaged. I do not say that all Suffolk people are of this individualistic character, but I suspect that you will find more of this kind in Suffolk than in most counties. I cannot say in all counties, because Norfolk and Yorkshire folk have ways of their own in all conscience!

Whether this kind of thing is praiseworthy or not I neither know nor greatly care, but it is at least honest. In an age of considerable humbug FitzGerald was an honest man. He genuinely tried to face the truth about life, about himself, and, most disconcerting of all, about his wife, who was the daughter of Bernard Barton, one of the "Woodbridge wits." He showed that the first two can be done, and that the third cannot. When the truth was hidden from him he was honest enough to say, "I do not know; I cannot help; and I distress myself as little as I can." Indeed, in studying FitzGerald's candour with himself it is difficult not to feel that even this admirable quality can be practised to excess. He knew his own weaknesses and freely accepted them. On his gravestone in Boulge churchyard he caused to be inscribed the words, "It is He that hath made us and not we ourselves." Most of us have an exaggerated conception of our own importance, but it does seem possible that FitzGerald would have done a great deal more in life if he could have had more faith in himself.

No doubt he was a little unbalanced. Even that he was ready to admit. All the FitzGeralds were mad, he said, and added that on the whole he thought he must be saner than his brother, because he knew he was mad and his brother didn't. One of the things that was usually set down as evidence of this lack of sanity in FitzGerald was his great admiration for a young fisherman, Joseph Fletcher, familiarly known as Posh. It was surely the opposite. FitzGerald saw in this drunken fisherman an exuberance of life that he himself lacked, and showed good sense in associating himself with it.

Again there was characteristic East Anglian common sense —lack of something, too, perhaps, but still common sense—in his dislike of the profound systems of philosophy and aesthetics then in vogue, most of them imported from Germany. Of these he wrote in a letter to Pollock, "Then there's an account of Hallam's literature, with a deal about aesthetics in it. Oh, Pollock! Let you and I and Spedding stand out against these damnable German humbugs! "

FitzGerald had the good sense to maintain the common touch, and it is part of the virtue of Suffolk that nowhere is it lost. The county has none of those extraordinary little settlements where superior people assemble to live what they conceive to be superior lives. We have seen how Ipswich maintains its relationship with the countryside, and that each little group of villages in the county is within reach of a sane and simple market town. This is because no part of Suffolk has been artificially industrialised. It has no mushroom cities, no business magnate's nightmare conception of Utopia. On the contrary it is a county in daily touch with the land and the sea, either of which will soon knock the nonsense out of a man. It is also a county with strong traditions and proud of its history, wearing its heritage lightly and holding the memory of its ancient riches in a thousand curious customs and prejudices. One of these is continued in the name of one of the houses FitzGerald lived in as a lodger, Farlingay Hall.

A strange tale hangs on this name. About the year 970 manorial lands in Woodbridge were granted by King Edgar the Peaceable to the monks of Ely as part of the Liberty of St. Etheldreda, who was also known as St. Audrey. The word tawdry is said to be derived from trinkets sold at fairs on St. Audrey's Day. It is related of a Woodbridge baker that he sold farthing gingerbread cakes cut in the shape of the saint on this day, and did so well out of his business that he was able to build himself a house, which he called " Farthing Cake Hall." In course of time this became Farlingay Hall.

Behind Woodbridge are lanes as quiet and villages as serene as any in the county. Most of them have one or two kindly old houses to remind us of Tudor or Stuart England. Great Bealings has Seckford Hall, a gracious old house with Tudor chimneys and crowstep gables. Above the door are the arms of Sir Thomas Seckford, a prominent name in Woodbridge history. Grundisburgh, a neighbouring village, has Basts, a fine old house, and Grundisburgh Hall, built in 1593, the seat of Lord Cranworth, which has been in the possession of the Gurdon family for two hundred years. The village stocks and whipping-post are preserved in the grounds. Otley, too, has a lovely old hall. All are within a few miles of Woodbridge.

In summer the Deben Yacht Club, which has its headquarters at Woodbridge, makes the river a most entertaining sight, for the river is the principal thoroughfare of Woodbridge, though an old sailor with whom I gossiped on the quay thought it far less interesting than when strange cargoes were coming in from foreign ports. "Fifty years ago," he said, " the shipping trade was still good. I have seen as many as fifty boats on the river at once. There would be Swedish and Norwegian boats bringing timber to Brown's there. Coal and grain would come in to the Mill docks, and Dutch tiles. There used to be four Trinity House pilots on the river. There isn't one now." He thought there was less interest in pleasure to-day than there was in work in his young days, and when he said this I remembered that FitzGerald was a fishmonger. There was character in trade before professionalism and slick efficiency killed it. As a port, Woodbridge always had a more exciting time than its larger neighbour, Ipswich, in the way that small tradesmen often get far more fun out of life than their more systematic and ambitious neighbours. Woodbridge seems to have got a considerable part of its trade through undercutting Ipswich. But it had its regular trade, too. It was also an important shipbuilding centre at one time, and boats are still built there. Peter Pett, a member of the famous shipbuilding family, settled at Woodbridge for a time, after marrying the daughter of the landlord of the "Crown," and built some fine boats from timber grown in the county.

There were three hundred and three mariners and thirteen ships from Woodbridge at the Siege of Calais; three of its ships went out to join the English fleet that assembled to intercept the Armada; and in the last war two yachts left Woodbridge as soon as the appeal was made for assistance with the evacuation of Dunkirk. Such was the seafaring fame of this old town that in 1844 there were thirty-five master mariners living in it. Much of that is changed, and I was inclined to agree with the old seaman that the quality of life has not improved as much as might be supposed with increased leisure and the multiplication of irrelevant accessories. We agreed that we have opportunities for making leisure more interesting than it used to be, but that most people find work burdensome now, which should be full of interest and happiness, and should promote health instead of destroying it.

Woodbridge, as we should expect, has produced its heroes. There was John Foxe, born at the "Crown" in 1528, who was captured by pirates twice, and the second time was sold into slavery, to be released from Alexandria after fourteen years. His story is told by Hakluyt, a Suffolk parson, who held the living of Wetheringsett.

Like all the smaller fishing towns and villages on the Suffolk coast, Woodbridge has long been a favourite resort for artists. In FitzGerald's day Thomas Churchyard found many subjects in the neighbourhood. Some of his paintings are to be seen in Christchurch Mansion, Ipswich. The most prominent of the modern Woodbridge painters has been Bernard Priestman, R.A.

Across the river we find Little Haddon Hall, built in 1914 by Sir George Manners in a style similar to that of his family's seat in Derbyshire. Behind it is Sutton Hoo, made famous in 1939 when the funeral ship of an East Anglian king was discovered in a tumulus there, after lying buried for nearly thirteen hundred years. Only three ship burials from Saxon times have so far been discovered, and all three were in south-east Suffolk, two at Sutton Hoo and one at Snape. By far the most valuable was the 1939 find. The ship itself was a boat more than eighty feet long, with a beam of fourteen feet, once

rowed by thirty-eight oarsmen. The British Museum experts
have now given it as their opinion that the harness fittings
—masterpieces of the art of both goldsmith and lapidary—
were made in East Anglia. With the helmet, mail-coat, shield,
and jewelled sword of the dead warrior a large ceremonial
whetstone was found, together with Byzantine silver dishes,
bronze bowls, and a beautiful gold buckle of English workmanship, showing Swedish influence in the design. Years of
careful study must be given to this remarkable and in many
respects unique discovery before a full report can be made
on it. When this is done, the discovery at Sutton Hoo may
prove to be as valuable for the light it throws on its period as
Stonehenge and Hadrian's Wall are for the light they throw
on theirs. When the burial ship was unearthed it was thought
to be that of the East Anglian King Redwald, but experts have
now been able to establish by their identification of some of
the gold coins found in the purse that the burial must have
been later than Redwald's. One interesting feature is the
Christian symbolism found on some of the objects, in spite of
the pagan character of the burial. Spoons are inscribed Saul
and Paul, in reference to the saint's conversion, and the hanging bowl has the Christian symbol of the fish on it. Some
of the objects found must have been old at the time of the
burial. They may have been heirlooms, and the warrior have
had Christian ancestors. Probably he had, though this is not
necessarily indicated, for the mingling of Christian and pagan
symbols was not unusual at this time.

From Woodbridge to Bawdsey the road runs through high
banks covered in summer with bracken and gorse, to emerge
on breezy Sutton Common, where golden ragwort and purple
ling blaze between belts of pine. After leaving Sutton we
run into a region of small fields and pleasant pastoral country,
with tall elms standing beside red brick cottages roofed with
Dutch tiles. Elm trees and hawthorn hedges form much-
needed screens when the east wind is blowing. Near Alderton, a plain little red-brick village, we find pines and heath
again. These East Suffolk villages a little distance inland are
for the most part plain and without any of the architectural
distinction that makes the West Suffolk villages so attractive,
but they are made delightful by the brightness of their

atmosphere and the exhilarating freshness of the breezes that
blow through them. Their beauty lies not in the eyes of the
beholder but in the blood that tingles in his veins and makes
him feel that all life is good and infinitely worth while.
Nearer the river is Ramsholt, with its curious church standing on a hill above the river. One of the favourite trips of
holiday-makers at Woodbridge is a trip down the Deben to
Ramsholt for tea; but the extreme difficulty of navigating
this river should be mentioned. It has a reach called
"Troublesome," where many a "foreigner" has been stuck
all night, waiting for the next flood.

The whole of this coastal heath is a glorious prospect, brilliant in colour as an enormous peacock's tail, and when we
reach the mouth of the river and sit upon the bank to reflect
upon the joy of the way we have come we may realise how
much of what is best in Suffolk we have been able to see
while following the course of this peaceful river—heath and
woodland, quaint old villages, Suffolk tales by the way, and
all the time the unspoilt river where FitzGerald sailed his
boat and discussed with poets, scholars, and quiet fisherfolk
the vanity of life's prizes and the value of its simple pleasures.

CHAPTER X

THE ALDE AND THE ORE

WE move easily from Woodbridge to Aldeburgh and find
ourselves in the same distinguished company in both places.
FitzGerald of Woodbridge confided that to him there was no
sea like the Aldeburgh sea, which, he said, spoke to him; and
Crabbe of Aldeburgh dabbled in medicine at Woodbridge
for about four years. It was at this time that he met and made
love to Miss Sarah Elmy of Parham, the "Mira" of his poems,
who first "with loftier notions fired" his soul, and relieved
him of some of the morbidity that already oppressed him,
though we are in error if we take a gloomy view of Crabbe's
personality. His muse had a heavy step, and the knowledge
that he was a parson seems to give many of his readers a serious
conception of him, though parson-poets are not on the whole
to be regarded as finding the burden of existence too grievous
a load. The truth is that in later life, when mellowed by
years and literary success, Crabbe was rumoured to be something of a ladies' man, which is certainly not the kind of
person to be deduced from most of his writings. Some of the
stricter members of his congregation are said to have looked
askance on his innocent gallantries. There is a story of two
maiden ladies who when asked about him used to smooth their
mittens prudishly and say: "*We* never thought much of Mr.
Crabbe." But even while at Woodbridge he was bold enough
to rhyme about the seamier side of life in a didactic satire
entitled *Inebriety*.

In Crabbe as in FitzGerald we are confronted with the
downright honesty of the East Anglian. Anyone who cannot
face the truth about life, or about himself, should keep away
from these uncompromising counties. Only last week I had
a letter from a lady of my acquaintance who had been called
home to nurse her aged mother in Norfolk. She wrote:
"Here no one is afraid of the truth, and I was told yesterday

by the shepherd of seventy, 'Oh, my dear, you *have* aged since you came here. But there, you've got a pretty daughter and you'll be a grandmother yet.'"

Crabbe served his native town as apothecary first, and later as curate. Though he never held a Suffolk living, he spent thirteen years in the Suffolk villages of Parham and Great Glenham, and in *The Borough* he described Aldeburgh and the people he had known there, who were, he said:

> a wild, amphibious race,
> With sullen woe display'd in every face;
> Who far from civil arts and social fly,
> And scowl at strangers with suspicious eye.

They are as tough to-day as they were then, though less crude, perhaps, in expressing it. Well-to-do visitors and the cultivated people who have settled in the town during the last fifty years or so have done something towards civilising it; but Slaughden Quay, a dreary waste of shingle between Aldeburgh Marshes and the sea, retains the sinister, foreboding atmosphere that Crabbe described.

> Here samphire-banks and salt-wort bound the flood,
> There stakes and sea-weeds withering on the mud;
> And higher up, a ridge of all things base,
> Which some strong tide has roll'd upon the place.

Here also the yellow poppy and the sea-pea, renowned in legend, grow.

Between this bank of bleaching stones and the sand-dunes to the north lies the town, with the ancient Moot Hall at the heart of it, though no longer at the centre as in the sixteenth century, when two rows of houses stood on its seaward side. North of it stood the market-cross, and two days each week the wide space in front of Wentworth Terrace used to be full of the stalls and booths of traders, upon whom the people of Aldeburgh had to depend for their supplies before their booths were replaced by permanent shops.

In seeking information about this sturdy little town, so full of Suffolk character, I was advised to call upon the mayor, Mr. S. H. Lewer, and was the more delighted to do so because he was the brother of a dear old friend of mine. I had previously regarded my friend, who was then eighty-eight, as the most vigorous octogenarian I had ever known. The mayor enquired about his brother's health, and when I said how wonderful he was for his years, I was cut short with:

"His years? Why, he isn't much older than I am." To my amazement I learnt that my genial and knowledgeable host was himself an octogenarian of several years standing. Clearly, I thought, the Suffolk coast is the place for long life and abounding health. I had further evidence in support of the view a few months later, when I found a Lowestoft man to whom I had been introduced seven years earlier, when he was ninety-two, still alive and enjoying his daily walk alone at ninety-nine.[1]

But I had called to learn something of the history of Aldeburgh, and as I sat with the mayor on the terrace of his beautiful garden, overlooking the marshes, I was soon presented with a different picture of the borough from that portrayed by Crabbe, where the wretched and wicked poor dragged out their unhappy lives in squalid hovels. The life described by the mayor was in no way stunted by poverty or frustrated by isolation. I heard about the men who left Aldeburgh to fight the Spanish Armada, the Cables, Wards, and Hakins, whose descendants enlisted in the wars of our own day.

"Yes," said the mayor, "the same old families have lived here for centuries, fighting the sea and hauling in their nets. And the courage of the Aldeburgh lifeboatmen—James Cable, for example—is proverbial."

I asked if he had noticed any change in the local character as the result of so many young men going to the war.

"Yes," he said; "but," he added, "I think the coming of the motor buses to Aldeburgh had an even greater influence."

"In what way?" I asked.

"Before they came," he explained, "there was a greater proportion of flaxen-haired, blue-eyed people in Aldeburgh than there is to-day. Many of the children are dark now as the result of marriages with the dark-haired girls inland."

---

[1] Mr. J. A. Ayers, who celebrated his hundredth birthday on the 29th March, 1948.

Aldeburgh had always been a seafaring place, he told me; but the character of its trade was changing. The last of the old cod boats, mentioned in records of Queen Elizabeth's day and in use up to the early years of the present century, could still be seen at Slaughden, a great hulk by the river, in use as a holiday home for orphan children.

I heard about the sufferings of Aldeburgh during the war years and the problems that faced it in the future, for the mayor was not a man who lived in the past.

"There is the serious water problem," he said. "The supply has sunk appreciably during the past few years. We get our water from the coralline crag, where the water is held up by the clay underneath. It is now so low that we may soon have to go several miles inland for an adequate supply."

This water problem is serious; and is also very interesting from a scientific point of view. The climate of East Suffolk has been affected by the drying up of the rivers. We discussed this until the mayor pointed out that we were wandering from the subject of Aldeburgh. At once I enquired about the Moot Hall.

"The Moot Hall. Ah, yes! You will be interested to hear that an American recently offered us twenty times its assessed value," said the mayor, "but of course we have no intention of parting with it."

Then we settled down on a garden seat with a pile of old books and papers between us, which the mayor had very kindly collected for me, and were soon reading out specially good bits to each other as we discovered them. But how can all these be condensed into the brief space at my disposal here? Perhaps there is a better service to be rendered than that of simply setting down every scrap of information I can lay hands on, namely to impart some sense of the pleasure to be derived from the search, and the rich harvest that can reward it. Matthew Prior was wrong in saying:

'Tis not how well an Author says,
But 'tis how much, that gathers praise;
Thus each should down with all he thinks,
As Boys eat Bread, to fill up Chinks.

As an example of some of the good things we turned up, there is an entry in the Aldeburgh Account Book recording that "Captain Fyrbussher, and others of his Company" were arrested on a charge of piracy and sent to London for trial. This was Martin Frobisher, the Elizabethan navigator, himself; and the mayor reminded me that this had been a famous coast for pirates. A parson of Hollesley named Richard Evans was mixed up with them, and the "King's Head" at Orford was a distributing place for contraband goods landed in the neighbourhood.

Another old paper turned out to be an order from Fairfax, dated 1647, relieving the town of the burden of quartering soldiers: "Forasmuch as the Towne of Aldeburgh in the Countye of Suff. stands upon the Sea and hath as I am informed beene at great chardges in fortefying and in furnishing Amunicon and other pvisions For the service of the Parlyment. Above any other place in Suff. and that being a Sea Towne is not soe capable to quarter Horse. . . ." From this we turned to the celebrations during this period, and found that the bells were rung for Fairfax, which cost the town ninepence in beer for the ringers. Tumbledown Dick Cromwell's proclamation was celebrated with half a barrel of beer, while for Charles II's proclamation there was a whole barrel.

Among the royalist parsons in the district at this time was John Fenn of Theberton, whose stone near the south door of the church has an inscription beginning with the sentence: "Here is a stone to sitt upon under which lies in hopes to rise, Honest John Fenn." But we also found the record of a much less worthy minister. This was a Mr. Violett, a curate who flourished shortly after Honest John Fenn. Mr. Violett was charged with being drunk and singing ribald songs. Among the papers in the Moot Hall referring to his case is the deposition of a lady staying in one of the inns he visited. She complained that at midnight he appeared at her bedside carrying a pot of beer which he tried to make her drink.

Aldeburgh never played an important part in the Suffolk woollen industry; but Mr. Lewer, as an ardent gardener, pointed out that it was the Flemish weavers who brought the appreciation of gardens to East Anglia, and that the Suffolk coast is specially mentioned as growing many root crops. The people of Theberton anticipated Turnip Townsend by growing turnips in 1674.

Like Dunwich, Aldeburgh has suffered much from the violence of the sea, and petitions were sent to Elizabeth's commissioners for assistance in bearing the charge of building sea defences. The fight still continues, and as recently as 1939 the appropriate authorities were petitioned in similar terms for the same purpose. Aldeburgh must have been of considerable importance in Elizabeth's reign, for one petition to Her Majesty refers to eight hundred mariners who took a thousand lasts of herrings annually, a last being approximately four thousand pounds, and three hundred men who annually took three thousand lasts of sprats. In addition, many ships sailed into northern waters cod fishing.

Such were the tales of old Aldeburgh that I heard one pleasant July afternoon from the gentleman who was then its worthy mayor, and as I wandered down into the town again, along the straggling streets described by Wilkie Collins in *No Name*, and the promenade or Crag Path as it is called, where the Aldeburgh fishermen lean against their boats drawn up on the shingle, with anchors, coils of rope, and all the gear of their ancient craft strewn about them, I could understand the fascination this old town has for the hundreds who return to it year after year, for like other places on the Suffolk coast it is so entirely different from the usual type of English watering-place.

Behind Aldeburgh, as behind Woodbridge, we run into bluff heathlands, with pine plantations and tumuli of early Anglo-Saxon date, similar to the tumuli Mrs. Pretty excavated at Sutton Hoo just before the Second Great War. They are to be found near the road from Aldeburgh to Snape. One of them was excavated in 1862 to disclose another ship burial. Upon a finger-bone of the chieftain's skeleton hung a golden ring; at his side lay a sword. We do not know what treasures may still lie hidden under the bracken and ling of this coastal heath. There are queer stories of buried treasure all along the coast, for besides tales of ancient treasure there are tales of smugglers' hoards. But as I motored along the coast after this particular visit to Aldeburgh, my mind was captivated by a field of blue flax, and later by the neatness of Snape

Maltings, before the sombre music of the restless ocean returned to me and I remembered that its brooding passion had recently found a voice in Benjamin Britten's opera, *Peter Grimes*.

Benjamin Britten bought a windmill at Snape in 1937, and converted the circular brick base into a study. In him we have another instance of the firm hold that Suffolk has upon its sons. He is the son of a Lowestoft dentist, but was not familiar with Crabbe's work when in 1941, under a warm Californian sun, he read in *The Listener* a report of a broadcast talk by E. M. Forster and felt such nostalgia for his native Suffolk, its hard-bitten life sharpened to him by contrast with the easy life about him, that he at once sought out a copy of *The Borough*, and was inspired to write his first complete opera, *Peter Grimes*. This was produced at Sadler's Wells when that opera house was reopened after the break of six years caused by the Second Great War. In the music of *Peter Grimes* we have an evocation of the Suffolk coast as realistic in its way as the poem that occasioned it. Benjamin Britten had always lived close to the sea. He had seen the lifeboats go out and the cliffs crumble before the roaring tides. As a child he had heard the sound of the fog-horn, like the lowing of a cow that has lost its calf. These he introduces into the various scenes of his opera as background to the dramatic story of Peter Grimes.

Mingled with the unrelenting realism of life in these old ports are strands of the supernatural and uncanny. You will hear of the birth of web-footed children who grow up to be different from other people and dangerous. They are usually girls, and when old enough to have lovers they lure them out on to the marshes and there destroy them. But the strangest of the unnatural beings reputed to have been found in East Suffolk was the wild man of Orford. The story goes that one evening, when the fishermen were returning home, a strange creature was seen disporting itself on the edge of the water. It was half man and half dog in appearance, and was covered from head to foot with reddish hair. The fishermen captured the creature, dragged him up to the castle and handed him over to the governor, who invited experts to examine him. He had all the organs of speech, but was incapable of uttering more than a small range of guttural sounds. When clothes were provided for him he refused to wear them, and when taken to church he was found to have no knowledge of how a Christian should conduct himself. In his room at the castle he would sit for hours on a settle drawn up to the fire, holding his head in his hands as though suffering intensely from either pain or remorse. One night he escaped. Fishermen saw him plunging madly through the waves. When they tried to recapture him he eluded them and dived into the sea, never to reappear.

The story has points of similarity with the Black Shuck legend, and probably no greater foundation in fact. Both are important as reflecting the similarity of mind between the East Anglians of several generations ago and their Norse conquerors of many centuries earlier. Such stories are strangely reminiscent of Scandinavian mythology.

To reach Orford by road you first cross a wide heath with a few old oaks growing among the heather, and then pass through miles of dense plantation until you emerge into a fragment of natural forest between Sudbourne Hall and the river. One or two small villages, such as Butley, where the famous heraldic gateway is to be seen, and Iken, are found on the heath; but Orford is remote and secluded. With its broad streets of low cottages standing behind well-trimmed greens and a number of larger, comfortable-looking houses, it seems to me an ideal place in which to spend the autumn of life. Great chestnut trees overhang the roads and cottages, making a brave show in spring. Places are often associated in mind with one particular season, even though we have known them in every part of the year. Perhaps at one particular moment we have been more sensitive than usual, and the character of the place has left an impression on our mind that is never effaced. I have such an impression of Orford in October, with the leaves on the chestnuts crimped and bronzed, many of them falling and blowing along the roads. This, of course, is personal; the scent of chestnut trees in autumn fills me with sensations of a past age reawakening and struggling to communicate something of its pride and sorrow through the straining branches. Just what it is in Orford that gives me that sense of belonging that we all feel

Parham Old Hall
Wingfield Castle

in certain places I cannot say. I have neither lived nor stayed there for any length of time, and so far as I know no ancestor of mine ever lived there, but this personal sensation is worth recording because it will remind others of similar mysterious intimations from the past.

The pride of Orford is the castle keep, which stands on an eminence to the west of the town. From the top we may look down upon the red roofs and garden squares below and across the marshes to the sea. Orford Castle was built by Henry II to safeguard Orford Haven from foreign invaders and to strengthen his hand in dealing with his own turbulent barons. Orford was then a thriving village, and the castle greatly increased its importance, turning it into one of the most flourishing boroughs in the county. The material used in building this massive fortress was London clay with a small quantity of coralline crag, both to be found in the neighbourhood, supported with quoins, parapets, door and window dressings of Caen stone. It took five or six years to build, and remained in use as a fortress until the fourteenth century. Afterwards it was occupied as a residence by the Pole and Wingfield families, and after them by Sir Michael Stanhope, Groom of the Chamber to Elizabeth and James I. Later it passed through the hands of several noble owners, among them successive Viscounts Hereford, Marquesses of Hertford, and Sir William Wallace, the patron of art who gave us the Wallace Collection in Manchester Square, London. It now belongs to the town through the generosity of Lord Woodbridge. Sudbourne Hall has another art association through Sir Kenneth Clark, late director of the National Gallery, whose father owned it. A later owner, Sir Bernard Greenwell, put new heart into the land in this neighbourhood. His Suffolk Punches, including a 2,500-guinea stallion, his cattle, pigs, and sheep were famous all over the world.

Orford Castle keep is an eighteen-sided polygon, described within a circle, flanked by three square towers, which rise several feet above the main building. Like all prominent buildings along this coast it has long served as a useful landmark for mariners, who when coming from Holland steer so as to make the castle cover the church in order to avoid the Whiting, a dangerous sandbank in these waters.

Framlingham Castle
The Moot Hall, Aldeburgh

Orford sent two Members to Parliament up to the Reform Act of 1832, and its history was similar to Aldeburgh's until it lost its importance as a port through the blocking of the harbour by a dangerous bar of shingle.

In the church, with the beautiful Norman arches of a ruined chancel outside, there is an interesting memorial to the Rev. Francis Mason, a learned divine who died in 1621. Underneath it a triangular tablet has been fixed, fitting neatly into the general design, but bearing a deceptive inscription. This reads: " In Justice to ye memory of so great a man who was Rector here 80 years & above 110 years old This Monument was Removed from ye ruinous Chancel: & Repaired and set up here at ye Charge of ye present incumb᛫. Josias Alsop B.D. Anno: 1720." An account of Francis Mason is to be found in Wood's *Athenae Oxoniensis*, which reports that he was born in 1566, and appointed rector of Orford in 1597. As he died in 1621 his age appears to have been about half the 110 years Mr. Alsop allows him.

The late Steve Harper, landlord of the " Jolly Sailor " at Orford, was painted by T. C. Dugdale, who lived at Iken, and the picture hung in the Royal Academy.

The convolutions of the two rivers on which Aldeburgh and Orford stand, the Alde and Ore, have so isolated the region between the Alde and Butley rivers that these marshlands now belong principally to the seabirds that nest in them. The Alde swells into a wide reach between Iken and Black Heath, and you imagine this to be the beginning of the estuary. Beyond Barber's Point, however, it narrows again and when within a few yards of the sea at Slaughden suddenly turns south-west to run approximately parallel with the coast for another ten miles before finding a narrow outlet in Hollesley Bay. On Orford Ness stands a lighthouse, and we have an entertaining account of a lighthouse keeper here in the middle of the seventeenth century. The lighthouse belonged at that time to Gerrard Goore, a wealthy coal merchant trading between Newcastle and London, where he lived. He appointed to this important charge a Mrs. Bradshaw, the widow of the late keeper, and daughter of the man who had kept it before him. In six months Mr. Goore received more complaints about the way this light was neglected than he had received in the whole of her husband's or father's time, and demanded her resignation. But he wrote more in sorrow than in anger: "I did not thinke you would have bin soe careless," he said, "but I excuse it because you are woeman."

The Alde is a trifurcated stream. One branch, the Ore, comes down from Framlingham, another from Bruisyard and Rendham, and a third from Kelsale by way of Saxmundham. Near the river Ore the most romantic of Suffolk's moated manor-houses, Parham Old Hall, formerly the home of the Willoughby family, dreams above the waters of its placid moat. Crabbe himself lived in another old hall at Parham for several years after the death of his wife's uncle, John Tovell, a yeoman of whom the poet's biographer said that "though he seldom went to bed sober, he retained a clear eye and a stentorian voice to his eightieth year and coursed when he was ninety." Another of the old man's nieces, Miss Tovell, lived in a cottage near the hall and was something of a trial to the family. She expected to be allowed to manage all her uncle's affairs without any interference from others, and took a wicked delight in teasing her relations. The highly strung poet was often her victim, and she boasted that she could "screw Crabbe up and down like a fiddle." For all that they were good friends and neighbours. During her last illness the poet attended her with great tenderness, though she still continued to threaten to alter her will if anything displeased her.

By far the most interesting town or village in this part of Suffolk is Framlingham, now a small market town on the slopes of two low hills, with a triangular market-place below that friendly old coaching-house, the "Crown." If you enter it from the south you may think there is no more to see than that. But Framlingham is not a place to hurry through. If you climb the market hill to the summit, leaving the church for later inspection, you come to the castle, the most noble and historic ruin in the county. It was here that Princess Mary took refuge from the supporters of Lady Jane Grey.

The summer of 1553 was a lively time for Suffolk. Edward VI lay dying, and Mary, alarmed at the support being given to the claims of her rival, Lady Jane Grey, fled from Hunsdon in Hertfordshire to Kenninghall in Norfolk, where news of the king's death reached her. At once she sent letters to the Council claiming the throne; but knowing the cunning of those who were plotting against her, she moved to Framlingham Castle, where she could have both greater security against a surprise attack and readier access to the coast if flight from the country became necessary. For the next three weeks Framlingham was the rendezvous of all who rallied to her standard, with messengers coming and going hourly and spies everywhere. The parish accounts of many Suffolk villages show how loyally the county supported Mary. Items incurred for her protection are common, and indicate the extent to which both peasantry and nobility were on her side. When, after Wyatt's rebellion, the country declared for her accession, she left Framlingham for Newhall, Boreham, Essex, before proceeding by way of Wanstead to her coronation.

Framlingham Castle is now in charge of the Ministry of Works, under the provisions of the Ancient Monuments Protection Acts. The date of the first castle is not known, but it was before the Norman Conquest. The oldest parts of the ruin are of Barnack rag, an oolitic limestone. An anchor, dug up in Fen Meadow, near the castle, in the seventeenth century, confirmed the tradition that the river was formerly navigable as far as Framlingham, and the material for building the castle would come by water. Tradition holds that after Edmund had been defeated by the Danes at Thetford in 870 he took refuge here, but was pursued and the castle besieged. At that time dense forest would surround it, and this would assist Edmund in making his escape when the castle fell. But we are assuming that the story is true, and there is, in fact, no reliable evidence for it.

Nothing is known with certainty about Framlingham Castle before 1100 or 1101, when it was granted by Henry I to Roger Bigod. His grandson, Hugh Bigod, who was created Earl of Norfolk by King Stephen, and with whom began the castle's association with the Norfolk title which lasted for five and a half centuries with small interruptions, either rebuilt or greatly strengthened it. In 1173 he made it his headquarters when he joined the rebel barons against Henry II, who stormed and took the castle the following year. A record is still preserved of money paid " to throw down the Castle of Framlingham" and "for filling up the fosse" after this capture. But a new castle seems to have been built directly. The king restored to the earl his possessions on condition that they should all revert to the Crown if ever there should be no heir. This happened in Edward II's reign, and the estates were then conferred upon the king's brother, who was also created Earl of Norfolk and Marshal of England.

After the deaths of both Thomas Plantagenet, the new earl, and his only son in 1338, the castle passed through the ownership of several noble families until it came to the Howards. The moulded brick chimneys and much of the architecture we see to-day is the work of Thomas Howard, second Duke of Norfolk, who lived here in great splendour in the reign of Henry VII, and died at the castle in 1524. His son, also Thomas, the third Duke of Norfolk of the Howard line, uncle of the two queens Anne Boleyn and Catherine Howard, was attainted a few days before the death of Henry VIII, and the castle again became Crown property. The king's death saved—by a single day—the duke from the executioner's axe, and when Mary became queen his possessions were restored to him. He returned to Framlingham, where he died in 1554. The fourth duke was executed for supporting Mary Queen of Scots, which again caused the property to revert to the Crown. James I restored it in 1603 to Thomas, Lord Howard de Walden and his uncle, Lord Henry Howard. The latter resigned his share in favour of his nephew, who by this time had been created Earl of Suffolk; and it was his son, Theophilus, who in 1635 sold it to Sir Robert Hitcham for fourteen thousand pounds. Sir Robert's name continues to be associated with the district through his many charitable bequests. He had been senior Sergeant at Law to James I, and it is recorded that "the title to the estate was so perplexed that, had he not had a strong brain and a powerful purse, he could never have cleared it, of which he was so sensible that, in thankfulness to God for his wonderful success, he settled it for pious uses on Pembroke College, in Cambridge."

Sir Robert Hitcham was a bachelor. He was reputed to be exceptionally ugly, though his portrait in the National Portrait Gallery does not bear this out, and is said to have had a "writhen face and sneering looke." One day when several lawyers were making merry together, one asked Hitcham when he intended to marry. "Never," replied Hitcham. "I'd rather lead apes in hell."

"Nay! faith," exclaimed Hoskins, one of the lawyers present, "if it comes to that I am sure thou wilt pose all the devils, for there will be such gaping and inquiring which is the man, which is the ape; and they can never distinguish unless thou goest thither in thy sergeant's robes."

Above the principal gateway to the castle are the arms of Howard, Brotherton, Mowbray, Segrave, and Brews, quartered in one escutcheon, with lions for supporters, and a lion passant above, resting upon a helmet. Though from the outside the castle appears to be so exceptionally well preserved, inside not a single room remains intact. The trustees of the estate of Sir Robert Hitcham cleared it completely, even to the dungeons and underground passages, in order to find material for the charity institutions prescribed by his will, and also to assist in the rebuilding of Southwold, which was nearly destroyed by fire in 1659. The site of the chapel can be identified on the right inside the walls, and close to it was the room called Princess Mary's Chamber. The dwelling within the precincts that is still occupied was built during the eighteenth century upon the site of the Great Hall. For nearly a hundred years this building served the town as a workhouse, and during the Napoleonic wars French prisoners are believed to have been housed here.

The church at Framlingham, of which the nave was built by the Mowbrays and the chancel by the Howards, contains the magnificent Howard tombs. The most remarkable is one of painted alabaster to the memory of the poet Earl of Surrey, son of the third Duke of Norfolk, and his countess, Frances de Vere, daughter of the fifteenth Earl of Oxford. Over his armour he wears robes of state, but his coronet is placed on one side to signify that he was beheaded. This tomb is a fitting memorial to the brilliant and splendid age he typified as well as to himself. Over the tomb of the third Duke of Norfolk hangs "the helmet of Flodden," believed to have been worn by the second duke, the victor of Flodden, on the field. This helmet was examined by the keeper of the king's armoury some years ago and pronounced to be a genuine helmet of the period, though the Cap of Maintenance and the crest surmounting the helmet appear to have been added later, probably on the occasion of the duke's funeral, when it would be laid on the coffin in the funeral procession. The sum of five hundred pounds was offered for this interesting relic, or four hundred and fifty pounds and a reproduction. The rector and churchwardens asked the then Duke of Norfolk for permission to sell, but he replied—very properly, I think—that it must not be moved.

In 1634 a Framlingham churchwarden named Nicholas Danforth and his son emigrated to New England and founded a new town in Massachusetts, which they named after their old home, but spelt it Framingham. In the "Crown" at Framlingham a frame of photographs of this daughter town is exhibited, bearing the greetings of the residents. In omitting the "l" from the name the Danforths were spelling phonetically, and residents in the American town may be interested to know that the name is still pronounced by natives in that way. This tendency to curtail words, which is so marked in the eastern counties, I have heard attributed to the east wind making it inadvisable for a man to open his mouth more than necessary. The same theory is advanced to excuse laziness of speech in the milder west, only there the mouth is closed to keep the damp out!

The most important building in the Framlingham of to-day is the college, founded in 1864 as a memorial to the Prince Consort. The prime mover in directing the county's patriotic sentiment into this enterprise was Sir Edward Clarence Kerrison, who had long been anxious to see greater use being made of the Framlingham estate in accordance with the educational provisions of Sir Robert Hitcham's will. He therefore proposed that the memorial should take the form of a college for providing "a scientific education to the middle classes at a moderate cost." A deputation waited on the Earl of Stradbroke, Lord Lieutenant of the county, on the 20th February, 1862, and within a week nearly seven hundred leaders of public life in Suffolk had signed a document in support of the proposition. This enthusiastic support for the scheme, so ably formulated, guaranteed initial success. The school opened on the 10th April, 1865, in a matter-of-fact Suffolk way, without any ceremony, but with full classrooms. All but thirty-five of the two hundred and sixty-eight admitted that first term were from the county.

The system by which the school was governed remained unaltered for forty-six years, until in 1910 the powers of the school corporation were restricted and a new body of fifteen governors set up, ten to be appointed by the school corporation, three by the East Suffolk County Council, and two by the West Suffolk County Council. In 1922 this was again altered. The number to be appointed by the corporation was reduced to six, and the number to be appointed by the East Suffolk County Council increased to seven.

In spite of the hopes and resolves that went into its foundation, Framlingham College had to wait twenty-two years for the man who was to establish it firmly as an English Public School. The man to whom it owes this service was Dr. Oliver Digby Inskip, headmaster from 1887 to 1913. In course of time it came to be said of him that he was the most powerful religious influence in the whole county. When he took charge of the school the number of pupils had fallen to seventy-two. By the summer of 1898 it had risen to three hundred and six, of whom all but twelve were boarders. Among the Framlingham boys of his day the most widely known is the President of the Royal Academy, Sir Alfred Munnings.

Dr. Inskip was succeeded by F. W. Stocks, whose memory is revered with singular strength by hundreds of men who even as boys at school regarded him with admiration. The influence of this man upon the character of the boys who were educated at the school during his headmastership is believed by many to be beyond estimation.

Another Framlingham personality who must be named with Dr. Inskip and Mr. Stocks is Mr. Alfred Pretty, who has been associated with the school in one capacity or another for nearly eighty years. He entered as a pupil in 1870, and spent most of his professional life there as a teacher. But Mr. Pretty's greatest contribution to the life of Framlingham has been through the Old Framlinghamians Society, of which he was the principal founder. Though long past his eightieth birthday at the time I write these words, he still continues his long-established practice of writing to an old boy of the college every day of his life, and as many of them are scattered over the world, Mr. Pretty is a most valuable link between them and the school.

With the coming into force of the recent education act, opportunities for the college's expansion will be available, and with able leadership it is likely to become increasingly valuable to the county. Unlike many other schools and colleges, it has no difficult land problems to solve. In 1943 the Society of Old Framlinghamians bought College Farm, and the college Little Lodge Farm, so the college is surrounded by land under its own control. Its farms are let to expert farmers who are under contract to afford facilities for agricultural training to students. In an agricultural county this is of prime importance. With these provisions the college should guarantee to the county an instructed farming community who will take care that rural Suffolk is as progressive and enterprising as the urban Suffolk we see in Ipswich.

CHAPTER XI

THE GARDEN OF SUFFOLK

YOXFORD, between Saxmundham and Blythburgh on the Yarmouth road, is known as the "Garden of Suffolk," a name given to it by Clement Scott after a visit to the "Three Tuns," which was then a fashionable hotel, sporting a page-boy, and enjoying the patronage of visitors who arrived with carriage-and-pair. It is true that the countryside does become kindlier in aspect about Yoxford, and the explanation of the richer vegetation and softer climate is simply that the road has gradually been drawn inland to avoid the estuaries that grow longer and broader with each succeeding river. By the time Yoxford is reached the road is five miles from the sea, and is protected from the east wind by the cliffs of Dunwich. Even to those who travel north the scenery about Yoxford is more pleasantly rural than that along any previous stretch of this busy road. It is when we think of some of the rich country inland that we wonder why Yoxford alone should have a name that might be applied with equal justice to many of the Suffolk valleys. At the same time we might reflect that no part of Suffolk can reasonably be described as a garden when compared to thousands of acres in Essex and Kent.

The glory of this part of Suffolk is in its trees. There are parts of the main road itself that are green, translucent tunnels in summer, a fact it may be foolish to record, for so often the lover of trees returns to a favourite grove only to be reminded of Cowper's lines:

> The poplars are fell'd, farewell to the shade,
> And the whispering sound of the cool colonnade.

For part of the sylvan beauty of this neighbourhood we are indebted to a former vicar of Benhall, the Rev. John Mitford, a cousin of the author of *Our Village*. It is gratifying to

notice that Cowper's verses on the fallen poplars were first
published in the *Gentleman's Magazine*, because John Mitford was the editor of that journal, and for seventeen years
contributed a scholarly article to its pages every month without a break. Cowper's poem appeared after Mitford's death,
but the association is none the less pleasant to recall.

John Mitford was a classical scholar of wide attainments.
He was a collector of Greek coins, cameos, miniatures, and
manuscripts. As for books, when he died the English portion
of his library alone realised nearly four thousand pounds. He
edited several of our poets, and wrote biographies. He was a
valued friend of many distinguished men. But since his death
in 1859 at the age of seventy-eight he has been remembered
in his old parish principally as "the wicked parson who
haunts Mitford Lane." What his sins were we do not know,
but his wife left him after a year of married life, and his
friends referred in their letters to "grievous errors of conduct." Whatever these were it is good to know that they were
not such as to estrange the goodwill of the Quaker poet, Bernard Barton of Woodbridge. Barton frequently mentioned
Mitford in letters to Charles Lamb, who purchased expensive vases for him from a friend in China.

This interesting man travelled extensively. One of the
cedars he brought back from Lebanon still flourishes in the
vicarage garden. Trees were his passion. Samuel Rogers
wrote to William Jesse, Deputy Surveyor of Royal Parks and
Palaces: "You ought to know Mitford, Jesse. He has as great
an affection for old trees as you have. Trees and butter,
those are what he lives for, it seems to me. He is in town
just now, so if you will meet him some Tuesday in St James'
Place I shall be glad to make you acquainted with him.
Poor fellow! His going into the Church was a great mistake.
He is no more fit to be a parson than I am to be the Angel
Gabriel."

The reference to butter in this letter is explained by
William Jesse's daughter, who published an account of the
wicked parson entitled *Letters and Reminiscences of the Rev.
John Mitford*. Rogers was in the habit of holding Tuesday
morning breakfasts, to which he invited his many eminent
acquaintances, Mitford among them. After one of these

meals it came to Mitford's ears that Rogers had complained about the amount of butter he spread on his toast. From that time forward Mitford took a malicious pleasure in engaging his host's attention while selecting the thinnest slices of toast and plastering them as thickly as possible with butter. It was at one of these breakfasts that Mitford and Jesse met, and Mrs. Houston says that her father came home in a state of enchantment and could talk of no one but Mitford. When the friendship of these kindred spirits ripened, delightful letters passed between them. In one of them Mitford writes:

" MY DEAR JESSE,

I was so influenza'd when your letter came that I thought of nothing but flannel stockings, warming pans and seidlitz powders. All this came of going to Church. Had I not gone to church I had not caught my cold. . . . The snipe are over in shoals, and the Bishop of Norwich is after them . . . and by the bye, I must tell you that a fine golden oriole was shot lately on our green. A very rare bird here. . . . All this time I am as mopy and miserable as a shepherd's dog. Wishing I was at Rogers' breakfast table, eating Rogers' butter, or anywhere where social and civil life exists; for here the parsons can talk of nothing but double duty, the XXXIX Articles, and the Bishop of Exeter. Fare thee well."

A selection of Mitford's letters, edited by C. E. Heanley, was published in the *East Anglian Magazine* in March, April, and May of 1937. Mitford, now forgotten as a scholar, was vicar of Benhall and Weston, and rector of Stratford St. Andrews in Suffolk for forty-nine years. Now, alas! he is only remembered in his parish as a wicked old parson who haunts a village lane.

Ghosts are not uncommon in this neighbourhood. Northeast of Yoxford is the haunted vicarage at Darsham, where the apparition of a woman walks abroad once a year, but appears only to members of her own sex, a restriction much regretted by a former vicar of Darsham, who was interested in occult matters, but was a bachelor.

Another haunted lane in this well-wooded part of Suffolk is found at Sibton, north-west of Yoxford, near the beautiful village of Peasenhall. Two grass-covered mounds by the side of a byway leading to Sibton Green are said to be the graves of these ghostly visitors, whose identity is uncertain. One report says that they are the graves of two suicides, another that they are of two gipsies who were hanged for horse-stealing.

Sibton has the remains of the only Cistercian abbey ever established in Suffolk—an attempt to establish one at Codden-ham failed. It was founded here in 1150. All that remains of it to-day are a few fragments of walls in the grounds of the lord of the manor's residence. Though not extensive, they are sufficient to show that the abbey was of considerable importance in the Middle Ages. Its fortunes declined, and before the Dissolution it passed into the ownership of Thomas, second Duke of Norfolk, the grandfather of Catherine Howard, fifth queen of Henry VIII.

The most important monastic remains in this neighbour-hood are those of the Premonstratensian abbey on the crest of a low hill about half a mile from Leiston station. This Order took its name from Prémontré in the north of France, and its clergy were known as the White Canons. The abbey buildings are now found scattered about a farmstead, but one or two windows remain—that of the north transept, for example, which is forty-five feet high and of fine proportions. The window in the north aisle of the choir also stands, and other walls and foundations remaining are sufficient to enable us to trace the plan of the buildings, though little care has been taken to preserve what is left of them, with the exception of the Lady Chapel, which was restored over twenty years ago, and in 1945 presented to the diocese for use as a Retreat and Conference House.

The buildings of Leiston Abbey were arranged round the four sides of a rectangular cloister. The church stood on the north, the chapter house and offices on the east, the refec-tory on the south, and the guest-house, along with offices for conducting the business of the abbey, on the west. Its founder was Ranulph (or Ralph) de Glanville, the founder of Butley Priory, which was an earlier foundation endowed with lands presented to de Glanville by Henry II. The manor of Leiston was among these lands, so when Leiston Abbey was founded in 1182 this particular manor was transferred to it by the older foundation. But the site of this first abbey was not that of the present ruins. The first abbey was built near the Minsmere river on low, marshy ground close to the sea, and moved from this unhealthy position to the higher ground where the present ruins stand by Robert de Ufford, Earl of Suffolk, in 1363. This second building was burnt down in 1389, and a third abbey built on the same site as the second.

The site of the first abbey is preserved in the ruins of Sizewell Chapel, and it seems possible that a few of the canons were left behind when the rest moved to higher ground. Perhaps one only would remain. There is, I believe, a record in existence of an anchorite being consecrated in the chapel of St. Mary at this old monastery by the sea.

Ranulph de Glanville, the founder of these two abbeys, Butley and Leiston, had special affection for the district because he was born at Stratford St. Andrew. He rose to be Lord Chief Justice, but the most active part of his life was spent in the north of England, where he was Sheriff of Yorkshire in 1163 and of Lancashire ten years later, leading the Lancastrians against the Scots at Alnwick.

Since 1778, Messrs. Garrett & Sons, the well-known engineers, have been established at Leiston. Most of that time the firm has been known throughout East Anglia and to engineers in every part of the country. In referring to trade in Suffolk, I have tried to avoid anything that might look like advertising, but the Garrett family, both in business and social life, has played so distinguished a part in the life of the county for so long a period that to omit their name would be discourteous. They are as well known as the Ransomes of Ipswich, who should be named for the same reason. The tendency in modern industry is towards the impersonal, and to those who value the personal above everything else, firms that have maintained their family character through many generations are entitled to respectful recognition.

But in this stronghold of individualism there will always be character in industry. Not until men are able to tame the winds and regulate the tides will the Suffolk character conform to authorised standards. One voice of Suffolk rises from the land, the voice of patient toil and steadfast faith. This part gives no trouble. But another voice rises from the heaths and cliffs, the voice of defiant individualism. You will hear it from the unknown wild-fowler who lives by his wits and his skill in a craft that can never be taught in schools. You will hear it from the fishermen of Aldeburgh and Lowestoft, and in modern literature it found one of its greatest voices in the works of one who was born in Theberton, the parish adjoining Leiston: Charles Montagu Doughty, author of *Travels in Arabia Deserta*, who was born in 1843 at Theberton Hall, which had been built by his ancestor, George Doughty, in 1792.

Doughty's epic journey was begun from Damascus in November 1876. He had heard stories of the ruined city of Medain Salih, which was said to have been destroyed like Sodom and Gomorrah as a punishment for the sins of its inhabitants, and he determined to visit it. The British consul at Damascus, with whom he discussed his plans, did all in his power to discourage this hazardous adventure, but Doughty was not to be held back. A train of six thousand pilgrims with ten thousand beasts passed by on their way to Mecca. Doughty joined them, and for nearly two years wandered in the desert, studying the customs of the people and the remains of their ancient civilisation. In venturing into this lonely wasteland, he was undertaking hazards as great as those of any Elizabethan voyager across uncharted seas. Others, though few, had been there before him, but protected themselves by pretending they had embraced the Moslem faith. No one before Doughty had crossed northern Arabia proclaiming his faith as he went. Few would have believed that any man could do this and return alive. To the wild Bedouin the Christian was accursed above all others. It was only the magnetism of his personality and the calm assurance of his bearing that brought Doughty through perils that would have broken the nerve if not the body of almost any other man. He was a man without fear. When brought before one who had him completely in his power, and from whom he could expect no mercy, he said calmly: "I have not so lived, Moslem, that I need fear to die."

After travelling for three weeks with the Moslem caravan

in which he started his journey, he went on alone till he stood among "mountains of fantastic rock," guarding the city he had come to find. As he gazed at the inscriptions chiselled on the ancient deserted buildings he asked: "What might be the sleeping riddle of those strange, crawling letters?" The rest of his travels might be said to be his search for the answer to that question. By living in the tents of the desert tribes he discovered that " two chiefly are the perils in Arabia, famine and the dreadful-faced harpy of their religion. . . . Here is a dead land, whence, if he die not, the traveller shall bring home nothing but a perpetual weariness in his bones." Under threat of death he was repeatedly called upon to confess Islam. Always he refused, and as though under some divine protection—as no doubt he was—always he escaped the fate that seemed inescapable.

Though he must by that time have known that he was attempting the seemingly impossible, he pressed forward until he came to Mecca itself, where no Christian could expect to survive. As he approached the sacred city an enraged chieftain rushed at him with drawn knife. Even here he was saved. An old officer of the Sherif intervened and persuaded the chieftain that the stranger must be taken before the Sherif himself to be judged. Doughty had no reason to expect mercy from the Sherif, and knew well enough that the tortures commanded in cold blood might be more cruel than the instantaneous death he would have had from the fanatical chieftain. Nevertheless at this moment he seems only to have felt pleasure in the thought that by being taken to the Sherif he would see the ruler's palace. The Sherif proved to be an enlightened man. He could find no grounds for condemning Doughty, and after entertaining him as an honoured guest gave him an escort to Jinna.

On a November day in 1878 this brave man, sick and gaunt with suffering and exposure, staggered into the European Hospital in Bombay and asked to be admitted as a patient. The House Surgeon explained to him that the hospital was for Europeans only.

"But I am an Englishman, and my name is Doughty," he said in his dignified, gentle voice. He was admitted, and those who enabled him to regain his strength, sapped away by

176

so many months of privation, little knew what a precious life they were saving.

The record of Doughty's adventures, and his invaluable observations, were published by the Cambridge University Press in 1888. The book was slow in winning recognition, but in course of time its author was accorded high and universal honour amongst scholars and orientalists the world over. In 1912 he received the Founder's Gold Medal of the Royal Geographical Society, and might have spent the remainder of his life enjoying the respect of his fellows in peace. But Doughty was not of that metal. His great ambition was to contribute something of permanent value to English poetry, and he gave the last part of his life to writing verse and poetic drama. Critics are divided in estimating the value of this part of his work, and we must leave judgment to posterity, though the splendour of his intellectual vigour must always be recognised. His ambitious epic, *The Dawn in Britain,* which deals with the coming of Christianity to Britain —an appropriate subject for a man born so near Dunwich— is too severely intellectual and archaic in its studied Spenserianism for the common reader. His style was a strange one. T. E. Lawrence, his great friend and disciple, explains that the syntax of his difficult but magnificent prose was Scandinavian, which is an observation of great interest in view of the character of East Suffolk. As a poet he had two masters, Milton and Spenser.

Whatever the final estimate of Doughty's work may be, his immense contribution to learning will stand, and still more the story of his great courage. He was the first Englishman many of those desert tribesmen had met, and that this introduction to English life should come through such a man as Doughty, the son of a line of Suffolk squire-parsons, uniting in himself the best traditions of both the English gentleman and the Christian scholar, a man of complete integrity, has been of great benefit to us ever since. It would be difficult to estimate the benefit we derived from it during the First Great War. This great and good man died at the age of eighty-two in 1926. He was undoubtedly a man of genius, and, as always with genius, in him an unseen force was expressing itself through a human medium.

Yoxford

Theberton church, which Doughty knew so well as a boy, has one of the curious round towers of Suffolk. All the Suffolk towers are of flint, but the larger ones have stone dressings. Flint was easily obtained even in poor parishes. Stone, on the other hand, was expensive and difficult to obtain, so this circular form may have been adopted to avoid the need for quoins. At Theberton, stone was in fact introduced when both tower and church were extended, with results that are far from pleasing.

Allan Jobson, in *Suffolk Yesterdays*, a book that gets inside the Suffolk character in a way that makes us feel almost shy at the intimacy, tells us that Suffolk people used to think these towers were the casings of wells left from the flood. When the waters subsided, they believed, the ground sank also, and what had been wells below ground became towers above.

We may wander about these towns and villages of East Suffolk, picking up old tales and legends in this way, but sooner or later we must come back to the Yarmouth road, which might be described as the principal artery of East Suffolk. We have crossed this road several times in tracing the course of each slow, meandering river in the southern half of the county, and we have loitered in several of its ancient towns. We might have followed it from the Stour to the Waveney and have talked our way through half the county's history in one or other of its inn parlours. If we had done so we should have had an entirely different impression of its scenery, for much of the Suffolk we see from the highways is flat and monotonous, while the Suffolk we see from the byways is pleasantly undulating. So much of the county's beauty is in its river scenery, that the little roads that run along their banks seemed the only ones to follow if we were to discover the best that Suffolk has to offer. Nevertheless, much will be missed if we do not give some attention to the main roads.

An ancient and historic highway so near the coast as this, however dull it may appear to-day, must have had many tales and legends associated with it. Most of them are now forgotten. Secrecy was their indispensable characteristic. Rumours of the escapades of soldiers who patrolled the road

when invasion seemed imminent must often have been whispered round the cottages. There would also be tales told
between intimate friends, with warnings not to let them go
further; of costly merchandise that had been landed in Hollesley Bay, and had passed through the village hidden under a
load of hay or straw. The firing of mysterious shots must
often have been heard, and villagers returning home late
must sometimes have turned down a byway because what they
saw ahead of them on the main road was none of their business. Along this road, more than along any other in Suffolk,
men learned to hold their tongues and keep their knowledge
to themselves. So the best tales of the Yarmouth road will
never be told; they can only be imagined, and when they are
imagined it will usually be in association with such old inns
as the "Bell" at Saxmundham or the "Three Tuns" at
Yoxford.

The Saxmundham "Bell" that confronts the modern
traveller is not an old building. It is, however, of special
interest because it represents the latest type of country town
coaching-house before the railways took the majority of
travellers off the roads for two generations. With the motor-
ing age its prosperity returned, and those who journey along
this eastern road are again grateful for its hospitality. It
stands to remind us of that comfortable age when Englishmen
took careful thought to provide themselves with good food,
warm beds, and well-appointed dining-rooms both at home
and at the familiar halts along their journeys. A popular
reminder of that flourishing age long remained in the yard
behind the "Bell" in the "Old Blue," a well-known Suffolk
coach that stood there until it became derelict and was broken
up. In its heyday the "Old Blue" ran between Ipswich and
London, but when a newer coach replaced it on the London
route it turned north and passed a serviceable old age plying
between Ipswich and Southwold.

Another regular caller at the "Bell" was the Yarmouth
Mail, which changed horses there four times a day. Long
after most of the traditional dangers had passed from the roads
the guard was still as necessary as the driver himself along
a road so near to sheltered coves as this, in any one of which
a boat might be hidden ready for an undetected escape, either

to the Continent or to another county. The "Red Lion" at Martlesham has an "iron room" where the mail was stored each night. The guard used to sleep across the inside of the door, so that any attempt to enter would rouse him. His blunderbuss was always at his side, ready for action. This, of course, is the inn with the well-known sign, formerly a ship's figurehead, which gave rise to the saying "as red as Martlesham Lion."

According to a reliable authority, Mr. Gerald Rickword, writing in the *East Anglian Daily Times* of 24th November, 1926, no record has been found of coaches travelling from Yarmouth to London via Ipswich before 1743. Until that time the Yarmouth to London coaches had made their journey to the "Green Dragon," Bishopsgate, by way of Bury St. Edmunds, Newmarket, and Bishop's Stortford. When the Ipswich to Yarmouth road became a coach route the calling places were the "White Lion" at Beccles, the "Three Tuns" at Bungay, the "White Hart" at Blythburgh, the "Three Tuns" at Yoxford, the "Bell" at Saxmundham, the "White Hart" at Wickham Market, the "Crown" at Woodbridge, and finally the "Great White Horse" at Ipswich.

Beyond Darsham the Ipswich to Yarmouth road runs through little fields with high hedgerows until Blythburgh church is seen in the distance, when a wide heath opens out before the traveller and continues until the road slopes down to the estuary of the Blyth, which here resembles a lake. The dykes were breached several years ago, and have not yet been repaired. From Blythburgh to Wangford the open heath is exchanged for high banks and woodland from which the road emerges on to uplands with extensive views of a countryside that here begins to resemble Norfolk in scenery. The air seems keener and the landscape more clear-cut in outline. Along most of the way to Lowestoft, tall trees flank the highway, and the farms look well-kept and prosperous. The road forks a short distance beyond Blythburgh, one branch going to Beccles, the other to Lowestoft. In the fork of these two roads stands Henham Hall, Lord Stradbroke's residence, and the home of his family for more than three hundred years. A few hundred yards beyond, on the other side of the main road, is a byway leading through pleasant open country to Southwold.

CHAPTER XII

THE BLYTH VALLEY

WHAT image comes first to mind when the River Blyth is mentioned? Is it of Southwold with its cliffs and commons, friendly bohemian Walberswick, or Blythburgh church, seen across the heath, more like a castle than a church in sombre twilight, with a herd of cattle grazing on the marshes below it? All three appear before me as I write the name at the head of this page, but the quay at Walberswick and the cliffs at Southwold fade and leave only the grey and massive pile of Blythburgh church against an azure sky, with purple ling spread across the heath before it. No other church in the eastern counties towers against the sky so nobly.

When the great church at Blythburgh was built the town was a flourishing port. Traces of its quays can still be found, but the development of trade with America, together with the advance of engineering skill, produced larger ships, and the Blythburgh quays were no longer serviceable. The trade of the town declined, and when it was visited by one of the fires that repeatedly ravaged the east coast towns, half its houses were destroyed, compelling the homeless people to move into Southwold or another growing town. The church was left, a sombre memorial with only a few villagers to attend its services.

Blythburgh church was built in the fifteenth century by monks from the neighbouring priory which, like the priory at Stowmarket, was an offshoot of St. Osyth's Abbey in Essex. The priory was founded in the twelfth century, and the building of the new church was begun in 1442 when the town was prosperous and growing. The Reformation, the Commonwealth, the decline of population after the disastrous fires of 1667 and 1696, reduced it finally to an empty shell, and when wind and rain tore through its broken windows in winter, the nave where Christian folk had knelt seemed like a heathen fane. So lifeless did the church become that for twelve years at a stretch there was not a single celebration of Holy Communion—not even at Easter. Throughout the eighteenth century the progress of neglect and decay continued until the building became unsafe and had to be closed. During recent years life has returned to it, and as fast as funds have permitted, the work of restoration has been carried out with care and skill.

Blythburgh church is not so rich in splendid tombs as many East Anglian churches, but one is of special interest because of a tradition attached to it. This is the tomb of Lady Anne Hopton, daughter of Sir Roger Swillington, lord of the manor at the beginning of the fifteenth century, and wife of Sir John Hopton, who was lord of the manor when the church was built. Tradition maintained that when Henry VIII dissolved the Priory the monks hid the church plate here. Some years ago the matter was settled by opening the tomb, and if it is examined to-day the place where it was opened can still be seen. Nothing, however, was discovered—nor could be, because the plate was in fact given by Henry to the lord of the manor, who pawned it for £20. New plate was purchased, but this in turn was stolen at the beginning of the nineteenth century.

We have already noted the prevalence of superstition along this storm-harried coast, and Blythburgh church could not fail to become a place of supernatural visitation. Everything about it was congenial to the presence of ghostly visitors. Its day of sinister glory came on the first Sunday of August 1557. While the second lesson was being read a terrible storm blew up and struck the church with such violence that it "drove down all the people on that side of the Church, above twenty persons; then renting the wall up to the Revestry, cleft the door, and returned to the steeple, rent the timber, brake the chains and fled towards Bungay," where we shall have further news of it. A man and a boy were killed and others present were scorched. So much is true. It is also carefully recorded that the spire was struck down, and in falling crashed through the west end of the roof and broke the font, bringing the bells and the Jack o' the Clock with it. To these details legend adds that the devil was in the storm, and that as he left the church he touched the door with his hand and scorched it. The strange sequel is that when whitewash was removed from that door in 1933 marks of burning were actually brought to light, and these can be seen to-day.

Another Blythburgh story—probably a true one—relates that Cromwell's soldiers stabled their horses there. Evidence of this is visible not only in the broken tiles where the horses stamped, but also in the remains of an iron staple in the end pillar. Perhaps the nervousness of the horses was caused by the sport of the soldiers, for while quartered in the town these amused themselves by shooting at the carved angels on the roof, whose outstretched wings were either shot away or pitted with lead.

Whichever way we turn in this remarkable church there is something to stir the imagination. In the admirable little guide to it a pretty story is told in connection with a robin embroidered on the linen lectern-cover. About 1880, we read, a Mr. Arthur Cooper of Blythburgh Lodge left the parish to reside elsewhere. For some time he had assisted the vicar each Sunday by reading the lessons, and during the last Sunday of his residence here a robin nested in the lectern. After she had hatched her eggs and raised her brood, she flew away, never to return. In 1931—that is to say, about fifty years later —Mr. Cooper died and his body was brought back to Blythburgh for burial. That same year a robin again nested successfully in the lectern. Since then no robin has returned or been succeeded by another. It was a happy thought to commemorate these two events in this way. "Be Thou praised, my Lord, with all Thy creatures."

This simplicity of the ancient faith is again illustrated at Blythburgh in the carved bench-ends. One represents Slander—Tell-tale-tit, with her tongue hanging out, and treated as the old rhyme required. Another represents Sloth, refusing to rise from his bed. Drunkenness sits in the stocks on another. Pride, smug and richly apparelled, on a fourth, and on a fifth Gluttony, too full for his own comfort, but less in pain than Avarice on a sixth, who endures toothache rather than open his purse-strings to buy relief. The country year is also symbolised in such figures as a man sowing and another pig-killing.

An interesting side-light on local history is seen in the inkwells cut into the choir stalls. The explanation of these is that early in the seventeenth century Dutchmen and Swedes were engaged here in dredging and dyking the river. They brought their families with them, and a local scholar—probably the vicar—opened a school in a side chapel where these stalls formerly stood. One boy, Dirck Lowenson van Stockholm, A.D. 1665, had the temerity to carve his name.

Three miles behind Blythburgh is Wenhaston, where a painting of The Last Judgment, probably the work of one of the Blythburgh monks, is to be seen inside the church. Its existence appears to have been quite unsuspected until the church was restored in 1892, when a whitewashed partition, which had almost completely shut off the chancel from the nave, was taken down and carried into the churchyard. By night the rain fell so heavily that the following morning much of the whitewash had gone and the outlines of painted figures could be discerned through the remaining film. The vicar at once collected the boards and had them carefully cleaned, with the result that a painting 17 feet 3 inches by 8 feet 6 inches came to light. It aroused widespread interest among antiquaries, because though paintings of The Last Judgment were at one time fairly common, such fanatics as William Dowsing, who must engage our attention presently, destroyed them so thoroughly during the Great Rebellion that only eight, painted on panels in this particular manner, remain to-day. A rare feature of the Wenhaston Doom is that the Holy Rood was actually attached to the panel. According to experts, the date of the work is about 1480.

Much of the merit of this painting is in the arrangement of the supporting groups. At the top we find Our Lord as Divine Judge, seated on a rainbow, His head encircled by a seven-rayed nimbus. Two fingers of the right hand are extended in blessing, and the whole attitude is one of invitation. On His right is the sun, balanced on the left by the moon. To the spectator right and left are reversed, of course, so below the rainbow we find St. Peter on the left, with St. Michael on the right. St. Peter holds the keys of the Heavenly Mansions, which are depicted on the extreme left. He is shown in the gracious act of receiving four redeemed souls, who appear to be a king, a queen, a bishop and a cardinal. Doubtless a scroll near him was formerly charged with the words *Venite Benediciti*—Come, ye blessed. St. Michael, on the other side, holds a sword in one hand and scales for the weighing of souls in the other. Doubtless a scroll on this side would be charged with the words *Descendite Malediciti* —Depart, ye cursed. In looking at the scales it is heartening to a Christian humanist to find that the good deeds are out-weighing the evil, a conception of human nature that is out of favour with so many of our modern theologians, who have the effrontery to credit the Devil with more power than God Himself. In this entertaining group we find the Devil hover-ing near, complete with horns and tail, and with bat's wings, and eyes in his legs. He has two scrolls, one probably bear-ing his indictment of the souls being weighed, the other St. Michael's reply. Beyond the St. Michael group, balancing the Heavenly Mansions group on the other side, are the Jaws of Hell, represented by a fish's mouth adorned with a pig's snout on which sits a demon blowing a ram's horn. Inside the threatening jaws a black demon drags one of the con-demned to perdition, while eight others, encircled by a chain, await a similar doom, to which they are pressed by a demon with a pronged fork. Another demon carries a female representation of Pride, chief of the seven deadly sins. In the spaces between these groups five figures are depicted rising from their graves.

The Wenhaston Doom is curious and interesting as an example of the religious art of its period, though it is remark-able neither for the beauty of its workmanship nor for the depth of the religious feeling it reflects. For these qualities the neighbouring church of St. Andrew, Bramfield, should be visited. Here may be seen one of the finest Perpendicular rood screens in the county, with panels depicting the four Evangelists and St. Mary Magdalene. And in the chancel is a most beautiful seventeenth-century recumbent figure of Elizabeth, the daughter and heir of Sir George Waldegrave, who was the wife of the third son of Sir Edward Coke, the great lawyer.

It would be interesting to know how these memorials escaped the attention of William Dowsing, the Cromwellian

Visitor of the Suffolk churches, whom the Earl of Manchester commissioned to demolish all superstitious pictures, images, inscriptions, and so forth, and who was so lamentably conscientious that he will be reviled by all right-minded people to the end of time. He did all that was required of him at Blythburgh, where the Churchwardens' Accounts for 1644 have entries for amounts paid to "Master Dowsing" for removing images and brasses. There were, however, ways of circumventing even so conscientious a Puritan as Master Dowsing. At Halesworth, the market town of the Blyth valley, I was curious to know how the font escaped disfigurement, and asked Mr. Lambert, the verger, who knows every stone in the church. He told me that according to an old tradition, the lord of the manor of that day entered the church while Dowsing was busy destroying the stained-glass windows, and at once invited the unwelcome guest to dinner. After plying him well with wine, the lord of the manor turned to Dowsing and said: "And now, sir, perhaps you will be good enough to leave the font alone," or a seventeenth-century equivalent of those words. Whereupon Dowsing obligingly rode away and did not return.

The church at Halesworth is well worth a visit. It has Saxon long and short work still visible, and in the sanctuary there is a remarkable Dane Stone, probably of the late ninth century. When the Danes under Guthrum became Christians they made use of the existing Saxon churches, but introduced their own style of memorials, of which this is a rare example. It represents arms and hands holding a wheel, an emblem of Eternity. Keble was a frequent visitor to the rectory when the Rev. R. Whately, the famous logician, afterwards Archbishop of Dublin, was rector, and is said to have written part of the *Christian Year* there. Halesworth has been the birthplace of many distinguished men, including John Kirby, author of the *Suffolk Traveller*, and—somewhat unexpectedly—George Lansbury, the Labour leader. Lansbury's father was working on the extension of the railway to Halesworth at the time. The family did not remain there long, but George Lansbury himself, always a sound churchman, visited the town where he was born and the church where he was christened on at least three occasions.

Of the brasses in Halesworth church one in particular delights me. It is to John Brown, "who lyved a quiet lyfe," though he left six sons, ten daughters, and sixty-five grandchildren. What a remarkable woman Mrs. Brown must have been to manage so large a family and leave her husband in peace! Perhaps he escaped from his crowded home to the "Three Tuns," the old inn in the market-place. It has now lost its licence and serves as a social club. When I remarked to a resident that this seemed a pity, he replied: "Don't worry. It is still the one bright spot in the town." Perhaps he, too, has a large family.

There is a special reason for thinking of Dowsing in the Blyth valley. Laxfield, near one of the sources of the river, had the misfortune to be his birthplace. The register there records that he was baptised in the church on the 2nd May, 1596, and buried on the 14th March, 1679. Evidently he was sustained in the faith to a ripe old age. His Journal has a record of instructions for the removal of superstitious images and inscriptions in Laxfield itself, but he seems to have shown more charity there than in most places, for some of the old stained glass remains, together with brasses, including one to a William Dowsing, dated 1614. Perhaps Laxfield even then was less offensively Catholic than its neighbours. Protestantism had already had another redoubtable champion in the village in the person of John Noyes, whom we must honour whether we agree with him or not, because he had the courage to die for his faith. John Noyes was a Laxfield shoemaker, and was burnt at the stake in his own village in 1557 after suffering imprisonment at Eye and Norwich. As the faggots were placed about him he blessed the hour in which he was born to die for the truth. Foxe says that one, John Jarvis, who was present, spoke words that were interpreted as showing sympathy with the martyr, and in punishment was sentenced to the stocks next day, as well as being whipped round the market naked.

The Blyth is not a long river, but it has a number of interesting associations. After flowing between Heveningham and Huntingfield it broadens into a lake, with Heveningham Hall overlooking it from an eminence on the south bank. The Heveningham family was of such antiquity that one of its members was lord of the manor in the reign of Canute. Another evidently entered into the eternal struggle of the warring sects, so lamentably active in this peaceful country-side, for we find Sir Richard Gipps, who lived in the seventeenth century, and who was evidently not in agreement with him, writing that he "was one of those daring Monsters who usurp'd the authority of God; to whom alone Kings are accountable, and impiously sat in judgement upon his Anointed; But soon after the Family wither'd and came to Nothing."

The original mansion of the Heveninghams stood on the Huntingfield side of the river, and was a building of romantic fame. Its great hall was built round six huge oaks, by which the roof was supported. On these stout trunks were hung many weapons and trophies of the chase. In 1531 the Huntingfield estate was granted by Henry VIII to Charles Brandon, Duke of Suffolk, who returned it to the Crown six years later in exchange for other lands. When Henry divorced the cleverest of his six wives, Anne of Cleves, he settled Huntingfield on her as part of her large pension, and after Anne's death Queen Elizabeth bestowed it upon her cousin, Lord Hunsdon, who made it a place of sport and revelry. Queen Elizabeth herself was entertained there, and on this celebrated occasion she is said to have shot with her own hand a buck, which fled to a hollow tree in the park, afterwards known as Queen Elizabeth's oak.

Such are the tales of old Huntingfield. To-day the principal attraction is the angel roof in the church, which is unique in the county in being painted in bright colours throughout the entire length of nave and chancel. The work is modern. It was done by Mrs. Holland, the wife of a former incumbent, who was himself responsible for extensive alterations to the church, including the introduction of new oak benches, some of which are exceptionally well carved. Mrs. Holland gave three and a half years to adorning the plaster and timber of the roof, and the result is not only entirely pleasing—to my own mind, at least—but is a remarkable achievement when we consider that the whole of the work must have been done at that great height, most of it lying on her back. She began the chancel roof in July 1859, and finished it by February 1860. In undertaking this important work she wisely obtained the advice of Mr. E. L. Blackburne, F.S.A., an authority on medieval decoration, and no doubt continued it under his direction. The bills for this part of the work include £30 for colours and £7 10s. for one hundred books of gold leaf.

The second and greater part of the work was not begun until three years later. Entries appear in the church accounts for gold leaf and colour from the autumn of 1863 to the autumn of 1866, when the scaffolding was finally taken down. The Hollands were pioneers in the field of church restoration, much of which was extremely ill advised in the middle of the nineteenth century. They might have done better if they had been working to-day. On the other hand, in our own age they would almost certainly have lacked funds for such work. Taking all things into account, they are surely entitled to the highest praise, and I cannot agree with those learned but prejudiced antiquaries who criticise them for tampering with an ancient structure. They acted in the light of the best knowledge available in their day, and what they did was done in love.

Another part of their work it would be impossible to criticise. The churchyard at Huntingfield is a glorious sight in spring, when white companies of snowdrops and a brave display of daffodils bring promise of the summer that country folk await so eagerly. Mr. Holland's accounts have entries for bulbs bought in cartloads from Wenhaston and Rumburgh. "Two hundred large bunches of daffodils and three hundred large bunches of snowdrops," reads one such entry, "planted in the Churchyard in addition to what was there before."

This part of Suffolk, though near the coast, is surprisingly well wooded, particularly in the neighbourhood of Huntingfield parsonage, which has a garden surrounded by a magnificent yew hedge. Mr. Holland must have been as proud of it a hundred years ago as Canon Dobson, the present incumbent, is to-day, and both deserve our gratitude for their care of beautiful things in this remote parish, from which so much of its former glory has faded.

The oaks are especially fine in this part of Suffolk. Nor

is Queen Elizabeth's the only one to which a romantic story is attached. Apart from hers, the most famous oak in East Suffolk was at Henham, where Sir John Rous, a loyal supporter of the Stuarts, took cover when a party of Cromwell's rebels called with a warrant for his arrest. This decayed but massive oak was used by the family as a summer-house. The trunk was hollow, but was fitted with a door faced with bark so that the tree looked perfectly sound to anyone passing it. Sir John, it is said, was persuaded by his wife to take cover here. The lady in question was the beautiful Elizabeth Knevitt, and the story relates that she stole out to him with food each night during the soldiers' stay, not daring to trust anyone else with their secret.

Later, this same oak was the scene of other loyal demonstrations by staunch supporters of the exiled House of Stuart, who used to meet here, and on bended knee drink to the " King across the Water."

The story of the Henham Oak was told to Suckling, the Suffolk historian, by Agnes Strickland, one of three clever sisters who lived at Reydon Hall, a plain, whitewashed house near Southwold. All three were writers. Kate went to Canada and wrote of life in the backwoods. Jane wrote novels. And Agnes surpassed them both in fame if not in earnings with her *Queens of England*. Her grave is pointed out in the churchyard at Southwold.

We are indebted to Agnes Strickland for several valuable notes on local history. In her story of *Dunwich Fair* she gives a moving account of a trip from Southwold to St. James's Fair at Dunwich on the 25th July, 1616, when the boat capsized and twenty-two people were drowned. The story was suggested to her by a pathetic entry in the Southwold parish register, made by the vicar, the Rev. Christopher Younges: " They were drowned in the haven coming from Donwich Fayer, on St. James's day in a bote, by reason of one cable lying overwharf the haven, for by reason the men that brought them down was so negligent, that when they were redie to come ashore the bote broke lose, and so the force of the tide carried the bote against the cable and so overwhelmed. The number of them were XXII, but they were not all found." Miss Strickland's imagination was kindled by reading later in the account the words: "Edward and Elizabeth Younges, daughter and son to me C. Younges, vicar and minister."

Southwold was long fortunate in having as its Town Clerk, Major Cooper, the man to whom we are indebted for so many records of life along the Suffolk coast. He recorded not only events of importance, but also numerous little incidents that a less imaginative chronicler might have missed, but which reveal in an instant the character of the people as well as their customs. It was Major Cooper who told us about the old seaman who lay dying while a storm blew up, but in spite of his condition insisted that it was time the lifeboat was launched, and that he must go down to give a hand. Only when friends were brought in to tell him that the snow was now so thick that all attempts at rescue had been abandoned could he be pacified. Another lifeboatman, a young man this time, left his bride on their wedding night to go out with the boat in a snowstorm. Such are the men of this coast—men so attuned to the elements that they seem to live in almost mystical communion with them, calm when the sea is still, restless when a wind blows up, and possessed by apparently superhuman energy when the lifeboat is being launched. They are a grand race, the product of the immemorial war that is waged along this coast against treacherous and tyrannical tides. The old port has always been proud of its sons. Of one, John Jentillman, or Gentleman, who flourished while Elizabeth was queen and died at the age of ninety-eight in 1609, the parish register says: "He lived above fourscore years in perfect sight and memorie and in his flourishinge time for building of shippes and many other commendable parts he continued in his place unmatchable." Old John's son, Tobias Gentleman, who described himself as fisherman and mariner, viewed with concern the loss of much of England's sea trade to the Dutch, and wrote a pamphlet appealing to his fellow countrymen to try to regain their old position. Of his own townsmen he said that they were a good breed of fishermen, sailing to Iceland for cod and ling, but suffering because the haven was so often blocked by shingle, so that they were frequently obliged to remain idle because they could not get their boats out to sea. His plain-spoken appeal seems to have been effective in attracting national attention to the Southwold fishermen, though the trouble was to recur at intervals throughout the history of all these Suffolk seaports. Milton himself, forty years after the publication of Tobias's pamphlet, in a State paper records the destitution of the Southwold fisherfolk, both from the impairing of the harbour and from losses incurred in several fights with the Dutch.

Of these encounters with the Dutch, the one which found its way into Suffolk song was the Battle of Sole Bay, fought on the 28th May, 1672, a dramatic incident in the third Dutch War. The English and French fleets, numbering 101 ships, of which 35 were French, were anchored in Southwold Bay when a Dutch fleet of 91 men-of-war, 54 fire-ships, and 23 tenders under De Ruyter's command, fell upon them in a north-west wind so unexpectedly that many were obliged to cut their cables in order to take up battle formation without undue delay. Count D'Estrées, the French commander, whose ships were lying at the southern end of the line, sailed out to sea on the port tack, while the English took the starboard tack. As the Dutch admiral attacked in the centre the allies were divided at once, and before they could unite again De Ruyter had inflicted heavy damage. The Duke of York's flagship, the *Prince*, was so badly damaged that she had to be abandoned, and the Duke's flag transferred to the *St. Michael*. The Earl of Sandwich was second-in-command, and his flagship, *The Royal James*, after a desperate battle lasting several hours, in which two-thirds of her crew were killed, had just succeeded in getting clear of the Dutch ships that had surrounded her when a fire-ship bore down, set her alight, and in spite of all efforts to subdue the flames she drifted towards Easton Ness and exploded, every man on board perishing. The earl's body was picked up three days later, but was so disfigured that he could only be recognised by the star he wore. In spite of this great initial advantage gained by the Dutch the fight lasted till nightfall with enormous loss of life on both sides. De Ruyter himself was wounded, and when he drew off at sunset neither side had strength to justify any claims of victory. The Dutch were forced to retreat, and the allies were too shattered to pursue them. The losses of the Dutch in men were never made public, but they were

certainly great. The allies lost 2,000 men, most of whom were English.

The story of this famous battle was recited all over the county long afterwards in the popular verses beginning:

> One day as I was sitting still
> Upon the side of Dunwich Hill,
>   And looking on the ocean,
> By chance I saw De Ruyter's fleet
> With Royal James's squadron meet;
> In sooth it was a noble treat
>   To see that brave commotion.

Southwold cannot claim the antiquity of some of its neighbours. Its prosperity came with the decline of Dunwich, following the accumulation of the bank of shingle that made Dunwich harbour useless. These banks of shingle that are so dangerous to mariners are, in fact, the sole defence from the tides of large areas of marshland. They are constantly, though imperceptibly, in motion, and are built up of sand and shingle borne down from the north until their progress south is blocked by cliffs. This is a general trend along the Suffolk coast, but has been most noticeable in the history of Dunwich haven, where we have records of the new cuts that had to be made as the shingle pushed the harbour farther north. It was this process that during the fifteenth century brought Southwold into rivalry with Dunwich as a port, and in 1489 the rivalry between the two towns was decided in Southwold's favour when Henry VII granted a charter to it, reciting: "That the navigation of the inhabitants of that Town by their industry exceeded and excelled above that of the ancient privileged Towns of these parts." We cannot question the industry of the inhabitants thus recognised, but there were in fact two other considerations that carried considerable weight. One was that the people of Dunwich had taken the wrong side in the Wars of the Roses; the other was the industry of the sea, which surpassed that of the people.

In the Southwold of the twentieth century, new and old are agreeably blended, both along the cliffs and about the nine greens that give so much character to this popular resort.

Wortham Mill

Its many open spaces are said to have been caused by the terrible fires that swept across it when most of its houses were built either entirely or partly of timber. The loss of these makes the architecture of all the East Suffolk towns uninteresting in comparison with those of the west and centre. There was little hope of saving a building when a fire was started and the bellows of the east wind began to play on it. Once they gained a hold, these fires travelled quickly because the cottages were built close together for protection against wind and rain. Hardly a town or village in East Suffolk escaped devastation by fire at some time in its history. Many suffered repeatedly. In the great Southwold fire of 25th April, 1659, two hundred and thirty-eight houses and every public building went up in flames. Three hundred families were impoverished. Three-quarters of the town was destroyed. The damage was estimated at forty thousand pounds, a high figure in the middle of the seventeenth century, though relatively low to-day.

It is no matter for wonder that the men of these East Coast towns should be built in heroic mould and lack some of the graces of a softer culture. Storm and battle have tried them in every century. Modern fire brigades have reduced the risk of loss from one old enemy, but during the last war these valiant little ports suffered severely. To those who knew it in the prosperous days before 1939 the Southwold of the early forties was a pitiful sight. It will recover quickly, and I should be doing Southwold and other coastal towns no service by describing the depressing, war-battered appearance they bore when I ran through them soon after peace returned. I mention this devastation only to pay tribute to the fighting spirit of these humble fisherfolk and their wives. The war scars will soon be hidden, and Southwold will again be a pleasant and unsophisticated town, invitingly situated on a hill above the marshes, with the sea on three sides of it.

Its church is yet another of the massive structures already described at Lavenham and Long Melford. The porch, with its groined ceiling and windows above the arch, is worthy of note; and the interior woodwork, which is both elaborately carved and painted, is the best in any church in the county. A resplendent rood screen extends across the entire width of the church, and even this is only part of what it was when its vaulted canopy and rood loft were complete.

In Lavenham we derived pleasure from the street names of the town; here in Southwold it is the names of the greens that arouse our curiosity. Gun Hill, the principal green, took its name from six ancient cannon which were presented to the town by the Duke of Cumberland, who captured them during the famous rebellion of 1745. The Duke landed at Southwold on his way home, and presented the cannon to the townsfolk in acknowledgment of their cordial reception. Butts Green is also easily explained. The butts stood there. But this again is interesting as a reminder of the days when the law required that every man should be proficient in the use of the bow. A more difficult name to explain is Tibby's Green. This was formerly a pasture for calves, and Tib or Tibby was the favourite name for them.

From Southwold we may ferry across the Blyth to Walberswick, a decayed port with an air of mystery about it from its smuggling and privateering past that is now a favourite resort of artists. Its cottages are strewn about wide greens, and along winding lanes, in a delightfully disorderly fashion. On a sunny day there is always either a cottage or a tumbledown shack on the quay that catches the light in a way that makes you want to sit down and try to give permanence to what you are convinced is a rare trick of the sun, giving beauty to something commonplace in a way that can never be repeated. The next time you visit Walberswick another nondescript scene will catch your glance no less excitingly. And always you will see one or two people wandering round Walberswick who have obviously learnt the art of happy living. Or is it only that among these rickety old sheds, coils of rope, and flying spindrift, all cares and responsibilities fall away, and once again it is enough to feel the wind in your hair, and be like the gorse on the commons behind you, inconsequently gay?

CHAPTER XIII

LOTHINGLAND

In Lowestoft a boat was laid,
    Mark well what I do say!
And she was built for the herring trade,
    But she has gone a-rovin', a-rovin', a-rovin',
    The Lord knows where!

KIPLING

M O S T of the people who live in large towns and cities leave them, I suppose, for only a fortnight each year. To these, and all who for various reasons lack opportunities for extensive travel even in their own country, each maritime English county is thought of in terms of its larger holiday resorts. Devon is summed up in Torquay, Sussex in Brighton, and Hampshire in Bournemouth. The truth of this is shown by the large number of people to whom Essex, a county of varied charm and scenery, is dismissed with a reference to Southend-on-Sea. To the same people Suffolk means Lowestoft, and when the county is named they see not Lavenham or Long Melford, or any of the places that hold the hearts of those who are able to go east and west along its valleys at will, but trim gardens on Kirkley Cliff, with tennis-courts, bowling-greens, and smart hotels above them, and below them a crowded beach; or perhaps the harbour, with its noisy and exciting fish-market. Later they see Oulton Broad, the fresh-water half of Lake Lothing, with house-boats along its quay and the graceful white sails of yachts blown across its breezy waters.

Suffolk has less to complain about than most counties in this tendency to identify a county with a holiday resort, because though Lowestoft is a large and sophisticated watering-place, it has both elegance and character. Here, however, as at Whitby in Yorkshire and other places, the two are kept apart. The true, historic Lowestoft is divided by the cut to Lake Lothing from the new town built for visitors on the

Kirkley side. Formerly, Kirkley and Lowestoft were separate towns, and some geographers believe that in the distant past the Waveney entered the sea between them. According to these, Lake Lothing was then an estuary, similar to the estuaries of the Deben and the Orwell in the southern part of the county. But in course of time the sea washed up a bar of shingle and turned the estuary into an inland lake, at the same time forcing the river to seek another outlet, which it eventually found in the river Yare. Other authorities deny that this can ever have been so. However that may be, the spring tides washed over the shingle into the lake, and flooded the low-lying marshland beyond it, until an embankment was constructed between Kirkley and Lowestoft, and these neighbouring towns were united. In 1885, when Lowestoft received its Charter, the new borough included the parish of Kirkley. To-day, Kirkley is an independent parish only for ecclesiastical purposes.

Early in the nineteenth century, however, Lowestoft ship-owners began to view this embankment with disfavour. They saw that much would be gained if it were cut to allow vessels to enter the lake, and pass through by a navigable channel to Norwich. In 1814 an engineer was employed to make a survey, but he did not report until seven years later, when he strongly recommended the plan, at the same time pointing out that it would be costly. Nevertheless, the scheme was adopted, and in 1827 a Bill permitting the work to be done received the Royal Assent. A channel was soon cut through the embankment, severing the old coach road, which since that time has been spanned by a swing bridge, and the object of turning the lake into a harbour was achieved. The second part of the enterprise—that of making a navigable channel to Norwich—was a failure, and for twelve years work was suspended, until in 1842 Sir Morton Peto, often described as the maker of Lowestoft, successfully advocated communication with Norwich by means of a railway between Lowestoft and Reedham, which would connect the port with Norwich and through Norwich with London. This line was laid, and since then Lowestoft has enjoyed remarkable progress, interrupted only—though seriously—by the two great wars of the present century.

If we could see Lowestoft from an aeroplane, approaching it from the sea, the cut and the lake behind it would look like the elongated body of a giant moth, with enormous wings on either side. But the wings would not match, for one would be brilliant with green and white and gold, while the other would be a warm, tawny brown, mottled with strong but sombre colours. As the land rises steeply on both sides of the water, we may add that the moth would appear ready for flight, and who could wonder, with that exhilarating sky and restless ocean before it?

The visitor to Lowestoft may bask in sunshine on the promenade to his heart's content, but before he leaves he should rise early on at least one morning—which should not be difficult, because the sunrise is so beautiful at Lowestoft, with the sea a lake of liquid gold—and make his way down to the fish-market. The transition from a sunrise to a fish-market may sound like bathos, but it is not, for Lowestoft's fish-market is as romantic and exciting a scene as a man could wish to see. Countless trucks rattle along the paved floors of the sheds. Baskets of gleaming fish are hoisted from the hold of each of the trawlers in the dock, then swung towards the quay and emptied into large wooden trays. From these they are pushed into baskets and packed into large barrels which are set in front of the auctioneer. Though the noise from trundled trucks, barrels, and screaming gulls is deafening, sharp as a chisel and hard as a hammer rings out the auctioneer's voice. No one could hear him without marvelling that such sounds could come from anything less resistant than steel. Starting with a few phrases that sound like a flourish of trumpets, he quickly comes to business and knocks down barrel after barrel to the wholesale fishmongers whose offices are ranged along the back of the shed.

Nearer the entrance to the same shed the fish already sold are tipped into small wooden crates that are tossed about like match-boxes. The lids are hurriedly knocked off, ice is splashed into them, and in a few seconds they are packed, nailed up, and labelled for dispatch.

Before the last war a babel of tongues increased the confusion, for fishermen of all nationalities could be found here. Russia, Spain, Denmark, and Belgium had their vice-consuls, and Norway, Sweden, France, and Germany their representatives. Lowestoft was then the third fishing port in the kingdom. At the time I write it is still striving to pull itself together after a war that brought its trade to a standstill. There was no fishing at Lowestoft during the war years. Many of the boats were used as mine-sweepers, others were taken to Fleetwood. Now it has to start again, but with sixty-three acres of harbour and quays for wharfage and berthage extending to 5,800 feet, its recovery is certain. The trawl basins have four and a half acres of water space, with over eleven hundred feet of quay available for landing; the Waveney Herring Dock has thirteen and a half acres of water space, with over sixteen hundred feet of landing quay; the Hamilton Dock eight and a quarter acres of water space, with over thirteen hundred feet of quay. But the boats to be seen in the harbour at the present time are all either English or Scots, and the vice-consuls have gone. For all that, the names of the old boats still reflect something of the pride and gallantry of the sea. Walking through the fish-market recently, I found there the *King Richard*, the *Lord Suffolk*, the *Lord Keith*, and the *Lord Collingwood* alongside the *Convallaria* of Banff and the *Lizzie West* of Milford Haven.

The most exciting time starts in October, when the herrings come south and with them the "kipper girls," as the braw Scots lassies are called who come to Lowestoft for the curing season. In the prosperous pre-war days they could be seen standing side by side in long rows along the large troughs of silvery fish, often with their wrists bound to strengthen them for the hard work of gutting the fish and tossing them into large bowls ready for curing, and sometimes because they had cut themselves. Cuts and small injuries were so frequent that the girls usually had a nurse in attendance. When they had finished work for the day these big, strong girls, with shawls over their heads, and wide, thick, navy-blue serge skirts on their sturdy hips, used to add much laughter to the old town as they strode along its streets. As may readily be imagined, they were not very popular with the local girls, who feared their attraction for the young fishermen.

The last war so effectively broke the life of Lowestoft that

at the end it was like an empty house awaiting a new tenant.
Inevitably we think of it in its heyday. My own memory of
the town goes back only for a little less than twenty years, but
I was happy to find two gracious, elderly ladies who had seen
through sixty years and more its gradual rise as a watering-
place. They were anxious, of course, for me to appreciate
that it had always been a more select resort than Yarmouth
—in Lowestoft you must never express appreciation of Yarmouth. In the days these ladies remembered first, the private
hotels we see along the front to-day were newly built private
houses, occupied during the summer months by well-to-do
families who owned them. The boarding-houses were then
along the back. With the rising fortunes of the lower middle
class, if the class term may be allowed for a moment, the
boarding-houses gradually displaced the private houses along
the front, but continued to be visited by the kind of people
who had previously owned them. These would now be content to hire a suite of rooms for a month or six weeks in
July and August. Many of these Victorian and Edwardian
boarding-houses had a graciousness about them from this
association with gentlefolk. Their landladies were proud that
their houses should be patronised by well-known families, and
took pains to maintain standards of hospitality and conduct
in keeping. However inevitable may have been the disappearance of that orderly if sometimes prudish mode of life,
and the rebellion of a new generation against it—as the new
generation has always rebelled against the old—it had a kindly
charm, and we who are old enough to remember those over-
furnished but welcoming establishments will always have
pleasant memories of the dignified ladies who presided over
them and received their guests so courteously.

We must not, however, exaggerate the respectable side
of Edwardian Lowestoft. Like all Suffolk towns it had its
"characters." There was one well-known citizen reputed to
be extremely clever, who had taken to drinking heavily and
was to be seen wandering round the streets with a bundle
slung over his shoulders at the end of a stick. Most of the
people who became impoverished in those days were supposed to have fallen through over-indulgence in strong
drink. Every town of any size must have had its example,

and what a valuable object lesson he was for the use of moralising parents and Sunday school teachers! Such men should have been generously rewarded for the edification they provided. There was also a strange little dwarf, as round as a barrel, whose name was Shelley Cook.

During the eighteen-seventies, the outstanding personality in Lowestoft was George Borrow, who lived in a pleasant cottage with a garden that sloped down to Oulton Broad, on the banks of which he had a summer-house. The cottage has gone, but the summer-house is still there. In this beautifully situated retreat *Lavengro* and *The Bible in Spain* were written. It was Borrow's custom, we are told, to spend his mornings there and write down the thoughts that came into his head on odd scraps of paper which were later passed to his devoted wife, who copied them on to sheets of foolscap. In those days Borrow's cottage was situated on a farm, which he owned, and where he allowed large gipsy encampments, much to the annoyance of his neighbours. With the lake in front, a pine wood at the side, a paddock for his favourite Arab, Sidi Habismilk, at the rear, and gipsy tents at hand, Oulton was as perfect a place of residence as could be found for a man of Borrow's temperament. Complete happiness was denied him by his religion, for he was a rigid predestinarian and believed himself damned eternally.

In appearance Borrow resembled "a colossal clergyman." He was tall and muscular, had snow-white hair, dark eyes burning fiercely in a smooth, innocently oval face; and with his arrogant, sonorous voice and aggressive manner, he was an intimidating figure. His attributes, as so often with men of genius, who are rarely at ease either with themselves or anyone else, were conflicting and difficult to follow. He was as wild as the gipsies with whom he was most at ease, and at the same time as much attached to his Bible as a Plymouth Brother. At one moment he was shrewd and scholarly, at the next as perverse as a child and absurdly gullible. One of his closest associates was a gipsy whom he believed he had converted to his own kind of narrow evangelicalism. This disciple of his, supported by Borrow, used to preach extraordinary sermons in a small conventicle in the neighbourhood. No doubt the gipsy found Borrow's friendship much to his advantage. After the death of his famous friend he relapsed into his natural paganism and left the district.

Sir Morton Peto's railway crossed Borrow's land, and Sir Morton was so foolish as to boast that he had made more money out of the gravel taken from it than the right of crossing it had cost him. Borrow heard of this, so when Sir Morton, by this time a wealthy man and owner of Somerleyton Hall, invited him to visit Somerleyton, Borrow replied: "I call on you! Do you think I don't read my Shakespeare? Do you think I don't know all about those highwaymen Bardolph and Peto?"

Sir Morton was not the only Shakespearian character in the district he claimed to have identified. One of his greatest pleasures was to take the distinguished people who visited him while they were staying in Lowestoft to Oulton church, and there show them the brass bearing an effigy of Sir John Fastolf, whom Borrow claimed to be the original of Sir John Falstaff.

Borrow was not a great reader, and had not a very high opinion of literature in general. To a well-known lady writer who expressed pleasure at making his acquaintance, and asked if she might send him a set of her books, he replied: "For God's sake don't, madam; I shouldn't know what to do with them." His rudeness was frequently disconcerting, and scandalised the respectable people of Lowestoft, who believed him to be a retired missionary. No doubt they would have liked him to open sales of work for them, and attend garden parties. One day a highly respected local doctor, named Dr. Ray, was returning from his round of visits when his coachman took a corner rather sharply and grazed the flank of Sidi Habismilk with Borrow on his back. The doctor's coach drove on with the Arab in pursuit; but the two were separated somehow, and the doctor reached home and was safely indoors before Borrow presented himself at the front door. He rang the bell without dismounting, and when the door was opened struck his heels into the Arab, which at once sprang through the hall while Borrow called for the doctor. When this worthy gentleman appeared, Borrow roared at him: "Where is that scoundrel coachman of yours, sir? Do you know what he has done, sir?"

"Mr. Borrow," replied the doctor quietly, "if you will be good enough to remove your horse from my hall and speak like a gentleman I shall be happy to attend to what you have to say." Borrow thereupon drew round his horse and rode out without another word.

He could be as unreasonable in cold blood as he was in hot. Sir Walter Scott was a favourite subject with him. He heartily detested him and all his works. Sir Walter, he said, was responsible for the lamentable revival of flunkeyism to be seen everywhere because he had spent his life preaching the worship of gentility. By this Jacobitism, according to Borrow, he was also responsible for the revival of popery. With the utmost satisfaction Borrow would recount the financial disasters that darkened Sir Walter's closing years, and explain how these were the punishments inflicted by divine justice upon one who had sinned so grievously in laying up for himself treasure upon earth.

On the other hand he had extraordinary powers of observation, and a gift for eliciting out-of-the-way information from the people he met on his solitary walks. His skill as a linguist enabled him to trace Scandinavian origins of words and customs found along the Suffolk coast. Of his passion for walking we have the testimony of his wife, that on a bright morning he would come downstairs and announce that he was going for a walk. For months nothing would be heard of him; then one day he would reappear and quietly report that he had enjoyed his walk.

Such were the humours and angularities of a great East Anglian "character." If you wish to find "characters" in the Lowestoft of to-day you must go down one of the scores into the old town. These Lowestoft scores are steep, narrow streets leading from the main street to what is called "The Beach." The name is derived from the Anglo-Saxon *scoran*, to score or furrow. They were channels scored into the face of the cliff by streams, and formed easy passages for ascent. In course of time houses were built up the sides of them and they are now to Lowestoft what the rows are to Yarmouth. As they are too steep for traffic they still cut off "The Beach" from the rest of the town, and those who live in that quarter still talk of going into Lowestoft when they climb a score to reach the shops. Some of the buildings in this part are interesting relics of a past age. South Fleet House at the top of Wilde's Store is one of the most notable of the old flint buildings of East Anglia, and has the date 1586 over its doorway.

The inhabitants of "The Beach" share only about a dozen names among them, of which Ayres, Mewse, and Yallop are the most common. One day I spent a pleasant hour gossiping with an old local character who was then living in the Fishermen's Hospital. When he first went to sea about sixty years ago, he told me, the boats might be away for as long as six weeks at a stretch, and even then the men would have to land the fish when they got back before going home for twenty-four hours' leave. To the end of his time, he said, if a boat had been away no longer than a week and docked before 6 p.m. the men would be expected on board again before 6 a.m. next day. Now the boats are usually away six or seven days only, according to how long the ice lasts, and as soon as they dock the men finish work and go off for forty-eight hours' leave. The "lumpers" then jump in and land the fish.

When I asked about pay he told me that he thought he was doing well when he got ten shillings a week as a cook. He married on seventeen shillings a week, and thought that his wife had managed quite well on it. Living was cheap. They had a good cottage for half a crown a week. He agreed that it was a hard life, but thought people were as happy then as they are now. He would not have left the sea for twice the pay he got. "But then," said he, "the sea ain't like other trades. It's in your blood, an' I still says it's a grand callin'. It's a Biblical callin', as you might say. It's not like this flyin' in aeroplanes. Devil's playthings, I calls 'em. Nerves won't stand that sort o' caperin'. It's agin nature." His prejudice was easily understood, for all round us was the evidence of enemy bombing. "They'n knocked it abaht a bit," said the old man when I referred to the damage done.

I asked if fishing was now subject to all kinds of new regulations. It was, he agreed, though punishments were less severe than they had been in his day. He grinned and said he had never known a time when fishermen wouldn't break regulations if it suited them. "We're fairly well behaved, mind you," was his way of putting it, "but if we can't find fish where we're supposed to, then we go after 'em. You can't make that old sea fit in with one-way traffic ideas."

This old fisherman, I thought, personified the spirit of Lowestoft all through its eventful history, for it has faced enemy attack with as much spirit in earlier centuries as it does to-day. During the sixteenth century it was plundered by Kett's rebels, and during the Civil War it challenged the greater part of East Anglia by declaring gallantly for the king —perhaps principally because Yarmouth was on the Parliamentary side. These two neighbours have long memories and never forget their ancient feud, so while most of East Anglia escaped the ravages of that unnatural struggle, Lowestoft and Yarmouth took advantage of the opportunity it provided for them to bring out a few private accounts for settlement. It was at this time that Cromwell surprised the Suffolk Cavaliers at Lowestoft after an abortive attempt had been made to secure the county for the king. The garrison at first resolved to resist, but when a local merchant showed them how hopeless their position was they laid down their arms, and Cromwell entered the town unopposed at the head of a thousand men. He took up quarters at the "Swan," the principal inn of the town, which stood on the east side of the High Street near Swan Score.

Twenty-two years later, on the 3rd June, 1665, a famous naval engagement was fought off Lowestoft between an English fleet of 114 men-of-war and 28 fire-ships commanded by the Duke of York and a Dutch fleet of 102 men-of-war and 17 yachts and fire-ships commanded by Admiral Opdam de Wassanaer. From 3 a.m. to noon the engagement continued without advantage to either side, then the Earl of Sandwich dramatically forced his way into the centre of the Dutch line, causing confusion and distraction from which no opportunity for recovery was allowed. The flagship of the Dutch admiral blew up in the middle of the action, and only five of the five hundred men on board—representing most of the best families in Holland—were saved. The fight continued until seven in the evening, with appalling loss of life for the enemy.

One of Lowestoft's most distinguished sons, Sir Thomas

Allin, who lived from 1612 to 1685, took part in this engagement, and must have been particularly useful, because no one knew the waters better than he. During the Civil War Sir Thomas, who was then a Lowestoft merchant and shipowner, commanded the forces of the port in their engagements with the Yarmouth recruits, and it was largely in consequence of his brave and skilful leadership that the Lowestoft men were usually victors. After the 1665 victory he was knighted and appointed admiral. In 1670 he was appointed comptroller of the Navy, and about this time he bought Somerleyton Hall, where he spent much of the remainder of his life in honoured retirement.

Another Lowestoft naval commander, Sir Andrew Leake, who died in 1704, took part in the Dutch war of 1690. He was known as " Queen Anne's handsome captain," and was as remarkable for gallantry as for good looks. Sir Andrew died from wounds received in the engagement off Malaga. After these had been dressed, he wrapped a table-cloth round him, and as he was by this time unable to walk he ordered the chair he sat in to be carried on to the quarter-deck. There he followed the fight until he collapsed and died.

Thomas Nash, who satirised Gabriel Harvey in " Have with you to Saffron Walden," and whose romance, *Jack Wilton*, introduced the adventure story to England—a writer who had much of the spirit of Rabelais in his constitution— was also a native of Lowestoft. His father is described in Lowestoft parish register as " preacher and minister." He was probably a Puritan, which may account for the son's hatred of that sect. Centuries later, Lowestoft gave us another novelist, for it was there that Joseph Conrad first set foot on English soil and decided to make this country his home. " Lowestoft was my spiritual birthplace," he said.

Memorials to many of Lowestoft's distinguished sons are to be seen in the old parish church which stands on a hill to the west of the town. In the graveyard, near the east end of the church, is a stone inscribed " Edmund Gillingwater, who died September 23, 1772, aged 79 years. The Historian of Lowestoft." Thousands of visitors who have attended service in the church must have read that stone and have believed that they were in fact standing at the grave of the man who wrote the *History of Lowestoft*. But if they are fortunate enough to be able to borrow a copy of that work they will discover that this is only another of the surprisingly large number of mistakes to be found on church and churchyard inscriptions. The permanence of stone should make those who are responsible for such inscriptions exceptionally careful. We have seen how a misleading statement was added to an inscription in Orford church, and it should be pointed out that here in Lowestoft churchyard there is another. The preface to Gillingwater's history is dated 1790, and the book was not in fact published until 1795. It contains references to events that occurred twenty years after the death of the gentleman who is wrongly credited with having written it. The truth is that the stone is above the grave of Edmund Gillingwater the father of the historian. Edmund the historian died at Harleston in 1813 and is buried in Redenhall churchyard.

There are pleasant circumstances about the life of Edmund Gillingwater the younger that are worth recording. He was of humble birth, and was apprentice to a Lowestoft barber when the Rev. John Bellward, for thirty-eight years rector of Burgh, discovered him—perhaps by visiting the barber's shop where he worked—and finding him a studious boy, undertook his tuition. How much good work of this kind has been done by country parsons in every generation! Edward FitzGerald commented on the advantage to the nation of having an educated man stationed in every parish in the kingdom. It was a wise observation. The mere going in and out among the people of a Christian gentleman has been a great civilising influence in the development of English social life. But in addition to this, countless boys of promise, whose gifts would have gone unrecognised if there had been no parson in the parish, have been encouraged and given practical help. There are few more beautiful sights to a man who esteems scholarship, than to see a young boy from a humble home, who by some happy chance has discovered the sweetness of knowledge, sitting by a study fire while an elderly scholar quietly draws back the curtain of his mind until the boy catches a glimpse of a vast and exciting country that may keep him occupied to the end of his life. We can imagine something of the thrill that Edmund Gillingwater must have felt when Mr. Bellward first invited him into his study at Burgh rectory.

The result of this association was that Edmund became a scholar, and as he lacked the means to take up a scholastic career, he did the next best thing; he became a bookseller, choosing for his little world the old market town of Harleston, just over the Norfolk border. There he not only prospered in business but became highly esteemed throughout Norfolk and Suffolk as an antiquary, and no less for his saintly character. All his life he was a devoted churchman, and found time among his many interests to conduct a class for the young men of Harleston. So excellent was the relationship between teacher and scholars that in later years, when enfeebled by age, the old man's scholars were like sons to him. In addition to his *History of Lowestoft*, he wrote a book on parish workhouses, a history of Bury St. Edmunds, and compiled material for a history of Suffolk.

All this makes a pleasant story, but there is an even more delightful circumstance in the life of Edmund Gillingwater. His best work was not his laboriously compiled history of Suffolk, which was never published, nor yet that of Bury St. Edmunds, which was, but his *History of Lowestoft*. And much of the material for this was provided by his brother Isaac, who remained a barber in Lowestoft to the end of his life. Barbers have always been noted gossips, and their shops are still used as sources of local information. Isaac Gillingwater's was no exception. As the Lowestoft people sat waiting for their hair to be cut and their beards to be trimmed, they would frequently compare notes about former days, and would sometimes recall things their fathers or grandfathers had told them. When this happened Isaac would say, " My brother would be interested in that," make a note of the facts disclosed and send it to Edmund. Isaac was also parish clerk, another occupation that gave him opportunities for historical research. He lived to be eighty-one and died in the same year as his brother. He was described by one who knew him as " singular in his habits, but very intelligent."

The *History of Lowestoft* was the work of these two men. It was the work of a barber and a bookseller. In thinking of this we may recall that Gardner's *History of Dunwich* was the

work of an exciseman. Suffolk is constantly reminding us that it is the county of the inspired amateur. FitzGerald himself was a fishmonger, and Bernard Barton, his friend, was a coal-merchant and bank clerk as well as a poet.

North of the old town we find a pleasant district for visitors along the crest of what used to be a cliff. The sea has receded here, and between the houses and the beach there is an expanse of sandy common called the Denes, which run out to Lowestoft Ness, the most easterly point in England. From here we may continue along the cliffs to Corton. There could be no better place to lie on a summer day than on these cliffs, amid fern and heather, listening to the sea pounding on the shingle below, gazing towards the bramble and gorse behind, or the ragwort, poppies and wild snapdragon growing on the Denes.

From the cliff the road continues through shady woods to Corton, where the parish church, half of which is in ruin, is a familiar landmark. Only the chancel, five pews in the nave, and a small gallery above, are now in use. The tower is nearly a hundred feet high, and on seeing it sailors recall the old rhyme:

> When you come to Corton,
> The way begin to shorten.

The use of the plural form of the verb is an East Anglian peculiarity. A coastal road continues from Corton to Gorleston, at the northern tip of the county, where another old rhyme goes:

> Gorleston was Gorleston ere Yarmouth begun
> And will be Gorleston when Yarmouth be gone.

Or sometimes:

> Gorleston great one day will be;
> Yarmouth buried in the sea.

Gorleston, it is claimed, is an older place than Yarmouth, with traditions going back to pre-Norman days, but there is so much rivalry between Yarmouth and its neighbours that many of their respective claims require careful scrutiny. Perhaps few now care about these claims to antiquity. However

P

Hoxne

ancient Gorleston may claim to be it has the appearance of
being the newest resort on the whole of the Suffolk coast,
and of having been built specifically for the pleasure-loving
twentieth century. Its hotels stand on high cliffs round a
shallow bay, where a fringe of sand is covered with beach
huts and holiday crowds, while along the top of the cliffs is
the Marine Parade, with its neat, artificial gardens and all that
is expected of so up-to-date a watering-place.

We cannot come so near to Yarmouth without thinking of
Charles Dickens and *David Copperfield*. Nor do we need to
step across the border and prove traitor to Suffolk by writing
about Yarmouth, because the important David Copperfield
associations are on the Suffolk side of the Yare. The story
of how Charles Dickens came to use a Suffolk village as the
setting of the early chapters of *David Copperfield* is worth
telling, especially as it is in keeping with the pleasure we
have already derived so often from noticing local place-names.
It would be interesting to know how many places have found
their way into literature on the strength of their names. There
are many beautiful villages that can never live down the
reproach of an ugly name, and plain villages that become
celebrated simply because their names are evocative in some
mysterious way. Blundeston, the reputed birthplace of David
Copperfield, found its way into fiction on the strength of its
name. Dickens was on a visit to Somerleyton Hall when he
saw the name of this village on a signpost. It had almost
exactly the sound he required. He repeated it to himself
several times, and in doing so an *r* crept in. With that the
name was perfect, so when he wrote *David Copperfield* the
village of Blundeston became the village of Blunderstone.

As Dickens so generously adopted Blundeston it only
remained for Blundeston to make capital out of the association, which it promptly proceeded to do. Over the "Plough"
Inn is an inscription stating that the willing Barkis, the car-
rier in *David Copperfield*, started from that house. On the
round tower of the church is the sundial David used to see
from his bedroom window at the "Rookery," or Rectory, as
Blundeston calls it. The meadow Peggotty ran across to wave
to Master David as he started out for school may be seen, and
the fence by which the infatuated Mrs. Copperfield stood to

talk to Mrs. Murdstone, whose name, especially when borne by his sister, is one of the ominous masterpieces of literature. Not far away, between Yarmouth and Blundeston, stands the inn where the same Barkis is said to have taken so long over the delivery of an iron bedstead.

The Somerleyton Hall visited by Dickens has been the great house associated with Lowestoft in all generations since it was built. Sir Morton Peto lived there. In an earlier house on the same site lived the Jerninghams, Sir Thomas Allin, and Sir John and Lady Wentworth. Like Henham Hall, it was a Royalist house during the Civil War and suffered damage in consequence. In Sir John Wentworth's day our worthy friend, Thomas Fuller, was a visitor. He noted the aptitude of the name in a characteristic reflection: "for here summer is to be seen in the depths of winter, in the pleasant walks beset on both sides with fir trees—green all the year long, besides other curiosities."

The district has lost none of its beauty since then. On the contrary, the plantations that were curiosities in the seventeenth century are now mature woodlands surrounding Somerleyton and Herringfleet halls, in the midst of which is the loveliest lake in all East Anglia, Fritton, a secluded stretch of water more than two miles long and about a quarter of a mile wide, the haunt of widgeon, duck, and teal. It is one of Suffolk's two large bird decoys. The other is at Orwell Park. With wild fowl so numerous the district is ideal for the purpose. In *The Borough* Crabbe wrote:

> High o'er the restless deep, above the reach
> Of gunners' hope, vast flights of Wild Ducks stretch;
> Far as the eye can glance on either side
> In a broad space and level line they glide,
> All in their wedge-like figures from the north,
> Day after day, flight after flight, go forth.

This profitable decoy at Fritton has been in use for many centuries. In 1576 John Jerningham "demised to one Godfrey, all that his fowling, liberty and royalty of fowling upon the waters of Ashby and upon the common of the town of Ashby, rendering 100 couple of Teals and two couple of Mallards yearly."

If it could be seen from above, a bird decoy would look like a starfish. From a quiet lake, closely fringed and over-hung by trees to guarantee seclusion, radiate arms of shallow water, artificially made and effectively disguised with reeds and water plants, each curving and narrowing to a point at its extremity. These pipes, as they are called, are not con-structed all the way round the lake, but are set to catch the birds flying inland, and also with an eye to the prevailing winds. It is necessary for several to be provided, otherwise only one direction of the wind would serve, because the wild fowl to be snared must fly against the wind in rising from the water. For a pipe to work successfully the wind must blow down it from the narrow end to the mouth.

Approximately half-way along each arm of water the pipe begins. To form it, an arch is thrown over the water, measur-ing about twenty feet across, and this is followed by a series of smaller arches as the pipe narrows until the last is no more than two feet across. These arches are covered along their entire length by a net, which forms a cage shaped like a long stocking with a hole in the toe. Additional disguise is pro-vided by a series of diagonal overlapping screens, arranged to allow a view through to the mouth of the pipe, but not back-wards to the broad entrance.

The fowl are decoyed into these traps by more than one means—sometimes by decoy-ducks, which may be hand-reared mallard trained for the purpose, but more often by a decoy-dog, which is mistaken for a fox. This dog is trained to run behind a screen, and the birds follow it either out of curiosity or to chase the intruder away.

Andrew Marvell has some satirical political lines that may come to mind here:

> I'll have a fair pond, with a pretty decoy,
> Where many strange fowl shall feed and enjoy,
> And still in their language quack *Vive le Roy!*

During the last war Fritton Lake was reserved for secret experimental work.

Those who prefer a larger expanse of water to this quiet, romantic retreat must go a few miles farther north and look out across the broad expanse of Breydon Water from below

Burgh Castle. Breydon is the estuary of the Yare and the Waveney, and has an area of over a thousand acres against Fritton's one hundred and sixty and Oulton Broad's one hundred and thirty, or to put it in miles, Breydon is four and a half miles long by two-thirds of a mile broad. Seen at sunset, when the flood waters are out, with windmills in the distance and cattle grazing on a tongue of land in the foreground, it is like a picture by a Dutch master. Above is that grand old ruin, Burgh Castle; and after admiring the view across Breydon we may climb the cliff to examine it. At present it has only three sides, but originally there must have been a fourth. Perhaps this may be thought a rash assertion. Archaeologists are divided on the point, I am told; but it is difficult to believe that any Roman would have left one side exposed to attack.

Canon J. J. Raven identified Burgh Castle with the Roman *Gariannonum*. The walls enclose a quadrangle measuring 620 feet by 383 feet (Canon Raven's measurements), and are between fourteen and fifteen feet high, nine feet thick, with foundations twelve feet thick. Four great bastions strengthen the eastern wall, two against the rounded corners and two between them. The north and south walls have one bastion each, both a little to the west of the middle. A peculiarity of these bastions is that for the first seven feet from the ground —that is to say, for approximately half their height—they are not bonded into the walls, which are built of flint-rubble and concrete laced with courses of tiles.

It was here, according to tradition, that St. Fursey, an Irish missionary who came to East Anglia, where the king received him gladly, built his tiny monastery of clay and wattles. He was a meditative man who loved solitude, and as we have chosen evening for our visit to this northern tip of the county, we may sit for a while on this escarpment as St. Fursey himself must often have done more than thirteen hundred years ago, gazing across Breydon, through which, three centuries or so earlier, the Romans had sailed in their galleys to this same Burgh Castle.

CHAPTER XIV

THE WAVENEY VALLEY

THE two rivers that separate Suffolk from Norfolk, the Waveney and the Little Ouse, rise within a few feet of each other near Redgrave, but flow in opposite directions. For this they are called "disagreeing brethren." Redgrave Hall, near the source of these two streams, is one of several historic houses in East Anglia associated with the Bacon family. The first mansion to be built on this site was a rest house for Abbot Samson of Bury St. Edmunds, who was lord of the manor. Henry VIII, in the last year of his reign, granted it to Thomas Darcy, and it was from him that it passed to the Bacon family. Sir Nicholas Bacon, Queen Elizabeth's lord-keeper, lived here, and after him his son, also Sir Nicholas, who was created premier baronet of England by James I in 1611. From the Bacons it passed to the Holts, and the present hall was built by Rowland Holt in 1770.

To the east is Wortham, a scattered parish of five hamlets with an inn called the "Tumble-down Dick," built to commemorate the fall of Richard Cromwell. Its church has the largest round tower in England, a curious structure when first seen, for though it is thirty feet in diameter it is only sixty feet high. Richard Cobbold was rector of Wortham, and *Margaret Catchpole* was written at the rectory. If he were alive to-day, that reverend gentleman would have trouble over both his honours as a novelist and his dues as a parson, for another Suffolk novelist now lives at Wortham—Miss Doreen Wallace of Wortham Manor, who, as Mrs. Rash, has exceptionally strong views on the subject of tithes, which are not such as the Rev. Richard Cobbold could ever have been persuaded to share. So if Redgrave is the home of "disagreeing brethren," Wortham is the home of disagreeing novelists.

At Palgrave, the next village along the Waveney, lived another Suffolk worthy, who said that it was his ambition to be known as " Honest Tom Martin of Palgrave." At the end of a useful life spent in collecting Suffolk books and records, and other things dear to his antiquarian heart, he was buried in the church porch, where a tablet to his memory may be seen. His collections were sold to a Thetford man for the modest sum of six hundred pounds, but enriched their purchaser, it was said, by many thousands. His valuable Suffolk collection was acquired by Sir J. Cullum and is now in the Cullum Library at Bury St. Edmunds.

Associations like these are to be found along every Suffolk valley. There is hardly a village that has not been the home of a fine old English family or of a kindly scholar whose name and virtues it is a pleasure to record. But the Waveney has prouder memories than these. After flowing through fens and marshes it reaches Hoxne, where it receives several feeders that reach it after they have united with the Dove, and this low-lying marshland, with the streams and undulating pastures around it, was the scene of the event that determined the course of Suffolk history for nearly seven hundred years. It was here in the year 870 that Edmund, King of the East Angles, was martyred after refusing to renounce Christianity and make terms with his Danish captors. It is not surprising to find that the event is as clearly remembered in the village as if it had happened a hundred instead of a thousand years ago, because it was, in fact, about a hundred years ago—in August 1848 to be precise—that an ancient oak, reputed to be the one to which St. Edmund had been bound and shot to death with arrows, fell by its own weight, and when broken up two months later was found to have an arrow head embedded in its trunk. The discovery roused fresh interest in the old tradition. When examined carefully, the tree bore evidence of more than a thousand years of growth, and the arrow was in the part that would be about four and a half to five feet above the ground. But in spite of this discovery doubt was cast on the authenticity of the story of St. Edmund's martyrdom at Hoxne by two able scholars, Lord Francis Hervey and Dr. M. R. James. The reason given for this doubt is to me far from convincing. Lord Francis discovered that a Bury scribe, writing before 1100, stated that Edmund was buried at a place called Suthtune (or Sutton), near the place of his martyrdom. As there is at present only one Sutton in Suffolk, the one near Woodbridge, Lord Francis concluded, and Dr. James concurred, "that we ought rather to look for the place of the final catastrophe in the south-east corner of the county."

But surely the name Sutton was formerly a common one. There were probably several if not many Suttons, or southern homesteads, in the land of the south folk. I am assured that there was one in the Hoxne district, and that there is much evidence for the antiquity of the tradition associating St. Edmund with the parish. There are old references to a field called "Kyngfelde," and St. Edmund's well in Oakley Park is of great age. In the "Compotus" or Account Rolls of the cell of St. Edmund, Hoxne, 1327-1545, items are to be found showing money paid for cleaning St. Edmund's well, and altogether, while admitting that the subject is one for the specialist, the evidence in favour of the traditional view still appears to be too great to be dismissed by that produced against it up to the present time.

On the other hand, we must freely recognise that much of Edmund's story is folk-lore rather than fact. Most of us have seen legends grow up in our own lifetime, and though we would not doubt the accuracy of events still earlier to which dependable witnesses bore testimony, the circumstances that led to St. Edmund's martyrdom, and the nature of the evidence, were not such as to give us complete confidence in the accounts, which in any case are conflicting. For this reason we are grateful to Lord Francis Hervey for sifting truth from legend in the main body of the story, even if we cannot accept his argument in favour of Sutton, near Woodbridge, and not Hoxne being the place of martyrdom. Readers who wish to have an accurate historical account should refer to Lord Francis's writings. Here we can only give a brief summary of the traditional story. According to this, Ragnar Lodbrog—lodbrog meaning leather breeches—a Dane of royal blood, while on a hawking expedition, was sailing near an island off the coast of Denmark when his boat, caught by a tempest, was driven across the North Sea and up the Yare to Reedham. On landing, the Dane was conducted to King Edmund, who was then at his castle at Caister in Norfolk, and was received so graciously that he accepted the king's invitation to remain for some time in England before returning to his own country. He enjoyed both the company of the king and the pleasures of the court, but above all else he enjoyed hunting, and much of his time was spent with Beorn, the king's huntsman, though whether for what he could learn from the huntsman or because he was attracted by the huntsman's wife is not certain. Some versions of the story say one, some the other. For whichever cause, Beorn the huntsman became jealous of the Dane and one day enticed him into a wood and killed him. There the body was discovered by Ragnar's faithful hound, which lay sorrowing beside it night and day, until hunger compelled him to creep up to the castle in search of any scraps that might have been left on the ground. By this means Ragnar's body was discovered, for one of the servants at the castle saw the dog and followed him to the wood. At once the huntsman was suspected of the murder. He was tried by the king's court and sentenced to be put to sea without chart or compass in the same boat that had brought his victim to England. The sentence was carried out, and by strange chance the wind carried the boat back to Denmark, where it was recognised, and Beorn the huntsman found himself for the second time charged with murder. When Ragnar Lodbrog's two sons, Ingwar and Ubba, stood before him and demanded to know the circumstances of their father's death, Beorn swore on oath that Ragnar had been killed by Edmund, his master, King of the East Angles, and that he had come to Denmark to inform the Danes of this crime. So completely convinced were Ingwar and Ubba that they acquitted the huntsman and immediately levied an army of twenty thousand men, and with Beorn to direct them sailed for the shores of England. But the wind carried them to Scotland, and they were forced to land at Berwick on Tweed, where they pillaged the district and then returned to Denmark.

In the following year, which was 866, the tenth year of King Edmund's reign, they landed in East Anglia, but without fighting any decisive battles withdrew again to their own country. A third time they crossed the North Sea, and this time, according to the legend, they encountered the king's army and drove the king himself into marshland from which escape seemed impossible. The king was thus compelled to decide whether he would surrender or fight his way out and probably die in the endeavour. He resolved to fight. The surrounding land was examined, and a ford discovered. Edmund and his army rushed across it and by the fury of their attack succeeded in cutting their way through the enemy, who withdrew in confusion and escaped from the country as quickly as they could. The ford where this dramatic encounter took place was at Barnby, which is said by some to take its name from Beorn, the name of the treacherous huntsman. The terminal *by* certainly signifies Scandinavian origin, though it is borne by only four Suffolk parishes.

In the year 870 the Danes again attacked in force, and this time succeeded in fighting their way to Ely, where Ubba was left to guard the spoil while Ingwar marched east through Thetford in search of Edmund, to whom he sent a message proposing that Edmund should renounce Christianity and become the vassal of Ingwar and Ubba, who would then allow him to retain the rule of half his kingdom. Edmund, on receiving this proposal, collected his army and marched towards Thetford, where a furious battle was fought, resulting in serious loss of life on both sides; but it was the Danes who at evening were compelled to withdraw from the field. Edmund then inspected the remnants of his army and crossed the field of battle. When he saw the wounded and dying, and heard their groans of distress, he was so moved with compassion that he withdrew to Hoxne, vowing never again to engage in battle with the pagans. Rather than bring such suffering to his people, he declared, he would offer himself as a sacrifice, and in doing so save his kingdom and vindicate his faith. In the meantime Ingwar had been joined by his brother Ubba at the head of ten thousand men, and with these combined forces the Danes marched into Eglesdune, which appears to have been in the Hoxne area, where they took the king by surprise, captured him, and when he refused to renounce his faith, shot him to death with arrows.

Much of this story may be legend; but it is at least true that the Danes pillaged eastern England under the commands of Ingwar, Ubba, Beorn, and also Guthrum, in 866, though there does not appear to be any evidence that they came into conflict with Edmund's army before 869. Of the course of the struggle all that is reasonably certain is the last phase. The records of this rest on the authority of Edmund's armour-bearer, who was present at his master's death and heard both his rejection of the enemy's terms and his refusal to renounce his faith. He gave testimony that the king was tied to a tree, scourged with whips and shot to death with arrows, and that finally he was beheaded. This man lived to a great age and gave an account of what he had seen to King Athelstan. A young man named Dunstan was present, and wept to hear the story. He never forgot it, and three years before he died he repeated it to the monk, Abbo of Fleury, who embodied it in his *Passion of Edmund*, recording there, in a dedicatory letter to Dunstan, the way the story had been handed down.

After his martyrdom Edmund was buried in a wooden chapel at Hoxne, and remained there for thirty-three years. A curious story is told about the burial. At first the king's head could not be found, so his men called out, "Where are you?" and a voice answered, "Here! Here! Here!" When they followed the sound of the voice they found a wolf holding the king's head in its paws. Many representations of this story are to be found in various places. We have noted one at Hadleigh, and the arms of Bury St. Edmunds, taken from those of the abbey, are of a wolf holding a king's head, in the terms of heraldry, "couped proper, crowned, or." The legend in conclusion relates that when the head and body were put together they were miraculously joined, so that the king's final humiliation might be cancelled.

This chapel at Hoxne was built of split logs set upright, similar to the ancient church which stands to this day at Greensted, near Ongar in Essex. Both are supposed to have been built by the same hands, for Greensted church was built where the body of the king, by that time canonised, rested while being carried back to Bury St. Edmunds about 1013. The Bury monks, fearing the Danes might steal their saint, had hidden his body in London during a period of danger.

After Edmund's body had been enshrined at Bury in the great abbey built to his memory, the chapel at Hoxne was con-verted into a small priory for seven or eight Benedictine monks, whose prior was nominated by the Prior of Norwich. At the Dissolution this Hoxne priory was valued at £40 per annum. The Bishop of Norwich held this manor until 1535, and frequently resided here. After it had been surrendered to the Crown, Henry VIII granted it to Sir Robert Southwell.

Another tradition connected with Edmund's capture at Hoxne is still fresh in mind in this most charming of all the villages of the Waveney valley. It relates that the king hid from his enemies under a bridge, and was discovered there by a newly married couple returning home late in the evening, who saw by moonlight his golden spurs reflected in the water. They treacherously reported their discovery to the Danes, and the information led to his capture. The king was so incensed at this betrayal that he put a curse on every couple who should pass over that bridge to their wedding. To-day, more than a thousand years later, the curse is still feared.

In social history a thousand years is a long period, but we have evidence of human life at Hoxne long before any period of which we have connected records. By singular good fortune a certain John Frere, who lived at Roydon Hall at the end of the eighteenth century, when little interest was taken in prehistoric remains, realised that the flaked flints he had discovered in a brickfield in 1797 were the handiwork of men, though "not of this present world," because obviously uninstructed in the use of metals, and at that early date produced evidence of social life in Hoxne rather more than half-way through the Old Stone Age.

The Waveney valley is as rich as any part of Suffolk in both archaeology and folk-lore, and in folk-lore it is richer than most. Perhaps the character of the river itself, with its twists and turns, its fens and treacherous marshes, has been conducive to fancy. The name Waveney is said to be derived from Saxon words meaning "waving water," or, less poetically, quaking bog. How likely to be true that suggested derivation is I should not like to say, but it is a pretty fancy and one we may adopt so long as we are not dogmatic about it. There are rivers that are merely taken for granted by those who live near them. They play no tricks, provoke no strange imaginings. The Waveney is not one of these. It is always in the minds of those who live near it, and rarely out of their sight. Its principal towns on the Suffolk side, Beccles and Bungay, glory in it. Some of its villages fear it, for it is more subject to floods than any other East Anglian river, and in a wet summer, like that of 1946, crops and even livestock may be borne away on its swirling waters. In winter the scene may be even more alarming. The Waveney will not allow herself to be ignored or slighted.

Before the marshes were drained, one of the strangest things about the Waveney to superstitious cottagers was the frequent appearance of ghostly lights in the valley. These were usually called Syleham Lights, after the village where they appeared, and sometimes the "lantern man." Often they led benighted travellers astray. "They fare to come out o' the ground," an old man who knew them well explained, "and run about and around. They tell me they're wepers (vapours) —I don't know." They were, of course, *ignes fatui*.

If you are visiting Suffolk specifically in search of folk-lore, the most profitable place to visit after Hoxne will be Bungay, and there we must go, but first we must note in passing, Flixton, where Margery de Creke founded an Augustinian nunnery in 1258. It is here that we recall that delightful reply made by Charles II. Whilst travelling this way to Yarmouth he noticed the hall, at that time occupied by the Tasburghs, a prominent Roman Catholic family, and asked who lived there. "A popish dog," was the surly reply. "The dog has a very beautiful kennel," replied the king.

The house that Charles admired, and with good reason, was built by John Tasburgh about 1615, but was burnt down in 1832 while the family were in London. Between 1888 and 1892 it was restored in Tudor style by Sir Hugh Adair and is now a handsome mansion standing in five hundred acres of deer park. The most notable of its treasures is an oak chest mounted in silver, made from St. Edmund's tree at Hoxne. In the park there is one of the six Suffolk heronries. These beautiful birds build their untidy nests in old oaks about a mile from the river.

A dog, much more sinister than any papist, haunted the Bungay district. This was the hell-hound or churchyard-beast, Black Shuck, whose acquaintance we have already made.

At Blythburgh we recalled a ghostly visitation on the first Sunday of August 1557, and promised further news of that morning's devilry when we visited Bungay. Here the account is as circumstantial as at Blythburgh. That same morning, while the people were at their prayers between nine and ten o'clock, "a sore and sodain feare, that they were in a manner robbed of their right wits," came over them, and straightway a black dog, "or the divel in such likenesse," rushed through the church to where two people were kneeling, and before they could rise or defend themselves seized their throats so that both died "where they kneeled." The creature also gave another man such a "gripe" in the back that he was "drawen togither" and shrivelled up like a piece of leather that has been thrown into the fire. The parish clerk, who was cleaning the gutter of the church at the time, was struck down but not hurt, though the church door was "mervelously renten and torne," and bore marks that seemed to be made by claws. The wires and wheels of the church clock were twisted and broken on this same terrifying occasion; but throughout it the parson kept his wits about him and continued to lead the people in prayer.

Perhaps even more frightening than the dog, because still unlaid, are the ghosts of the wicked Bigods, the feudal lords of Bungay and the builders of its Norman castle. At Geldeston, just across the river from Beccles, there is a place called Bigod's Hill, where the phantom Bigod coach with the headless driver is seen or heard on the wildest nights of the year. It is said that in penance for their unshriven sins, the more dissolute members of this turbulent family are doomed to ride abroad in a coach that some who have seen it say is of leather and others say is of wood. Four steeds, with flames of fire and clouds of smoke streaming from their mouths and nostrils, draw it, and the coachman carries his head under his left arm. This coach leaves Bungay by Lover's Lane, proceeds to Geldeston by the high road and returns by the low road. It is never both heard and seen by the same person at the same time, and is heard more often than seen. It is heard most alarmingly as it rumbles down Bigod's Hill, first as a faint murmur in the distance, then gradually increasing to a roar, though the coach is completely invisible, until it seems to be coming straight at you, before tearing past and gradually fading away.

Another instance of local superstition may be given here before we turn again to the Bigods. The people of the Waveney valley are for the most part blue-eyed and flaxen-haired, and in consequence a brown-eyed person is much admired. All children, of course, are born with blue eyes, but every Waveney mother hopes that these will soon turn brown, and in the hope of inducing the change some of them tie hazel twigs to the child's back, or hang them in the bedroom.

The ruins of the Bigod's castle are within a few yards of the market square, where a fine market-cross stands, but are not visible from it. They are behind the " King's Head " hotel. At the present time the strategic advantages of this position may not be obvious, but at the time it was built a broad and swiftly flowing river provided strong means of protection, and Bungay Castle, built in a loop of the Waveney, also commanding a good view south, was admirably situated for defence. Hugh Bigod, who fought with the barons against Stephen, boasted of its security:

> Were I in my Castle of Bungaye,
> Above the Water of Waveney,
> I would ne care for the King of Cockneye,
> And all his meiny!

Later he had to change his tune, for the old ballad tells us that:

> Sir Hugh took three-score sacks of gold,
> And flung them over the wall;
> Said he " Go your ways, in old mischief's name,
> Yourself, and your merry men all;
> But leave me my Castle of Bungaye,
> Upon the river Waveney,
> And I'll pay shot to the King of Cockneye."

Bungay was one of a hundred and seventeen manors granted to Roger Bigod by William the Conqueror. This Roger was the father of Hugh Bigod celebrated in the ballad, who was created first Earl of Norfolk on Stephen's accession, but was often in rebellion against him. In 1140 Stephen proved to him that his favourite castle was not the impregnable fortress he had believed it to be. He brought an army to Bungay and took it, afterwards restoring it to the earl, who fought with him at Lincoln in the following year. In 1153, however, Hugh Bigod was fighting for Henry of Anjou, and for a time held Ipswich against Stephen; but when the town fell he contrived to escape punishment. He was no more loyal to Henry than he had been to Stephen, and in the revolt of the king's sons against their father, Hugh Bigod garrisoned Norwich Castle with imported French and Flemish soldiers. Again he was on the losing side, for Henry raised an army at Bury St. Edmunds and brought his rebellious barons into submission. For this treachery Henry ordered the Bigod castles at Walton, Framlingham and Bungay to be dismantled.

The Bigod lands were restored to Roger, the second earl, by Richard I, and a new castle was built. It is the ruins of Roger Bigod's castle that are now to be seen behind the "King's Head." They are not extensive. Two round portal towers remain, built in the usual East Anglian manner where stone dressings were not employed. There are also portions of three sides of the keep and other fragments scattered about neighbouring property. After Roger Bigod's death his castle of Bungay passed to the Ufford family. William de Ufford, second Earl of Suffolk, married Joan de Montacute, and an interesting story is told of her sister, Katherine de Montacute, who was a nun in a convent founded in Bungay in 1160. For some reason unknown to us, Katherine de Montacute was absent from the convent without leave, and a scandal was caused when the Bishop of Norwich had a warrant sent out for her arrest. She was stated to be "fleeing from parish to parish, in divers parts of our kingdom of England, in secular dress to the contempt of the dress of her Order, in peril of her soul and to the manifest scandal of her said Order." Canon Raven thought she was probably no farther away than her sister's castle. Some little dispute had probably arisen among the ladies of Bungay as they were pleasantly called, and Katherine, being a lady of high degree and some spirit,

walked out of the convent and did not return until affairs were more to her liking. It was probably the bishop who caused the scandal. Four years later a lady of the same name became prioress, and in view of the nobility of that name it can hardly have been other than the same lady.

The remains of this convent are seen in the churchyard near St. Mary's church, which was formerly the conventual church. Bungay's three churches, dedicated to the Holy Trinity, St. Thomas, and St. Mary, the convent and also a Benedictine priory, all stood in the one churchyard, which must have been a lively scene on the occasion of a church-ale, or when an interlude was being performed.

Around the ruins of these ancient foundations the Bungay of to-day has grown up and is now itself showing signs of antiquity. Mr. William Dutt, whose opinion on East Anglian subjects was always worthy of respect, paid a high compliment to Bungay. He said: "After having seen almost every town in East Anglia, I am ready to maintain that none of them can compare with it in old-world charm and pleasant surroundings." Most people, I think, not prejudiced by personal associations, would be inclined to agree with him, though many would give it second instead of first place. Below the town, in a loop of the river, is Outney Common, an open space that is protected, but not owned, by the National Trust. Recently Bungay has come into fame as the home of the Norfolk poacher whose books were edited by Lilias Rider Haggard.

The natural advantages that Bungay undoubtedly enjoys have long attracted to it people of means and culture. Throughout the eighteenth and nineteenth centuries it was second only to Bury St. Edmunds in elegance and pride. Much of its early reputation was due to the enterprise of a Mr. King, who described himself as an apothecary of Bungay, and who, about the year 1700, conceived a plan for turning the town into a watering-place, after persuading himself that the chalybeate spring in the castle grounds possessed unique medicinal properties. In order to reserve for himself a proper share in the profits that would accrue from his scheme, Mr. King built a bath-house on the Norfolk side of the river, and planted a vineyard where visitors might disport themselves

Beccles

both to Mr. King's advantage and to their own. Having made these preliminary arrangements he inserted the following advertisement in the *Gentleman's Magazine*:

"Mr. King, Apothecary in the pleasant town of Bungay, in Suffolk, has finished, after Sir John Floyer's plan, a cold bath there, in a delightful situation and healthful air; every thing is compleatly and handsomely provided for the reception of such gentlemen and ladies as shall be advised, either to the use of the cold bath, or of mineral waters, of which there is an excellent sort at that place."

The advertisement is simple enough, but Mr. King reinforced its appeal with a pamphlet couched in the most florid language, which he called *An Essay on Hot and Cold Bathing*. Here is a passage from it: "Those lovely hills, which incircle the flowery plain, are variegated with all that can ravish the astonished sight. They arise from the winding mazes of the river Waveney, enriched with the utmost variety the watry element is capable of producing. Upon the neck of this peninsula, the castle and town of Bungay (now startled at its approaching grandeur) is situated on a pleasing ascent to view the pride of nature on the other side, which the godesses have chose for their earthly paradise; where the sun, at its first appearance, makes a kindly visit to a steep and fertile vineyard, richly stored with the choicest plants from Burgundy, Champaigne, Provence, and whatever the East can furnish us with. Near the bottom of this is placed a grotto, or bath itself, beautified on one side with oziers, groves, and meadows; on the other with gardens, fruits, shady walks, and all the decorations of a rural innocence. The building is designedly plain and neat; because the least attempt of artful magnificence would, by alluring the eyes of strangers, deprive them of those profuse pleasures which nature has already provided. As to the bathing, there is a mixture of all that England, Paris, or Rome could ever boast of: no one is refused a kind reception: honour and generosity reigns throughout the whole; the trophies of the poor invite the rich, and their more dazzling assemblies compel the former."

After such eloquence as that, the most carefully considered compliments that such poor, pedestrian topographers as Mr. Dutt or myself might pay must appear feeble and dull. It is perhaps churlish to record that Mr. King's scheme proved abortive, and that the honest townsfolk of Bungay have never been moved to erect a statue to his honour in their pleasant market square.

A hundred years later this quiet Suffolk town again made overtures to fame when it became the retreat of Chateaubriand, an exile from revolutionary France. He lived for several years in a large red-brick house in Bridge Street. It is whispered that the last months of his residence in Bungay were made uncomfortable for him by the indiscreet affection of Charlotte Ives, daughter of the rector of St. Margaret's, Ilketshall, who lived in the town.

During part of his residence at Bungay, Chateaubriand was French master at Beccles College in the Waveney's other and larger town. Though Beccles has never been so highly praised as Bungay, it is a kindly old town, and even Bungay does not possess a street to equal Baileygate in Beccles, where dignified Georgian houses look out across the marshes. Below the town is the Pool, well known to holiday makers, where every kind of pleasure craft may be seen on a summer day.

As Bungay is built round a castle, Beccles is built round a tower. It is true that the present tower beside St. Michael's church dates from the fifteenth century only, but there was a watch tower here more than a thousand years ago, when Beccles was a port and subject to invasion. Its early prosperity came from the herring industry, but when Henry VIII caused sea walls to be built at Yarmouth and the tides were thus held back from Beccles, another industry had to be found. The town was partly compensated for its loss by the conversion of large stretches of fen into excellent pasture, but much of its new prosperity came from the revival of the hemp industry, for which the district was particularly suitable. Before the fibre could be beaten out it had to be soaked, and ponds for this purpose were easily found. This industry continued to flourish in Beccles until the nineteenth century.

Celia Fiennes visited Beccles in William III's reign, and noted that it had "a pretty bigg market Cross and a great Market kept." Of the church she wrote: "There is a handsome stone built Church, and a very good publick Minister, whose name is Armstrong; he preaches very well they say,

notwithstanding the town is a sad Jacobitish town." Perhaps
it was under Parson Armstrong that the saying "Beccles for
a Puritan" came into use.

But the parson to recall in this district is not Parson Armstrong of Beccles but Parson Lewis of Gillingham on the Norfolk side of the river. Mr. Lewis spent so much of his time
in the saddle that in old age his limbs became so stiff that he
could no longer either stand or sit in a chair with any comfort. The only place where he could be at ease was in the
saddle, so when he was too infirm to stand in the pulpit while
he delivered his sermon he had a saddle-shaped contraption
set up there. Another amusing story is told of this same
parson. A certain pew in his church was always reserved for
"churching" mothers. One day two Beccles ladies walked out
to service at Gillingham and by mistake took their seats in
this particular pew. The rector promptly "churched" them,
and the mistake was not discovered until the clerk held out
his hand for the fee.

Beccles had for centuries a leper house, or Lazar house, as
it was called, because Lazarus is believed to have been a leper.
This was built as the result of a leper named Ramp finding
himself cured after bathing in a spring of water on St. Mary's
Hill. This house continued in use until sometime after the
Dissolution.

The most interesting house of the district is Roos Hall, just
outside the town, close to the Bungay road. It is a tall, red-
brick house, finished about 1583, and is a good example of a
manor-house of its period. The turrets and chimneys are
of moulded brick, and every step of the staircase is a solid
block of oak. Barsham, one and a half miles away, has a
beautiful Jacobean rectory, in which Nelson's mother was
born in 1725, and a church rich in associations with the Suckling family, many of whom held the living. Few churches have
been better served over so long a period, and evidence of the
devoted care of a long succession of scholarly rectors is to be
seen on every hand.

Chapter XV

HIGH SUFFOLK

If ever you are asked the question, "Do you know Suffolk?" you will, if you are wise, reply: "No one knows Suffolk." It has the same kind of mysterious fascination as Mona Lisa, and nowhere is this haunting, enigmatic charm felt so inexplicably as in the lonely region between Eye and Halesworth, where the landscape has neither the verdure of the valleys nor the gay and multi-coloured beauty of the coastal heaths. Most of it is plain, undemonstrative corn country, with some grazing land on the east. You may pass through it a dozen times and only marvel that so lonely a tract of country should be found within a hundred miles of London, until one day you chance to see it in the glow of an autumn sunset, when the sheaves are ready at harvest, and suddenly find yourself conscious of an unimagined beauty and of presences you had never suspected were there.

In such a mood this dull and heavy clay land becomes again the land of St. Felix, and the man who has anything of the pilgrim in him will resolve at once to visit that neglected shrine, the Old Minster at South Elmham. But to resolve is one thing and to accomplish is another. There are no signposts to direct the pilgrim to this ancient shrine that Suffolk appears to have forgotten. You can be within fifty yards of it without knowing it is there, yet this is one of the oldest churches in the county and an important historic relic. There is, it is true, some doubt about its date. Charles Reed Peers, Chief Inspector of Ancient Monuments, writing in the *Archaeological Journal* in 1901, dated it *c.* 670; Baldwin Brown believed it to be post-Conquest. A. W. Clapham, in *English Romanesque Architecture Before the Conquest* (1930), argues in favour of a tenth-century dating, which seems reasonable, because the Minster would then be a product of the revival of Christianity in East Anglia after the Danish invasions, the period in which we hear of other ministers in the Waveney valley at Hoxne and Mendham.

My own first visit to the Old Minster was singularly fortunate. I was leaning over the font in Fressingfield church, reading some notes on its history made by a son of Dr. J. J. Raven, the Suffolk historian, when a lady came up to me and said, " I see you are interested in my brother's notes."

"Your brother's notes? " I replied, " then you must be Dr. Raven's daughter." She was indeed, and a worthy daughter, for when I told her that I was collecting material for a book on Suffolk, she volunteered more information in ten minutes than my brain could have assimilated in an hour, and all with the natural ease of one whose entire life has been spent in a family with whom archaeological problems are daily topics of conversation. I was as much interested in Dr. Raven as in the history of his church, for he was, I should explain, vicar of Fressingfield from 1885 till his death in 1906. Whenever I had heard his name spoken it had been with respect and enthusiasm. Before becoming vicar of Fressingfield with Withersdale in 1885, he was headmaster of Bungay grammar school from 1859 to 1866, and of Great Yarmouth grammar school from 1866 to 1885, so a large number of boys passed through his hands. Many hundreds more remembered him as a popular visiting examiner at Framlingham College for many years. One proof of his success as a schoolmaster is the large number of boys whom he inspired with his own love of historical and archaeological research, subjects that were full of exciting adventure as he taught them. In addition to his *History of Suffolk* and many archaeological pamphlets, he wrote two important books on church bells, *Church Bells of Suffolk* and *The Bells of England*. He studied the subject from boyhood to old age and was, I suppose, the best campanologist of his day.

At the end of this ten-minute conversation, Miss Raven asked if I had visited the Old Minster. I said I had not, and that I understood it was difficult to find. At once she offered to be my guide, and so after ordering lunch for ourselves at the " Fox and Goose "—formerly the guildhall, of which the earliest document is dated 1394—we went in search of it, crossing several fields after getting as near as we could by road, then threading our way between ripening corn and low hedges, breaking down nettles and thistles at almost every step. Not until we were within twenty yards of the fosse did the grey walls become visible through the trees that screen them. But the journey had been enlivened by tales of people who believed they had heard monks chanting among the ruins, by reminiscences of other enthusiasts who had been piloted to this secluded shrine, and by accounts of amusing incidents in the life of a Suffolk parson.

It was that same morning, I remember, that I heard tales about Sir Alfred Munnings as a boy at Mendham, a few miles from Fressingfield. His name was introduced into the conversation as we passed through Whittingham, where the first Derby winner, a grey, was trained. I noticed long, narrow fields along the roadside in which, I was told, horses were trained for Newmarket. Was it possible, I wondered, that the young Alfred Munnings had stood in those fields as a boy, and tingled with excitement as the beauty of those proud, swift animals fired his imagination? Miss Raven also told me an amusing story about her father's first Sunday at Fressingfield. At his first celebration of Holy Communion he noticed an odd-looking woman in the congregation. She conducted herself with propriety until the end of the service, and then puzzled the new vicar by continuing to kneel at the altar rail instead of returning to her pew. At the close of the service Dr. Raven mentioned this curious behaviour to the clerk. "Oh, sir," said that worthy official, "I forgot to tell 'ee. T'owd vicar allus gave her sixpence for comin'." This reminded me of an incident recorded in *Kilvert's Diary*, but by this time we were scrambling through the fosse to the Minster ruins, built, it used to be said, on the site of a Roman camp. Some of the dykes we crossed were part of a defensive system, but they did not appear to be Roman. Perhaps they are late Anglo-Saxon, built for protection against the Danes.

The square enclosure in which the Minster stands is about four acres in extent, with a fosse on each side about three hundred feet long, banked by the clay dug out to form it. The ruins are approximately a hundred feet by thirty feet, and consist of nave, chancel, and a portion of the tower. No part of the chancel wall remains, but the foundations can be traced. The broken walls still standing are built entirely of flint collected in the neighbourhood, firmly compacted with mortar. There is no evidence of dressed stone anywhere, though this may have been used.

Of the theory that South Elmham succeeded Dunwich as the seat of the bishop, it may be presumptuous to write in view of the learned authorities who have discussed the question. But one purpose of such a book as this is to give to the reader who lacks time to study the proceedings of learned societies the conclusions that the author thinks an impartial mind would be likely to reach after sifting the evidence produced by scholars. It is incorrect to say that either of the two Elmhams succeeded Dunwich as the see. Dunwich was divided, but continued, reduced in size, alongside the new see until 869. But in the tenth century only Elmham was revived. That South Elmham Minster was not the cathedral is fairly certain. It was probably a collegiate foundation, consisting of a group of priests commissioned to preach the gospel in the neighbourhood. Remains of the churches of such foundations are rare in East Anglia. At the Old Minster, and perhaps there only, we can trace the plan of one, unaltered by later rebuilding. What is even more interesting and unusual is that this *matrix ecclesia* is surrounded by a cluster of what appear to be daughter churches. Locally these are known as "The Saints," and together with Homersfield (also known as South Elmham St. Mary) and Flixton, they form the ancient deanery of South Elmham.

Though South Elmham appears not to have been the seat of the bishopric, it was a seat of the Bishops of Norwich during the twelfth and thirteenth centuries, and it may have been this residence of the bishop that led people to believe that it was the headquarters of the see. South Elmham Hall is still known to older residents as Palace Farm.

This entire region, like the Waveney valley on its northern border, is rich in legend and folk-lore. In the church at South Elmham St. James, for example, there is—or was—a gilded figure of a cuckoo, and formerly there was a series of carved panels in the chancel representing the men of St. James's building a hedge round a cuckoo in order to keep its song to them-

selves. It is also told of the men of St. James's that one harvest
time they cornered the Devil. He was first seen by the village
children as he entered the church by what is called the Devil's
door. The children informed the harvesters, who ran into
church with their forks and drove the Devil into the porch,
where they held him prisoner till the parson arrived with
candle and book. When the Devil heard the parson's step
outside, and heard the bell begin to toll, he screamed like a
soul in torment and disappeared through the wall. The
place where the porch is said to have been repaired after the
Devil's escape is still pointed out.

In this part of the county you may hear also a story called
The Suffolk Miracle or *The Suffolk Wonder*, related in the
form of a ballad that seems to have been printed first as a
broadsheet. The verses themselves have no merit, but the
story is interesting because it is similar to the many tales of
ghostly horsemen found in German, Breton, and other folk-
lore. It tells of a rich farmer who found the joy of his life
in the possession of a beautiful daughter. When a young man
came to court her, this selfish father was so jealous that he
did all in his power to keep the young people apart. Love at
first appeared to have the greater power, for the young people
gave their hearts to each other without waiting for the father's
blessing. But an old man's jealousy is a cruel thing. The
father sent his daughter to stay with an uncle forty miles away,
and told her to remain there without sight of her lover until
she had changed her mind. The young man, distressed to
have brought so much sorrow to his beloved, and seeing no
hope of a happy life, became ill and died. The girl was kept
ignorant of this, and was still at her uncle's house when, a
month later, her lover appeared to her in the middle of the
night and called her to dress and come quickly, for her father,
he said, had relented and given his consent to their marriage.
At first she was unable to believe this good news, but when the
young man showed her that he had come on her father's
horse, and that her mother had sent her own cloak for the
journey, she was completely convinced. At once she collected
her possessions and sprang up behind her lover on the horse.
Two hours later, after a furious gallop, they were safely home,
and while the young man stabled the horse the girl, excited

and jubilant, hammered on the farmhouse door to rouse her parents from sleep.

As soon as the old man saw his daughter he charged her with disobedience and demanded to know who had given her permission to return home. Had he not given permission himself? she asked, surprised at the question. Had he not sent his own horse for the journey? And had her mother not sent her own cloak? He had done no such thing, he said, and neither had her mother. But the story frightened him, because he knew that the young man was dead and he feared that his daughter was out of her mind.

"Where is your lover now?" he asked more quietly.

"He is in the stable, attending to the horse," she replied. Then the old man told her to go indoors while he went round to the stable. There, as the ballad relates:

> He stared about, but there could he
> No shape of any mankind see,
> But found his horse all on a sweat;
> Which made him in a deadly fret.

The old man then called on the father of the dead lover to make sure that he had not been deceived about the death of his daughter's lover, and when he had satisfied himself on this point he took the young man's father home with him, so that he, too, could question the girl. She still maintained that the story she had told was true, and added that her lover's head was bound with a handkerchief.

The grave was then opened, and in it lay the body, with a handkerchief tied round the head exactly as the girl had described it. The truth could no longer be kept from her. She was told the whole story, and on hearing it she, too, died of a broken heart.

But the district has a love story that owes nothing to legend. While Prince Edward, son of Henry III, was hunting in the Forest of Framlingham, he rode into Fressingfield and there saw a village girl, Margaret of Fressingfield, whose beauty captured his heart. News of the prince's attentions to this village beauty reached the king, who at once summoned his son to return to the court. The prince was obliged to obey, so with a heavy heart he rode away from merry Fressingfield, promising to return, and in earnest of his good faith he left behind him the Earl of Lincoln to be at his lady's command. The earl, as we should expect, himself fell under the spell, and Margaret of Fressingfield eventually became his countess.

It would be impossible for such a story not to accumulate additional romantic details in the course of repeated telling. It was the gossip of the court, and Robert Greene made use of it for his play *The Honorable Historie of Frier Bacon and Frier Bongay*, in which two Suffolk yeomen, Sersby of Cratfield and Lambert of Laxfield, are also involved in the love tangle and slay each other in single combat. In Greene's play this tragic event is exhibited to the sons of the combatants by Friar Bungay in his magic glass, whereupon the two young men, both students at Oxford, draw their swords to avenge their fathers and kill each other.

Each of Fressingfield's five manors seems to have had its story. Chepenhall had a hostel where pilgrims travelling along the Broad Road from Dunwich to Bury St. Edmunds might pass the night. The manor had been presented to the abbey of Bury St. Edmunds by its Saxon owner. Ufford Hall in the same parish was the home of the Sancroft family and the birthplace of William Sancroft, the Archbishop of Canterbury who crowned James II, but refused to read the same king's declaration of liberty of conscience, and led the six bishops who with him presented their petition against it. The petition was written by Sancroft in his own handwriting, and he and the bishops who supported him were committed to the Tower. After refusing to take the oath to William and Mary he retired to Fressingfield and lived there quietly for the remaining two years of his life.

Stradbroke, a neighbouring village, was the birthplace of Robert Grosseteste, Bishop of Lincoln, a man of humble birth who rose by ability and force of character to high position in the Church. He had the forthrightness of the typical East Anglian, resisting Henry III's demand for a tenth of church revenues, and even refusing to induct the Pope's nephew to a Lincoln canonry. Besides being the first mathematician and the first physicist of his age he wrote well on husbandry, and in his *Castel of Love* he maintained in the thirteenth

century, when scholars used only Latin and the court spoke
French, that poetry must be written for the common people
in their own tongue, or, as he said, "for lewde mennes
byhove":

> Nouther French, ne Latyn;
> On Englische I chulle tullen him
> Wherefor the world was, I wroht;
> Thereafter how he was bitaught
> Adam, ure ffader to ben his
> With al the merthe of paradys . . .

Suffolk has produced few greater men than this scholarly and
courageous prelate.   He wrote no fewer than three hundred
learned treatises, and Robert Manning's picture of him, under
the title, "bysshop seynt Roberd," has been my own delight
so long that I must share it here:

> He lovede moche to here the harpe,
> For mans witte yt makyth sharpe.
> Next hys chamber, besyde hys study,
> Hys harper's chamber was fast the by.
> Many tymes, by nightes and dayes,
> He hadd solace of notes and layes,
> One askede hem the resun why
> He hadde delyte in mynstrelsy?
> He answerde hym on thys manere
> Why he helde the harpe se dere.
> "The virtu of the harp, thurgh skyle and ryght
> Wyll destrye the fendys myght;
> And to the cros by gode skeyl
> Ys the harpe lykened weyl—
> Thirefore, gode men, ye shall lere
> When ye any gleman here,
> To worshepe God at your power,
> And Davyd in the sauter.
> In harpe and tabour and symphan gle
> Worship God in trumpes and sautre;
> In cordes, yn organes, and bells ringying,
> In all these worship the hevene kyng. . . ."

It is always good to find a sound churchman praising the arts and exhorting his fellow Christians to enjoy and not churlishly refuse the pleasant things that God has provided for them. They may, of course, take excessive pleasure in these good things, as, indeed, did James Buck, vicar for nearly twenty years of this same village of Stradbroke. He suffered so acutely from gout that his physician gave him only two years longer to live. That was at the beginning of the Great Rebellion. But the Rev. James Buck was cast into Ipswich prison and so benefited from the plain diet that he was completely cured of the gout and enjoyed good health until over eighty years of age.

About two miles north of Stradbroke, and the same distance west of Fressingfield, lies the scattered village of Wingfield, home of the de la Poles, one of the most powerful families in medieval England. William de la Pole, Duke of Suffolk, who lived here during the fifteenth century, is sometimes said to be the knave who figures after the king and queen on our packs of playing-cards. He was extremely unpopular and was often designated Jack the Knave or Jackanapes by his enemies, many of whom believed him to be the secret paramour of the queen.

The de la Poles came to Wingfield from Hull, Yorkshire, in the fourteenth century, after the marriage of Michael de la Pole with Catherine, daughter and heiress of Sir John Wingfield. It was this same Michael de la Pole who was created first Earl of Suffolk in 1385, succeeding the de Uffords in that title. Sir William de la Pole, the earl's father, had assisted the king with a large loan, and in return had received various offices of state. His son was no less astute in using his wealth to promote his political ambitions. Both knew the value of their sovereign's need of money, and Michael de la Pole gained such ascendancy over the young king, Richard II, that in 1383 he was appointed chancellor without the consent of Parliament. The Commons never trusted him, and in 1386, the year after he had been created Earl of Suffolk, the king's uncle, the Duke of Gloucester, brought this distrust to a head and persuaded both Houses of Parliament to demand his dismissal. Reluctantly the king acceded. Articles of impeachment were drawn up against the earl, and when tried he was convicted on three charges and imprisoned. When the Parliament that demanded his dismissal was dissolved, the earl was restored to favour for a while, but the succeeding Parliament was no less bitterly opposed to him. He was compelled to flee the realm and died in Paris. Sentence of death had been passed on him in his absence, and his title and lands had been forfeited.

The title was restored to his eldest son, also Michael, who fought in France with Henry V, and died at the siege of Harfleur. With him was his son, the third earl, who was killed at Agincourt when no more than twenty-one years of age, and thus made way for his brother, William de la Pole, to become the fourth earl, and in 1448 the first Duke of Suffolk. The fourth earl commanded the English forces in France after the death of the Earl of Salisbury in 1428 and later married the latter's widow, Alicia, a grand-daughter of the poet Chaucer. It was she, according to tradition, who had the beautifully carved oak benches installed in Fressingfield church, where the south porch is believed to have been erected as a memorial to the two Michael de la Poles.

William de la Pole negotiated the marriage of Henry VI with Margaret of Anjou, with whom he was alleged by his enemies to be on intimate terms. The Duke of Gloucester, Humphrey the Good, the king's uncle, desired a different marriage, with the result that Suffolk and the queen on the one side and Gloucester on the other were continually plotting against each other. It is in connection with the final overthrow of Gloucester that William de la Pole enters literary as well as national history, for in *King Henry VI*, the second part, Shakespeare makes dramatic use of the Duke of Gloucester's last days at Bury St. Edmunds, where he was arrested and died, though not, it appears, through foul play, as Shakespeare, following popular opinion, would have us believe.

In consequence of his great power over the queen, and of the unpopularity of the terms he had agreed upon with France at the time the marriage was arranged, Suffolk was the most detested man in the country. When, in 1449, war again broke out between England and France, with severe loss of life among the English forces, Suffolk, now duke, was accused of having sold the realm and was committed to the Tower. In March 1450, he was banished from the country for five years, but this was regarded by his enemies as an evasion of justice. The boat in which he sailed was intercepted off Dover, and the duke's head was struck off on the gunwale of the boat. The body was thrown into the sea, but was washed ashore, and it seems probable that it was buried in the church of the Carthusians at Hull.

The castle of the Wingfields and the de la Poles stood about half a mile from the church. The south front, with its fine gateway embellished with the arms of the two families, is still in good preservation. Over the gateway is the guard-room, entered from one of the two staircase turrets that flank it. This entrance was guarded by a portcullis and was approached across a drawbridge that spanned the moat. The walls are pierced with mullion windows, and there are smaller turrets at each end of the strong curtain walls. The remains of Wingfield Castle occupy about one and a half acres and are surrounded by a square moat. The present house, built about 1532, stands on the west side. No doubt much material from the original castle went to its construction. The original park must have been extensive, for long after the de la Pole estates had been forfeited to the Crown, Henry VIII granted to Thomas, Earl of Surrey, a licence giving him permission to cut down a hundred oaks in the park at Wingfield Castle.

The Suffolk dukedom was restored to John, son of the first duke, whose monument is to be seen in Wingfield church, but who appears to have been as unpopular as the rest of his family. At all events he figures discreditably in the *Paston Letters* through attempting to seize the Paston manor-house at Hellesdon in Norfolk.

The church at Wingfield became collegiate in 1362, when a college was founded here by John de Wingfield and built in the south-west corner of the churchyard. The stalls in the present chancel were formerly the seats of the priests, and their panels and poppy-heads are worth inspecting. Over the vestry is the chamber which was probably occupied by the priest whose duty it was to watch the light perpetually burning upon the altar. There are two slits in the wall through which it could be seen. Little remains of Wingfield College to-day, but in two field names, Priest's Croft and Priest's Meadow, the memory of its existence is preserved.

There was a similar college at Mettingham Castle, near Bungay, where a tall gatehouse and a few ruins remain of a castle which formerly occupied five acres surrounded by a moat, with the college buildings enclosed by an inner moat. Mettingham College continued to prosper until the Dissolution, when the estate was granted to Sir Anthony Denny, who appears in Shakespeare's *King Henry VIII*.

Another Shakespearian character claimed for the district, though probably of Eye, Westminster, was Margery Jourdain, the Mother Jourdain of the second part of *King Henry VI*, who was said to have aided and abetted the Duchess of Gloucester. " Mother Jourdain, be prostrate and grovel on the earth," commands Bolingbroke, and there are times in this lonely part of England when we can still imagine that superstitious atmosphere at

> The time when screech-owls cry, and ban-dogs howl,
> And spirits walk, and ghosts break up their graves.

Mother Jourdain was accused of having made a waxen image of the king with the intention of causing it to waste away. She was sentenced to be burned at Smithfield.

Late in the eighteenth century Eye had another witch in Old Nan Barret, who was consulted by people from all the surrounding villages. A pool in the Waveney near Harleston is still called The Witch's Pool, and without doubt gets its name from the practice of "swimming" witches in it when Matthew Hopkins was doing his devil's work in this part of the country.

Eye is another of the ancient towns of East Anglia. It is said to have been a borough by prescription before King John granted its charter. To the east of the town are the ruins of a Benedictine monastery at one time under the patronage of the abbots of Bernay in Normandy. When a prior died here the abbot of Bernay used to order a porter to keep guard at the gate until the next prior had been appointed. When the new prior was installed the porter received five shillings with

Norman Tower, Bury St. Edmunds

which to buy himself an ox. Richard II set this priory at Eye free from its dependence upon Bernay, and after the transfer of the East Anglian see from Dunwich, the site of the episcopal seat there became the possession of the monks of Eye. When Dunwich fell into the sea the monks of Eye removed to their own monastery St. Felix's copy of the Gospels, written according to Leland, who claimed to have seen it, in great Lombard characters. This came to be known as the *Red Book of Eye*, and people of the neighbourhood were in the habit of swearing their most binding oaths upon it.

Several important archaeological discoveries have been made here. Hundreds of Roman coins were dug up in a field at Clint Farm, south of the town, in 1781. The latest in date of these coins was of Constantine III, the usurping emperor who crossed the Channel with the Roman forces of Britain to win Gaul and Spain for himself (407-411). In July 1818, while a pit was being sunk north of the town, an Anglo-Saxon burial-place earlier than A.D. 500 was found. All except three of the urns were broken while they were being dug out, but they appear to have formed a circle of nine or ten feet in diameter. They varied in height between five and nine inches and no two corresponded in either design or size. The ornamentation was the inspiration of the moment with the potter, and took the form of line, dot, or angle as his fancy dictated. Thus Eye has produced one of the latest Roman and one of the earliest Anglo-Saxon finds in the county.

In the church at Thornham Parva, two and a half miles south-west of Eye, there is an early fourteenth-century retable, an important example of medieval painting which was exhibited at Burlington House in 1934.

While recording historic associations and notable persons who have lived in these remote and tiny villages, we cannot help feeling that the impression they give is hardly true to the character of the land as a wayfarer would see it to-day. Its representative figure is not William de la Pole, Duke of Suffolk, nor Archbishop Sancroft, nor yet Robert Grosseteste, the good Bishop of Lincoln, but the stout yeoman farmer whose ancestors have ploughed these acres for more centuries than anyone can trace. The Wingfields and the de la Poles enjoyed a brief glory, the farmer is always there.

The Abbey Gate, Bury St. Edmunds

But another character comes to mind. Suffolk is not gipsy country in the same way as Essex and Norfolk, but it is congenial to the wild flowers of humanity, and from the proud names of medieval Suffolk we may turn to a wandering bard, a poor vagrant who slept in sheds and lived on such odd scraps of food as he could pick up in his wanderings, yet who was highly esteemed by the cottagers as a poet. His name was James Chambers, and he hawked his poetical effusions from village to village until, when old and in need of comfort, a Mr. Corder wrote to the press about him. A subscription list was opened, to which, among others, the Countess of Dysart and the Duchess of Chandos contributed. A cottage was obtained for the old man, but all this well-meaning help was of no avail. After living in the cottage for two or three months, Chambers took to the road again, and was discovered living in squalor in a cabin behind Framlingham. There is a picture of him surrounded by dogs in the *Suffolk Garland*. Everybody knew him. Bernard Barton wrote a letter about him. He was a Suffolk institution in his day, and though filthy and dressed like a scarecrow, the villagers liked to have him about.

All these varied strains of life and character are to be found in this lonely region, but the impression that remains is of large open fields that move through the seasons with the steady rhythm of an old poem, and of little pastures that have the lilt of folk song. There is something Biblical about their beauty. This is the land of the saints, the immemorial land of plough and flail. "A sower went forth to sow," I find myself murmuring as I stride across these broad acres in springtime, and I see in mind again the slow procession of the seasons, the ancient ritual of the year, which the ancients may have understood better than we do, and which poor Jemmy Chambers may have been better versed in than most whom the world would consider his betters.

CHAPTER XVI

BURY ST. EDMUNDS

"AND this," said Mr. Pickwick, looking up, "is the 'Angel'! We alight here, Sam."

The words are symbolic. Bury no less than the "Angel," its grand old inn, is recognised at once, and to alight in Bury is to feel you have arrived, a feeling much rarer than it used to be. Modern towns, with uniform brick and stucco houses sprawling in every direction, tend to become indistinguishable from each other, and most of the older towns are similarly —though perhaps inevitably—disfigured. Their few remaining buildings of historical or aesthetic value are photographed and sketched until they are known everywhere, yet half the people who live near never see them. Wolsey's Gateway in Ipswich is an instance. Practically everyone in East Anglia must have seen a sketch of it at some time, but there are thousands of people in Ipswich itself who have never seen the actual building. A schoolboy once looked at me curiously while I was examining it. He didn't know what it was, and when I tried to simulate shocked surprise he said, "We don't bother much about those things now, sir."

That would not have been said in Bury St. Edmunds, because Bury does bother about those things. And so it should, for few towns of its size are so rich in ancient memorials, or have been able to preserve them in so congenial a setting. To stand on Angel Hill, with Mr. Pickwick's "Angel" on your left, those dignified eighteenth-century houses facing you, and on your right, at the foot of the slope, the precinct wall of St. Edmund's abbey with its noble gateway, is to be aware in a moment of all the pride and character of a fine old English town, and that town Bury St. Edmunds.

The hill is dominated by the Abbey Gate, an imposing and beautiful example of fourteenth-century Decorated architecture that now gives access to formal gardens sloping down to the sedgy river Lark, a tributary of the Ouse. In monastic days it was the entrance to the great courtyard in front of the abbot's palace. An earlier gateway was destroyed in 1327 when an insurgent mob, fired to rebellion by agitators from London, broke into the abbey, and after destroying every precious thing that lay in their path, retired, bearing with them five hundred pounds in money, twenty chests, three gold and forty silver chalices, as well as many other objects either of intrinsic value or sacred association. When reinforcements reached the town, the rebels were put to rout and thirty cartloads of prisoners, shouting defiance, were hurried through the North Gate bound for Norwich.

In 1381, some years after the present Abbey Gate had been completed, an even larger mob rushed through it to plunder and destroy. The ringleaders were again from London. Wat Tyler was killed at Smithfield by a son of Sir John Cavendish, chief justice of the king's bench, who lived in the village from which his family took their name, and fifty thousand people marched into Suffolk to take their revenge. They captured Sir John, robbed and set fire to his house, then carried him to Bury and beheaded him. The ruling abbot was away at the time, so the prior was in charge of the abbey; but when he saw the mob approaching he fled to Mildenhall, only to be captured by the rioters there, and at Temple Bridge to suffer the same fate as Sir John Cavendish. The prior's head was carried back to Bury and exposed to the derision of the townsfolk. After despoiling the abbey, the rebels, led by Jack Straw, withdrew from the town, but were overtaken and dispersed by Henry Spencer, the fighting Bishop of Norwich, after a bloody engagement.

Such violent scenes seem entirely out of keeping with the sedate and orderly aspect of Angel Hill to-day. Turning from the Abbey Gate, which provoked these memories, towards the "Angel" Inn or the houses facing us, we may imagine a different scene. For hundreds of years the famous Bury Fair, which Thomas Shadwell made the subject of a popular comedy, was held here. Bury had three fairs during the year. The first, the Calf's Tail Fair, was held on the Tuesday, Wednesday and Thursday of Easter week; the last was held on the 2nd of December, and was for the sale of farm produce.

It was the middle fair, which lasted for three weeks from St. Matthew's Day, 21st September, that was the fashionable season in Bury. When Mary Tudor, who was buried in St. Mary's church, was living at Westhorpe, she would ride into Bury, attended by her husband, the Duke of Suffolk, to receive the compliments of the nobility and gentlefolk in a specially built pavilion, lavishly decorated in her honour. At that time most of the now famous families had not been long seated in the county. The fair reached the height of its fame in the eighteenth century, the heyday of the English nobility. Most of the best Suffolk families had houses in the town, to which they resorted at this season. Throughout the day they enjoyed the entertainment provided on Angel Hill. In the evening they attended a comedy, and afterwards disported themselves at an assembly in one of the larger houses.

If scenes such as these are only memories in the pleasant old town of to-day, they are not alien to it. They seem remote but not incredible, as the adventures of a gay youth and a vigorous middle age may seem remote, but not incredible when recounted by a benign old gentleman no longer concerned with the fever and passion of life. The stories that Bury recounts are written in stone, from the Norman Tower and Moyses' Hall to the admirable modern offices of the West Suffolk County Council. And near those offices, squeezed into a corner of Angel Hill, there is a lovely eighteenth-century, red-brick house, recently acquired by the National Trust, which represents one of the best chapters in the town's history. When this has been restored and given the publicity which the Trust is able to give to its properties, we may find the right kind of attention being drawn to the many fine examples of domestic architecture, particularly of the eighteenth century, to be found here and in neighbouring streets.

Age has come kindly to Bury St. Edmunds. It has none of the bustle of Ipswich, and has been more successful than most towns in avoiding the more disastrous results of commercial progress. While the population of Ipswich has increased most rapidly, that of Bury has remained stationary. The town has not declined as so many of the smaller Suffolk towns have. It is alive. Nowhere within its boundaries do

we find that decayed kind of picturesqueness so dear to sentimental visitors, but the despair of residents. Bury knows that
to preserve is not enough; that beauty is something alive and
positive, and that to deny a place a sane and wholesome life
in the present is a poor way of rewarding it for the vigour
and beauty of its past. Briefly, then, Bury preserves in a
world that often appears to have lost both chart and compass
the graces of orderly life, disciplined by custom yet free and
enlightened.

It is sometimes said to have been the site of a Roman villa,
but no Roman remains have ever been found inside the town.
That it was an inhabited place from an early date cannot
be doubted. Its situation at a fertile point on an ancient
highway would guarantee some kind of settlement. As late
as the fourteenth century the only highway crossing Suffolk
and Norfolk, the road from London to Norwich, was the one
through Bury St. Edmunds. In the two great periods of English social life, the monastic, which lasted till the Dissolution,
and the aristocratic, which lasted from the fall of the monasteries to the Industrial Revolution, Bury enjoyed a remarkable degree of prosperity. More than once it was the scene of
historic assemblies. In 1214, after John, smarting from the
humiliation of having been put to flight by the dauphin and
the defeat of his army at Bouvines, had become outrageously
tyrannical, the barons met at Bury to defy him. It was known
that he would be there for the Feast of St. Edmund. Archbishop Langton was also present, and received in the abbey
church the protestations and oaths of the barons. It is said
that he rose in a crowded church and read aloud the draft of
a charter of liberties which he and the barons had drawn up
together, and that afterwards the twenty-five barons present,
starting with the eldest, walked to the High Altar, laid their
hands upon it, and swore that they would stand together until
the king had ratified their charter, and that if he refused they
would make war on him. Thus Runnymede, it is claimed,
was reached by way of Bury St. Edmunds, and of no incident
in its long history is the town so proud.

It is to be regretted that we cannot know with certainty
what part Langton played in this revolt of the barons. The
records are inconclusive. He has often been represented as

their leader, but this appears doubtful when we observe that at Runnymede itself he was a commissioner on the king's side, unless he attended the king only to make certain that the king attended the conference, which is not unlikely. Langton assisted in the drafting of Magna Charta, but to what extent we do not know. The clauses relating to the liberties of the Church, which he is most likely to have framed, are characterised by moderation. We cannot doubt that his sympathies were with the barons, and that it was he who held them together; but his attitude towards the king was never openly one of direct opposition, and on this occasion he was in a difficult position because he had been commanded by the Pope to excommunicate the barons as disturbers of the peace. All things considered, it seems probable that at Bury St. Edmunds he played a statesmanlike part in formulating for the barons a policy which John could not defy without openly showing himself the tyrant that at heart he was. In advising the barons to take their stand on the charter of Henry I which embodied the old Saxon laws, he was simply urging them to uphold the constitution.

What, we may wonder, would have been the issue of that eventful day if Abbot Samson, the greatest of St. Edmundsbury's thirty-three abbots, had still been alive. He had been dead only between two and three years. Samson feared neither king nor commoner. When Richard Cœur de Lion demanded the hand of a ward for one of his nobles he was respectfully informed that the abbot had already chosen a husband for her. When Richard repeated his demand, reinforcing it with threats, Samson stood firm, saying that the king might take his ward away from him by force, and might even burn down the abbey as a punishment for his apparent disobedience, but that he would not do what he believed would be a betrayal of trust. He added that he resisted the king's will on behalf of succeeding abbots as well as on his own behalf, because he believed that to yield on this occasion would be to establish a dangerous precedent. Richard continued to rave against the "proud priest" for a time, but when his anger cooled he acknowledged the justice of the abbot's attitude.

In *Past and Present*, Carlyle, who is surely unsurpassed in pen portraiture, drew a convincing though not a strictly historical picture of this worthy abbot, who ruled for thirty years and raised the abbey to the height of its power. He described no less graphically the town. "A prosperous brisk Town," he called it, "beautifully diversifying, with its clear brick houses, ancient clean streets, and twenty or fifteen thousand busy souls, the general grassy face of Suffolk; looking out right pleasantly, from its hill-slope, towards the rising Sun; and on the eastern edge of it, still runs, long, black and massive, a range of monastic ruins."

Samson of St. Edmundsbury had a Boswell in his chaplain, Jocelin of Brakelond, whose Chronicles were the source of Carlyle's lively sketches. Jocelin himself was a character. He had that delightful combination of genial simplicity and sharp-witted shrewdness that is sometimes found in a clever man who never quite grows up. Carlyle found him an agreeable and companionable author, but complained that Jocelin did not always tell him what he most wanted to know. For example, he said little about the first visit of King John to the abbey. Carlyle was more fortunate than most of us in that he could supply these omitted portraits from his own imagination, as he did most notably in this instance. Perhaps Jocelin's reticence was dictated by prudence, for what he would have written could not have been complimentary. The king and his retinue lived well on the abbey during their visit, yet when they departed, left only a silk cloth, which one of the courtiers had obtained from the sacrist for nothing, and thirteen pence sterling for a mass to be said for the king on the day he rode away.

Abbot Samson was a Norfolk man, stiff-set, vigorous, with a large strong face, bushy eyebrows, and "a very eminent nose" above his grizzled beard. The abbey was in a sad state when he became abbot. Poor old Abbot Hugo, his predecessor, had been a kind and pious man but a weak ruler. He had allowed his officials to plunder both the abbey and the town, and when repairs had become necessary he had met the charges by borrowing. Towards the end of his life Hugo had been so deeply in debt that he had rarely dared to go outside his own gates for fear of meeting his creditors. It was little wonder that Jocelin, who was a monk at the abbey in Hugo's time, wrote: "If I should live so long as to see the abbey vacant . . . I shall then advise . . . that we choose not too good a monk, nor yet an overwise clerk, neither one too simple nor too weak." He had learned from experience that while piety and learning are admirable qualities in a monk they can be indulged in to excess by an abbot.

Jocelin describes how Samson arrived at the abbey to take up his duties as abbot, and was received with "great solemnity, with ringing of bells inside the choir and without." He dismounted at the gate, paused while his shoes were removed, and with the prior on one side and the sacrist on the other, entered the abbey he had come to rule while the monks chanted the responses *Benedictus Dominus* in the office of the Trinity.

The thoughts of the monks must have been busy with both hopes and fears even in the midst of these impressive celebrations. Could the abbey be saved when it was so deeply involved in debt? Would Samson dismiss the treacherous officials who had impoverished it in Abbot Hugo's reign? Would Abbot Samson, too, have his favourites? The answers were quickly forthcoming. Within four years all debts were paid, and the abbey was prosperous. The power of the abbot was absolute. And this state was reached by the way he provided answers to the second and third questions. He ruled without fear or favour. His policy was to appoint the best man for each office without regard to either his friendship or his enmity towards himself, but he did not forget his friends when appointments were to be made that did not require particular qualifications. If they failed, however, he dismissed them at once.

This stout-hearted monk was a true East Anglian. "An eloquent man he was," says Jocelin, "both in French and Latin; but intent more on the substance and method of what was to be said, than on the ornamental way of saying it." He preached to the people "in the English tongue, though according to the dialect of Norfolk, where he had been brought up."

There were both stern and lively scenes in the years of his rule. On one occasion some of his monks plotted against him and threatened to take his life. The plot was discovered and the abbot restored order. Then he went away until his anger had cooled. "I would have taken vengeance on thee, had I not been angry," he said on his return, quoting a philosopher.

For a lively scene we have the story of the twenty-four young noblemen who met near Bury to engage in a tournament and afterwards rode into the town to pass the night there. Samson had forbidden tournaments, so when he heard that the young men had defied him and were now in the town, he ordered the gates to be bolted. The following day was the Vigil of St. Peter and St. Paul. The gates remained locked, but the young men were invited to be the guests of the abbot. After dinner, when Samson retired, they became merry, carolling and singing popular songs and even sending into the town for wine. So wild did they become that at nightfall they left the abbey grounds and broke the bolts on the town gates, riding away into the country, a gay and roystering company. The abbot promptly excommunicated them. Excommunication was a powerful weapon in the Middle Ages, and most of the young men were soon back at the abbey ready to do penance.

Before the end of Samson's thirty years as abbot the abbey reached a high level of prosperity. Wealth was still measured in terms of flocks and herds and Samson, through his cellarer, could draw on three large flocks. There was one of a thousand sheep at the grange nearby, and others at Risbygate and Hardwick. The town was encompassed by fields where the flocks of the lord abbot could graze. The cellarer, who managed the abbey's estates, was a powerful official. Samson was a just man, and granted privileges to the townspeople against the advice of his monks, but he declared that neither king nor judiciar had the right to alter anything in the banleuca without his consent. The restrictions he imposed applied to everyone from the poorest to the richest. The cellarer, acting on the abbot's behalf, even decided where and when the women should do their washing in the river, and where the fullers should wash their cloths. If these people defied him he would seize the women's washing or the fullers' cloths, and perhaps the webs and drying props of the latter as well, until he received compensation. No man could erect a mill without the abbot's consent. Jocelin has an account of the scene between Samson and Herbert the Dean after Herbert had been detected erecting a mill, though this was for his own use and on his own free fee.

Inside the borough the sacrist was as powerful as the cellarer was outside. As he appointed and controlled the two bailiffs, he had virtual control over the administration of justice in the courts.

Such an abbey as Bury became under Samson's rule—second only to Glastonbury in power in the whole kingdom—seems a strange development from the little wooden church, built to contain the holy shrine in which the martyr's body was laid when it was brought from Hoxne in the year 903.

There were two distinct monastic foundations at Bury. Sigebert, King of the East Angles who was baptised while an exile in Gaul and subsequently helped both St. Felix and St. Fursey in their attempt to convert his kingdom to Christianity, built the first monastery at Bury St. Edmunds, or Bedericsworth, as it was then called, and retired to it himself about 633, resigning the crown and receiving the tonsure. A few years later he left it to lead his former people against Penda, King of the Mercians, the champion of the pagans. In defending the faith, Sigebert was defeated and slain. We know little of the history of this foundation. The second owed its early development to the veneration in which the martyr's body was held when the miracles, alleged to have been performed at his grave at Hoxne, became widely known. About twenty-two years after the body had been enshrined at Bedericsworth, a college of priests was founded and attached to the shrine, but towards the end of the century the priests fell into disfavour "on account of their insolence and irregularity." But the foundation was to be saved by another miracle. Sweyn, the Danish invader, father of Canute, had conquered England and levied a heavy tax on the people from which the priests at Bury St. Edmunds, as Bedericsworth had now become, claimed exemption. Sweyn, it is said, had spoken in derision of the saint, when, one evening, in an assembly of his nobles, he suddenly exclaimed, "I am struck by St. Edmund." An arrow had pierced him, though no visible hand had directed its flight, and shortly afterwards he died, killed, it was believed, by the martyr-king. Canute was

so terrified of Edmund's vengeance that he made special gifts
and concessions to the monastery at Bury, which had been
reconstituted as a monastic foundation when, in 1020, the
priests in charge of the shrine were removed and twelve
Benedictines installed in their place. Canute granted to
this Benedictine abbey a charter confirming its right to all
the grants and privileges enjoyed by the college, and added
new sources of revenue, notably the right to retain the
Danegelt collected from the townspeople of Bury.

A new church was built, and to the martyr's shrine the
frightened nobles brought gifts of jewels, the king himself
offering his crown. Under royal patronage the abbey was
bound to prosper, and when Edward the Confessor increased
its endowments by granting it the town of Mildenhall with all
its produce and the royalties of eight hundreds and one half-
hundred it was already rich. With so many permanent
sources of income the monks felt the time had come for them
to dismantle the wooden monastery and replace it with one
of hewn stone from the Barnack quarries. When this plan
was mooted the abbey was fortunate in having as abbot a
Frenchman, Baldwin, because at the Norman Conquest he
was immediately in favour with the new ruler. He was even
reputed to be on friendly terms with him, and it is true that
the Conqueror's daughter, Constance, was buried in the new
abbey that Abbot Baldwin began to build. Thus, by a
sequence of fortunate circumstances, the great abbey of St.
Edmund came to be planned on the large scale to which the
ruins along the banks of the quiet river Lark bear testimony.

Abbot Baldwin built the eastern portion of the abbey,
including the magnificent Norman tower, erected about 1090
and so admirably restored in 1846-7 at a cost of about £3,400,
which is generally admitted to be the finest piece of architecture of its kind in England. Later abbots extended the buildings westward until when Leland saw it shortly before the
Dissolution he could write of the town and the abbey that
had made it: "A city more neatly seated the sun never saw,
so curiously does it hang upon a gentle descent, with a little
river on the east side; nor a monastery more noble, whether
one considers its endowments, largeness, or unparalleled magnificence. One might even think the monastery alone a city;

so many gates it has, some whereof are brass; so many towers; and a church, than which nothing can be more magnificent; as appendages to which are three more of admirable beauty and workmanship in the same churchyard."

The great abbey church has gone, but two fine churches remain; St. James's, which is now the cathedral church of the diocese of St. Edmundsbury and Ipswich, and St. Mary's, one of the most beautiful churches in the county, which has what is, I believe, the finest hammer roof in England. It would be unwise to go into the circumstances that led to the choice of St. James's as the cathedral when the new diocese was formed in 1913. Most of it is fifteenth-century work, but the original part was in the church built by Abbot Anselm about 1125. St. Mary's church is also fifteenth-century, with remains of an older church, and is a noble example of Perpendicular architecture, with too many interesting features to be enumerated here. It has often been described, and anyone who wishes to read a worthy account of it should refer to Mr. H. Munro Cautley's fine work, *Suffolk Churches and their Treasures*. Mary Tudor's tomb is in St. Mary's, which contains also the Regimental Chapel, refurnished in 1935 to commemorate the 250th anniversary of the Suffolk Regiment. A white alabaster cenotaph was unveiled here on 15th March, 1920, by General Sir Thomas Morland "to the glorious memory of 360 officers and 6,513 warrant officers, non-commissioned officers and men of the Suffolk Regiment who made the supreme sacrifice in the Great War."

Just before the Dissolution the Commissioners found in the old abbey "much vanity and superstition, as the coals that St. Lawrence was toasted with, the parings of St. Edmund's nails, St. Thomas of Canterbury's penknife and boots, and divers skulls for the headache, pieces of the Holy Cross able to make a holy cross," and many relics for superstitious uses. Among these was a pardon bowl which was believed to have the power to relieve whoever drank from it "in the worship of God and St. Edmund" of the sins of five hundred days.

Perhaps the most interesting of the superstitious customs of monastic Bury St. Edmunds was the oblation of the white bull, which seems to have been one that survived from pre-Christian days. It was for the benefit of childless wives. A white bull, garlanded with flowers and gaily bedecked with ribbons, was brought to the south gate of the abbey, then led along Churchgate, Guildhall and Abbeygate streets, to Abbey Gate on Angel Hill. On one side walked the lady who desired offspring, while the monks and townspeople followed in procession. They dispersed at Abbey Gate, and the bull was taken back to his pasture while the lady entered the abbey to make her offering at the shrine. Foreign ladies were allowed to make the oblation by proxy.

The field where the bull was kept is called Haberdon, and it was formerly let on the condition that the tenant always kept a white bull for the ceremony.

The revenues of the abbey at the Dissolution were set down at £2,366 16s. per annum, which was a considerable sum in the middle of the sixteenth century, but the abbey historians have thought it a low estimate considering how vast the abbey estates were. Like others in the same predicament the last abbot, John Reeve, foresaw the impending disaster and tried to win favour by bestowing abbey lands upon influential people. Thus in 1536 Abbot Reeve settled an annuity of £10 upon Secretary Cromwell and his son, payable out of the rents of the manor of Harlow in Essex, where the abbot had a rest house at which he could break his journeys to and from London. In this attempt to make his own lot easier, Abbot Reeve was no more successful than others, and he died heartbroken in a house in Crown Street. The Rev. A. F. Webling, rector of Risby, wrote a good historical novel about him, entitled *The Last Abbot*.

At the Dissolution, the abbey had been held by the Benedictines for five hundred and nineteen years and had been ruled by thirty-three abbots. During that half-century it had enjoyed a considerable share of royal favour. After the kings already mentioned, the first two Henrys visited it, and Richard I made a pilgrimage to St. Edmund's shrine before leaving for the Holy Land. John was at Bury early in his reign, as Jocelin records, and it was not his only visit. There was the visit already mentioned when the barons united against him. The monks also defied him, for it was on his visit in 1214 that he tried to assert his right to nominate a successor to Abbot Samson, whose place had not yet been filled. To his great annoyance the monks voted against his nominee. Shakespeare, in *King John*, sets the scene of John's last engagement outside the walls of Bury St. Edmunds, but for this he had no warrant in history. Henry III is said to have died of an illness contracted while holding a parliament at Bury St. Edmunds, and it was of another parliament held there that Shakespeare wrote a memorable scene in *King Henry VI*. This was the parliament that assembled in the abbey refectory in 1447, drawn to the town by the powerful William de la Pole, Duke of Suffolk, who had plotted to impeach his rival, "the Good Duke Humphrey" of Gloucester. Henry on this occasion was met at Newmarket by five hundred men of Suffolk, supporters of the Duke, all clad in red, and escorted to Bury. Gloucester followed, and was arrested one Saturday by several lords, friends of de la Pole, as he alighted from his horse. The following Thursday he died, according to report, at St. Saviour's Hospital which stood just outside the North Gate.

Other parliaments were held at Bury in 1272 and 1296, and in 1278 Edward I, accompanied by his queen and the greater part of the English nobility, visited the town.

Apart from its abbots, the outstanding personality in the history of the abbey was John Lydgate, born in the Suffolk village of that name about 1370, who enjoyed the patronage of Duke Humphrey, a fine scholar himself and a patron of learned men. Lydgate had been a gay youth who, by his own confession, was fond of "jangling and japing" with his fellows and of telling cherry stones when he ought to have been in church. He became a monk of Bury when he was fifteen, and a memorial of his association with the abbey is still seen in the Clopton chapel at Long Melford, which has a painted scroll round the cornice inscribed with verses by Lydgate. Perhaps his most famous work was his translation of Boccaccio's *Fall of Princes*. A first edition of this work by Lydgate was sold in 1926 for £1,750, and was bought by a neighbour of mine, Mr. Henry Davis of Loughton, in 1941 for £880.

A town so dependent on the power of the Church as Bury St. Edmunds had always been must have suffered a hard blow at the Reformation, whether we believe that the abbots had been oppressors or that, as the old saw has it, there had been "good living under the crook." It survived, however, and received a charter from James I, about whom an old ballad relates:

> King Jamie once in Suffolk went
> A hunting of the deer,
> And there he met a Bury blade,
> All clad in finest gear.

This ballad was founded on a hunting excursion which James made into Suffolk. A rich townsman of Bury, a stranger to the king, joined the chase, "very brave in his apparel, and so glittering and radiant that he eclipsed all the Court." The king asked his name, and on being informed that it was Lamme facetiously replied, "Lamb, call you him? I know not what kind of lamb he is, but I am sure he has got a good fleece upon his back."

Such gentlemen as Mr. Lamme seem to have gravitated towards Bury St. Edmunds, for in course of time it came to be as much the preserve of the gentry as it had formerly been the preserve of the monks, until in the eighteenth and nine-teenth centuries it was renowned for the elegance and bril-liance of its social life. It was thus that Defoe saw it when he visited the town, though whether his visit was long or short no one appears to know. A tablet with an ambiguous inscrip-tion upon it was placed on the Cupola House, a building that symbolises the period in its more flamboyant aspect rather well. There was a local tradition that Defoe lived in this house, but there is no written evidence to support such a belief. Of the town he found, Defoe wrote: "the beauty of this town consists in the number of gentry who dwell in and near it, the polite conversation among them, the affluence and plenty they live in, the sweet air they breathe in, and the pleasant country they have to go abroad in." With such noble-men in the district as the Duke of Grafton at Euston, the Marquess of Bristol at Ickworth, and Lord Cadogan at Cul-ford, with others of noble rank all round, Bury St. Edmunds became a centre of fashionable life and continued as such until the order of the state was undermined and broken by the Industrial Revolution.

Mildenhall

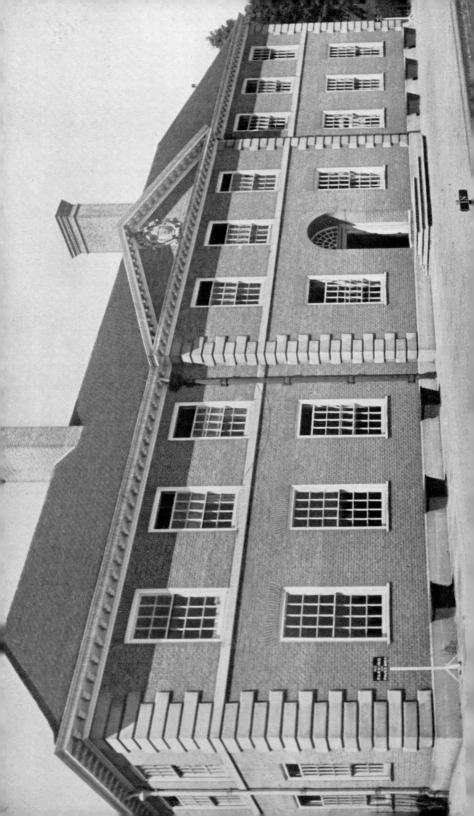

The town's roll of fame is too long to tell here. Louis Philippe of France lived as a child in the house adjoining the "Angel." He was there in charge of Madame de Genlis, while the very next house was the residence of Dr. Hyde Wollaston, who discovered the malleability of platinum. Dr. Wollaston was the secretary of the Royal Society from 1804 to 1816. The Wollastons were a distinguished East Anglian family. There is a memorial at Great Finborough to the William Wollaston who wrote *The Religion of Nature Delineated*. Most notable—and appropriate—is the large number of bishops either born or educated here.

With so many associations with learning in the past it is fitting that Bury St. Edmunds should have such excellent reference libraries. I envy the man who has daily access to the Cullum Library, presented by Mr. Gery Milner Gibson Cullum in 1923 and housed at the School of Art, together with the library of the Suffolk Institute of Archaeology and Natural History.

Architecturally the town has maintained good styles throughout its history. The new offices of the West Suffolk County Council, the Shire Hall, is a modern building in Renaissance style that agrees well with its neighbours. But apart from the ecclesiastical remains the most remarkable building in Bury St. Edmunds is Moyses' Hall on Cornhill, where the ancient ecclesiastical seat becomes a busy market town. There have been many theories about the origin of Moyses' Hall. One theory is that it was a Jewish synagogue. As Cornhill is some distance from what was the Jewish quarter of the town, this does not appear probable. It may have been occupied by a Jew at one time, though this again does not seem likely. The earliest reference to it, so far as I am aware, is dated 1328. It was then a tavern, and in 1441 it was still a tavern. There is a considerable body of informed opinion in favour of the view that it had some sort of Jewish association. The name supports the theory at first glance, but on further enquiry it is seen to be inconclusive. There were two householders named Mose in Bury St. Edmunds in the fourteenth century, one of them a butcher. Perhaps it was he who kept the tavern. Recently Moyses' Hall has come to be regarded by many good antiquaries as probably a pil-

County Council offices, Bury St. Edmunds

grims' hospice connected with the abbey. This seems to be the soundest theory of its origin, but whatever view is favoured it is certainly an excellent and rare example of Norman domestic architecture.

No one would be likely to miss Moyses' Hall on a visit to Bury, especially as it is now an admirably conducted museum, but the town has many objects of unusual interest that might easily be missed. For example, there is a stone in Risbygate that was formerly the base of a cross. The top of this stone has been scooped out to form a basin, and when smallpox was raging in the town in 1677, this hollow was filled with vinegar each day so that country folk coming into town to market their produce could dip their money in the vinegar on their way out again and thus disinfect it.

It is on Angel Hill, however, and in the public gardens beyond the Abbey Gate, that past and present come together most agreeably in Bury St. Edmunds. These gardens are enjoyed by the public through the generosity of the Marquess of Bristol. In the gate itself there is a useful plan of the original abbey buildings for the guidance of visitors. The broad walk crosses the abbot's courtyard and the site of the palace. Gaunt fragments distributed about the lawns are all that remain in view of the old monastic buildings. Instead of the chanting of monks we hear the laughter of children, who find so much pleasure on the greensward and in the river, which is spanned by a modest reminder of all the power and pride of Abbot Samson, the early thirteenth-century Abbot's Bridge, connecting the monastery wall with the wall of the vineyard on the opposite bank of the river Lark. As pleasure gardens these are all that the people of Bury St. Edmunds can desire, but Dr. M. R. James's words are worth remembering. "No monastic site in England," he says, "needs investigation more or, probably, would repay it better." Such investigation is already being planned, and we shall await discoveries and reports with unusual interest.

CHAPTER XVII

BRECKLAND

NORTH-WEST of Bury St. Edmunds lies a unique region called Breckland, a sandy waste of a hundred and forty-five square miles that is more like an African desert than a stretch of this green and merry island. Beyond it lie desolate fens on the Cambridgeshire border, where Ely's great tower dominates the landscape for miles. No one could fail to be astonished on visiting Breckland for the first time. That a county so fertile and highly cultivated as Suffolk appears to be—apart from its coastal heaths—should have this vast acreage that is neither ploughed nor sown seems incredible. Yet there it is, the loneliest bit of England between Northumberland and the New Forest. Its average population is only eighty to the square mile, whereas the average per square mile for England as a whole is about seven hundred. The figure would be even smaller if the Forestry Commission had not acquired a large part of the region and turned it into forest in order to replenish the timber resources of the country after the ravages of the First Great War.

Before this new use was made of it, Breckland had been chiefly favoured in modern times as shooting country. Every road that approaches it from Bury St. Edmunds crosses parkland and runs through trim villages associated with noble families, before reaching the great heaths and warrens. At Barton Hall, off the Ixworth road, noted for an art collection including portraits of the Bunbury family by Sir Joshua Reynolds, and paintings by Rubens, Van Dyck, Veronese, Corregio, Watteau, and other masters, Oliver Goldsmith was a frequent visitor. His biographer, Forster, tells us that he loved to play the fool there, and was often the butt of the party in social frolics. "Tricks were played upon his dress, upon his smart black silk coat and expensive pair of ruffles, above all upon his wig, which the valets as well as the guests at Barton appear to have thought a quizzical property; yet all this he suffered with imperturbable good humour. He sang comic songs with great taste and fun; he was inventive in garden buildings and operations, over which he blundered amazingly; and if there was a piece of water in any part of the grounds, he commonly managed to tumble into it."

At Ampton, on the Thetford road, we pass by a park in which such unexpected trees as cedars of Lebanon, Chilian pines, cork-trees, and tulip-trees may be seen, and between this park and the neighbouring one of Livermere lies the lovely Livermere Lake. Near the Brandon road stands Culford Hall, now a public school, an eighteenth-century mansion built by the first Marquess Cornwallis in place of the original hall built by Sir Nicholas Bacon, the premier baronet, in 1591; and on the Mildenhall road is that sumptuous example of Tudor architecture, Hengrave Hall, which, though only about one-third its original size, has an elaborate bay window, almost ecclesiastical in the splendour of its stonework, and a turreted gatehouse that seems to symbolise the flamboyant and adventurous spirit developing in English life at the time it was built by a rich merchant, Sir Thomas Kytson. It is also evidence of the confidence such men must have had in the power of the Tudors to bring peace and prosperity to the land. John Wilbye, who composed some of the best of our English madrigals, was a member of Sir Thomas Kytson's household. Later, Hengrave was to have a long association with the Gage family.

North-east of these large, well-timbered parks, which make the desolation beyond them so surprising when we reach it, lies Euston, the Duke of Grafton's seat, with a park still more extensive and noble.

Instead of taking the shortest route to Breckland, we may take the Ixworth road and visit Honington, the birthplace of Robert Bloomfield, author of *The Farmer's Boy*. Although on the edge of Breckland, the Honington district is like High Suffolk in character: level ploughland that would be dull and uninspiring if it were not for the streams that grace it with their loops and bends, and the willows that grow along their banks. Away from these, as across so much of North Suffolk, large fields of sugar-beet stretch monotonously between vil-

lages of no particular beauty. Occasionally a screen of elms
is found to break the wind, but most of the villages are
exposed to all the rigours of the weather. Here and there,
however, the road drops into a valley, as it does at Fakenham
just beyond Honington, and then we find again those thatched
cottages and mellow old manor-houses that are so attractive in
the old wool towns.

Both Fakenham and Honington are closely associated with
the Bloomfield family. The poet was born at Honington in
December 1766, the son of the village tailor, who died of
smallpox and was buried at midnight while Robert was still
a child. His grandfather, a draper in Fakenham, was a quiet,
studious man who neglected his business for books until his
family lost patience with him. And when Mrs. Bloomfield,
the poet's mother, was left a widow with six children to support, she opened a dame school in a Honington cottage, the
gift of her father, a Fakenham farmer.

Robert learnt his letters in his mother's school, which was
held in a clay-lump cottage with brick additions at the rear
of the blacksmith's shop. When old enough to write he was
sent to a school at Ixworth. At eleven he was put into farm
service with a Mr. Austin of Sapiston, with whom he gained
the experience described in the poem of which everyone who
has heard of Bloomfield knows the title, and hardly anyone
a single line that follows it. *The Farmer's Boy* was actually
written in a London garret. Robert was a frail boy, and after
four years of farming in this bleak, unkindly country he was
sent to London to work for his brother, who had settled there
as a shoemaker. In his leisure hours he rhymed of his old
home, his work on Mr. Austin's farm, and the changing
seasons until this long poem was written. When finished it
was sent to a literary farmer named Capel Lofft, a pleasant
but sentimental man whom Byron, envious of the young
poet's success, described as " the Maecenas of Shoemakers and
Preface-writer-General to distressed Versemen." To the amazement of the literary world *The Farmer's Boy* became so
popular that within three years of publication twenty-six
thousand copies had been sold. Several translations were
made, and the Suffolk ploughboy found his English home-
spun converted into the peasant costumes of France and Italy

and other European countries. But the Muses can be cruel as well as kind, and Bloomfield died a poor and worried man.

The Farmer's Boy will never again be widely read outside Suffolk, but there it will not be forgotten. Minor poets are often useful for their records of social life. Bloomfield is not very helpful in that respect. He has, however, a few poems of interest to the social historian, of which *The Horkey* is perhaps the best. The horkey was the last load of harvest, and was followed by the Harvest, or Horkey, Supper, to which the farmer would invite his harvest men, their wives and families, for an evening's jollification. He has also a ballad based on the story of the Fakenham "ghost," which terrified an old woman by following her home. She thought it was the Devil, but it turned out to be nothing more sinister than a young ass that had strayed from its dam in Euston Park.

The district has several good ghost stories. A much more alarming apparition than the ass's colt at Fakenham was that of the headless horseman at Icklingham. This was probably John de Cambridge, the prior of the abbey of St. Edmundsbury, who fled from the rabble in 1381, as described in the previous chapter, and was murdered near Temple Bridge by the people of Mildenhall.

But a more gruesome story than either of these was revived in 1936 when an aerodrome was constructed near Honington. While the ground was being prepared, an iron cage containing a skeleton from a gibbet was dug up. The cage itself is still to be seen at Moyses' Hall, Bury St. Edmunds. The skeleton was believed to be that of John Nichols, who appeared at the Suffolk Assizes in March 1794, along with his son, Nathan, who had been compelled by the old man to murder his sister. Both John and Nathan were sentenced to death and executed at Bury St. Edmunds. Nathan's body was afterwards handed over to a doctor for surgical dissection; his father's was hung in chains near the lonely spot between Honington and Fakenham, where the murder was committed.

In the Honington and Fakenham district this horrible story is given an amusing sequel. One night while the usual assembly of farmers and labourers were sitting drinking in the

"Fox" at Honington, one of the company brought the conversation round to the story of the crime.

"I'll dare 'ee," said he, "to cross the fields and ask that ole corpse how he fares."

"Your money's as good as mine already," said another, as he put on his hat and stumbled out into the darkness, where he found his way by listening to the creaking of the gibbet chains until the corpse swung above him in the cold night air.

"Well, Naabour Nichols, how d'you fare?" he asked, and a gruff voice answered:

"Wet, cold and hungry, and tired o' bein' here."

The man who had laid the wager had taken a short cut to the gibbet and had reached it in time to supply the voice.

Many of the local ghost stories, as Mr. Clarke informs us in that admirable book, *In Breckland Wilds*, arose from the custom of tying a pig's bladder at the end of a piece of string and suspending it in the chimney to prevent smoking. In a high wind the bladder would keep up an alarming battery on the walls of the chimney and terrify new tenants who did not know it was there. Mr. Clarke also has the story of the white rabbit with large flaming eyes that haunted Thetford Warren and was probably the Breckland manifestation of Black Shuck.

From Fakenham to Euston the road keeps close to the Little Ouse, which, like all East Anglian streams, is full of weeds and rushes, with tall grasses along its banks to provide nesting-places for the kingfisher, the moorhen, the little grebe, and the warblers that are so numerous here. Euston Hall itself can be seen clearly from the road where the unfenced park comes down to the opposite bank of the river. The present hall is a modern building, replacing a seventeenth-century mansion largely destroyed by fire in 1902, which was built by Lord Arlington in the reign of Charles II. It became the seat of the dukes of Grafton by the marriage of Henry Fitzroy, the first duke—son of Charles II and the Duchess of Cleveland—with Isabella, Lord Arlington's heiress. The original hall, like most of those built at the same time, showed much Continental influence in the style of its architecture. Evelyn, who visited it in 1671, called it a noble pile, but found it situated on a "soil dry, barren, and miserably sandy, which flies in drifts as the wind sets."

Evelyn was present at the marriage of Arlington's daughter, "a sweet child if ever there was any," with the king's son. This engaging child was then only five years of age. The king was determined on the marriage, which everyone appears to have thought would come to nothing. Seven years later, however, these children were re-married, and Evelyn hoped that "this sweetest, hopefullest, most beautiful child," would "find it to her advantage." From the death of Lord Arlington to the present day, Euston has continued to be the seat of the dukes of Grafton, who have maintained the estate with so much care that this is still one of the most beautiful parts of Suffolk. Cedars and oaks of magnificent girth ornament the grounds, though "the dappled herd of grazing deer" that Bloomfield described has gone. The poet found a generous patron in the third duke, perhaps the most splendid of the line, who was accustomed to ride about the park in a long, peach-coloured coat and a three-cornered, gold-laced hat.

Beyond Euston, approaching Breckland from this side, we get the first of the series of surprises that everyone must associate with his first visit to the district. For a short distance even the river assumes a character entirely alien to East Anglia, as it ripples over stones with a merry jingle that sends the mind dancing down a Yorkshire dale for a few seconds. But the river takes us to Thetford, which is in Norfolk, so we turn left to Barnham with its windmill, passing along avenues of oak and pine with bracken springing everywhere from the heath below. After we have crossed the main Newmarket to Thetford road at Elvedon the real breck begins, with Parsonage Heath on one side of the road and Wangford Warren on the other. Parsonage Heath is now a dense plantation, but between belts of conifers, golden broom and purple ling grow from the soft turf, and on a warm day the air is full of the hum of insects and the aromatic scents of the heath.

At the heart of this gaily coloured but solitary region is Brandon, the small grey town where the prehistoric craft of flint-knapping survives. Brandon is all flint. It is old—we find that a weekly market was granted to it in 1542—but it never mellows. That is the worst of flint. It is hard and bony like the face of an old man who has found neither kindness nor peace in his passage through life. It never endears itself to us as plaster, old brick, or stone may do. But it keeps fresh and serviceable to a great age. Even centuries old cottages look as though they were built not more than fifty years ago. The only place where the face of Brandon softens is on the river bank, where an inviting inn has smooth green lawns and a view of a bridge that has long been the delight of artists. This bridge, alas! is doomed to early destruction.

The principal interest of Breckland to scholars is in the evidence it provides of the life of primitive man. This sandy waste, now so sparsely populated, is one of the oldest inhabited regions in Europe. It was here that prehistoric man found some of his first instruments of progress in the flint that has been worked in the same place, and practically by the same method, ever since. The process of flaking and knapping flint, which is found in such pits as Grimes Graves, a short distance over the Norfolk border, gave those early settlers their knives and axes as well as their spear and arrow heads. In the war against Napoleon the Brandon flint-knappers supplied the whole British army with gunflints, and became so prosperous that they played pitch and toss with guinea pieces. Their largest order in recent years came from the Ethiopian government in their war of defence against Mussolini. Smaller orders come for flints to barter with the tribesmen of Africa. But the craft will almost certainly die out with the present generation of knappers. It would be inhuman to regret this. Not because the flints are used for weapons of war—deadlier weapons have replaced them—but because flint-knapping is a hard and unhealthy occupation. Fans have recently been installed to carry away the fine but gritty dust that used to penetrate the knapper's throat, and sometimes his lungs. The shed is now clean and well ventilated. But after every precaution has been taken, few would consider flint-knapping a desirable occupation.

Briefly, the process is this: the knapper lays the nodule of flint against his left knee, which is protected by a leather pad, and with sharp blows of a blunt hammer halves and quarters it. A worn hammer is preferred and little force is used in striking. By attacking the nodule in the right place and at the right angle a flat surface is obtained. This is essential for the next process, that of flaking. An interesting point arises here. The traditional flaking hammer was oval, but to-day a French flaker is used, and this, it is believed, was introduced by French prisoners of war captured in the Napoleonic war.

Flaking is highly skilled work, and depends for success upon the precision of the stroke. The flakes can be either thick or thin as required, and can be cut off at the rate of five to seven thousand a day. For the final process, that of knapping, the workman binds his right wrist tightly and selects a light, sharp hammer made from a cast steel file. With one hand he holds the flakes against an iron stake, which serves as a small anvil, and shakes and trims them by working the hammer at great speed, bouncing it off a thick leather pad on to the edge of the flint.

While the pits of Breckland provided primitive man with weapons, the woods and warrens provided him with the animals he required for food. At the same time the river gave him fish and such means of communication as he needed. But when the Iron Age came, and man discovered that he could not subdue the earth to his will by inducing the ground to yield crops, the poverty of the Breckland soil became apparent; even so, Breckland continued to be perhaps the most thickly populated part of East Anglia and was certainly cultivated up to late Anglo-Saxon times. There can still be found small, dark-haired people unlike those in any other part of East Anglia except the neighbouring fens, who may be the last of the Iceni. With the coming of the Forestry Commission many Scots have settled in the district, and the character of the people is undergoing modification.

The other peculiarly local occupation in Brandon is the result of the thousands of rabbits that burrow and breed in the sandy warrens. Many of the small farmers pay their rents by selling rabbits and rabbit skins. These skins are prepared for the cheaper kind of fur garments and in enormous quantities for the manufacture of felt.

The production of timber in Breckland by modern methods of afforestation probably began towards the end of the eighteenth century. In some parts the trees are now of immense proportions, and their serried ranks have a gloomy grandeur. There was a Scots pine at Santon Downham in 1909 that measured sixteen feet in girth two feet from the ground. It had six branches each as large as a fully grown tree and towered to a height of sixty feet. But the first large scale plantation was made in 1840.

It is true that much of the characteristic beauty of Breckland was lost when these plantations were made, but in the present century the Forestry Commission have tried to reconcile beauty with utility by planting poplars and other trees along the edges of the great blocks of conifers. The principal difficulty about planting hardwoods is that they are so often killed by frost, from which Breckland is free for only three months of the year. If you look round the plantations you can see how far the frost has gone up the trunks of the oaks and beeches. Even when protected by conifers they still suffer from it.

The great twentieth-century movement for the afforestation of Breckland began in 1922 on Lord Iveagh's land near Wangford. Other large tracts were acquired for the same purpose in rapid succession. The process was accelerated by the high taxation and the burden of death duties that was already impoverishing the landed classes. These estates were maintained solely for sport. There was no profit to be gained from them. Within a few years massed ranks of conifers, each block covering from fifty to a hundred acres, had come to form a vast forest, with a smallholding for a forestry worker created for each two hundred acres of plantation. Each of these smallholders is guaranteed at least a hundred and fifty days employment on the plantations each year.

The Forestry Commission has a district office at Santon Downham, now the centre of the important area that has been given the name of Thetford Chase. It was here in the seventeenth century that James I hunted the deer from his lodge, "The King's House" at Thetford. It was always a barren tract. We gain some idea of the nature of the soil from the story of the Santon Downham farmer who when asked where his farm was, replied: "Times thass in Norfolk, bor; times thass in Suffolk. That dew dipind which way the wind's a blowin'."

In 1668 this parish was nearly buried in a sandstorm. A Santon Downham farmer of the day found the sand in his yard up to the eaves of his outbuildings. To protect his land he went to the great expense of having banks nearly twenty yards high constructed. Yet in spite of all the endeavours of such determined men as he, it was almost impossible to get a living from the land in this district except when prices were exceptionally high. Only where trees had been planted to fence in the fields and protect the light soil from the wind could crops be raised with any confidence, and when everything possible had been done the yield was still pitifully small.

There are few records of the condition of Breckland in the past. For centuries it was lost to the rest of England. Those we have are the more valuable by their rarity. William Gilpin toured East Anglia in 1769 and recorded that between Brandon and Mildenhall "nothing was to be seen on either side but sand and scattered gravel without the least vegetation; a mere African desert. In some places this sandy waste occupied the whole scope of the eye; in other places, at a distance we could see a skirting of green with a few straggling bushes which, being surrounded by sand, appear'd like a stretch of low land shooting into the sea. The whole country indeed had the appearance of beaten sea-coast, but without the beauties which adorn that species of landscape." The young Duc de la Rochefoucald, travelling across the eastern part of Breckland in 1784, wrote: "You go across the Duke of Grafton's estate, notable for the large number of rabbits which you see and for the foxes which you do not see; this, combined with the poor quality of the soil, gives the Duke little chance of agricultural prosperity. Also the whole of the country through which the road runs for a distance of eight miles is covered with heather in every direction as far as the eye can see—not a shrub, not a plant, except in the little valleys which one sees in the distance."

There seem to be fewer arguments against the work of the Forestry Commission in this arid tract than in most districts. There are certainly none with the force of those used by defenders of the natural beauty of the Lake District. But Breckland has its defenders. One large area, Lakenheath

Common, is not likely to be acquired for afforestation. The Norfolk Naturalists' Trust will see to that. Some years ago an ancient common law was discovered, which laid down that no common can be sold unless all the tenants who have the use of it give their consent. Shortly afterwards, a trust was created to see that the one refractory tenant required should always be provided at Lakenheath. It must, however, be added that during the Second Great War the Air Ministry forcibly acquired the Common or Warren, over-riding the rights of the commoners.

It is not uncommon for the plainest child in a family to inspire the greatest affection, and Breckland, this region so desolate and forsaken, inspired a tribute that few of the most beautiful parts of England have equalled. *In Breckland Wilds*, a book written by the late W. G. Clarke and revised and rewritten by his son, Mr. R. Rainbird Clarke, covers this field in a way that can never be surpassed. I doubt whether I should ever have discovered so much beauty in Breckland as I do if I had not read—and re-read—Mr. Clarke's book. He knew it in every mood and at every season; he understood it with the sensibility of a poet and the precision of a naturalist. The solitude to be found in its spacious heaths was life to him. The winds are unleashed here, and he rejoiced in their freedom. His heart was with the wild and carefree creatures that rode them. He rejoiced, too, in the rank profusion of the golden ragwort that burns here so fiercely—with lady's bedstraw, bird's-foot trefoil, and knapweed throughout the summer months, and heather in the autumn. Gold and purple are the colours of the breck—proud, defiant colours that match its primordial nature.

A district with so many peculiar features inevitably has a number of plants and birds not widely distributed elsewhere in East Anglia. Generally speaking, the flora of Breckland is maritime. "The special Breck species," Mr. Clarke tells us, "number twenty, and include the conical and Spanish catch-flies, the sickle and bur medicks, the fingered, vernal and spiked speedwells, the umbellate holosteum, *medicago sylvestris*, the mossy tillaea, the wall bedstraw, Jersey cudweed, field southernwood, common rupture-wort, perennial knawel, grape hyacinth, star of Bethlehem, early speedwell, *carex erice-*

torum, and Boehmer's phleum. Many of these rare plants are typical of steppe conditions, and as Breckland provides the nearest approach to these found in Britain, it is reasonable to conclude that this steppe flora has survived from the dry, warm, Boreal period after the last glaciation."

Mr. Clarke also informs us that within six miles of Thetford one hundred and ninety-six species of birds have been recorded. Wheatears nest in the rabbit burrows, as also do stock-doves and occasionally short-eared owls. Sand-martins, as we should expect, are everywhere. One of the commonest birds is the nightjar, whose churring notes are particularly associated with Breckland by solitary walkers, because they are often the only sounds heard for miles in the late evening. Sometimes you will hear also the keening of the curlew and the plaintive notes of lapwings. The ringed plover and the stone-curlew are the two most characteristic Breckland birds. Most of the meres are in Norfolk. On these, many species of duck breed regularly, and the beauty of their plumage adds to the multi-coloured garment of the entire district. The Great Bustard had its last stronghold in the district. Ray, in 1678, mentioned that it was found in Suffolk, and was so expensive that it served only "to furnish Princes' and great men's tables at public entertainments." Its last breeding-place, I believe, was near Icklingham.

Bloomfield provides us with useful information about the wild life of the breck. He writes:

> Where noble Grafton spreads his rich domains
> Round Euston's water'd vale, and sloping plains
> Where woods and groves in solemn grandeur rise,
> Where the Kite brooding unmolested flies,
> The Woodcock and the painted Pheasant race
> And skulking foxes destined for the chase.

The hunting of the kite was the favourite sport of Lord Orford and Colonel Thornton, familiar figures in the district at the end of the eighteenth century. They hunted with falcons. Hawking had been a popular sport in England in the seventeenth century, but had practically died out when Lord Orford founded his Falconers' Society. Mr. Claud B. Tycehurst, in *A History of the Birds of Suffolk,* quotes an interesting notice that appeared in a newspaper dated Swaffham, 5th February, 1783: "The gentlemen of the Falconers' Society are hereby acquainted that the hawks will be in England in the first week in March and will begin Kite and Crow hawking immediately on their arrival. The quarters are fixed at Bourn Bridge, Cambridgeshire . . . until the first April meeting when they will go to Barton Mills and Brandon till the 31st of May when the season will finish. The hawks to be out every Saturday, Monday and Wednesday in each week at ten o'clock provided the weather is favourable."

Breckland seems to be a land of strange survivals. But lonely as it is, and desolate as its few farmhouses appear, each in its stockade of fir trees, there is always an exhilarating atmosphere about it that is to me entirely lacking in the neighbouring fens. If we take the Mildenhall road from Brandon we cross Wangford and Lakenheath warrens, and as we approach Eriswell a wide vista presents itself, with fine old English trees in natural formation and Mildenhall's church tower between three and four miles away, dominating the landscape. The fens look cool and refreshing from here; and if we leave the Mildenhall road to run down to Lakenheath village, where Lord Kitchener's ancestors are buried, we may feel that Fenland is a much maligned region. The air is so clear at Lakenheath, and the streets are so like those of a fishing village, that at every turn of the road we expect to hear the roar of the sea. But beyond the village lies a wide expanse of low, flat marshland that may have charm for some, but which, I confess, has none for me. Life is in a minor key here. Coming from the east we miss the wild flowers of the breck, the pines and the keen air. The fens belong to Cambridgeshire rather than to Suffolk, and no one is better able to interpret them than Dr. Ennion, who has written the Cambridgeshire volume in this present series. To appreciate them we must have something of the delight that he has in the wild life of the fens, or an interest in fen farming.

Life must be lonely on a fenland farm at any time of the year. It must be deadly in winter. Yet these fenland farms are eagerly sought. They yield big crops at small expense.

The soil has not lost its humus content, so the application of animal manure is not essential. The worst enemy of the fenland farmer is flood, and such a winter as that of 1946-7, when thousands of acres were inundated, might have made the land useless for two or three years if an unusually dry summer had not followed it.

Although fenland farming has proved so remunerative, the draining of these low-lying areas by Cornelius Vermuyden for the Duke of Bedford in the seventeenth century was bitterly resented by the fenmen, who had previously gained a livelihood by rearing geese and shooting wildfowl. They had no desire for their fowler's paradise to be turned into rich, alluvial soil. They were sportsmen, not farmers.

But whether we find the fens dreary or full of life, we shall probably agree that Mildenhall, the market town of the Suffolk fens, is one of the most attractive small towns in the county. Its pleasant old houses, broad square with a beautiful hexagonal cross of great antiquity, and its grand old church make it a town on which the mind dwells fondly. There is about it an atmosphere of prosperous contentment not particularly noticeable in any other small Suffolk town. This appearance is not deceptive, for Mildenhall is, I believe, one of the richest small towns in East Anglia.

This genial old town, now prospering with the fenland farmers, and from the nearby aerodrome, has a long history of well-being behind it, as the church bears witness. It had six guilds in the Middle Ages. There were two guild altars in the church. But the principal features of the church are the great tower, which Abbot Samson began to build in 1189, and which was heightened at the end of the fifteenth century, and the roof of the nave, with its moulded tie beams adorned with carved figures of angels holding scrolls, which represent, of course, the glorious words of the *Te Deum*, "To Thee all angels cry aloud."

The most interesting memorial in the church is one to Sir Henry Barton, the lord mayor of London who introduced street lighting into the capital. His order was for lanthorns to be hung out between All Saints and Candlemas.

Outside East Anglia, Mildenhall has now come to be known principally in connection with the "Mildenhall Treasure," a

Morning exercise at Newmarket
High Street, Newmarket

hoard of silver declared to be Roman and probably of the fourth century, that was turned up by a plough at West Row during the winter of 1942-3. Its existence did not become widely known until the summer of 1946, when the discovery was announced by wireless and long, illustrated articles on the importance of the find appeared in the press. At an inquest held on it in July 1946, the collection was acquired by the Crown as treasure trove and exhibited at the British Museum, where the Sutton Hoo treasure had already made Suffolk pre-eminent among English counties as a place of buried riches. The fact that the Mildenhall treasure was found within thirty yards of the site of a Roman villa led to hasty conclusions being drawn, and a number of premature and unguarded statements were made about its probable origin. Whatever the experts may decide about its age and the way it reached Mildenhall, all who have seen it must have marvelled at its beauty. The most remarkable piece is the "Neptune Dish," which has the head of the sea-god in the centre, with dolphins in his beard, and around it two circular panels. It weighs about 18 lb. and is beautifully engraved. In the inner panel, bordered by a circle of shells, sea-nymphs and monsters are entwined in a flowing design; in the outer panel Bacchus, with a panther at his feet, is the principal figure. On his left is Hercules, supported by two satyrs; on his right, Pan, with maenads and other satyrs, dancing and playing with pipes and cymbals. Other bowls ornamented with embossed designs were found, a covered bowl surmounted with a figure holding a cornucopia, or horn of plenty, and shallow dishes embellished with classical figures in repoussé work, together with drinking cups and spoons similar to those found at Traprain. No discovery of buried treasure can ever have aroused greater public interest.

If we leave Mildenhall to return to Bury St. Edmunds we cross breezy heathland again and pass through flint-walled villages sheltered by pine woods. Wild flowers again delight us, particularly orange kidney vetch and bluish-purple viper's bugloss. Along the whole way from Mildenhall to Bury St. Edmunds we are close to the river Lark, which forms the western boundary of the county for a few miles in fenland before flowing into Cambridgeshire.

T 273

Little Saxham Church
Kersey

Icklingham, the first village we pass through on this road, was situated on the war-path of the Iceni, and Palaeolithic and Neolithic implements have been found here in great numbers. Extensive excavations have been carried out in the district, some of them superintended by Mr. H. Prigg, who collected all the available information about them in his *Icklingham Papers*, which were edited and published by Mr. V. B. Redstone.

As we approach Bury St. Edmunds we run into the circle of stately parkland again, with such lovely villages as Flempton and Hengrave. North-east of Flempton is West Stow Hall, which I omitted to mention at the beginning of the chapter. It is one of the most remarkable mansions in West Suffolk. Formerly quadrangular and moated, it was rebuilt by Sir John Crofts, who died in 1557, and was later occupied by "gay Prodgers," the Hon. Edward Prodgers, ex-groom of the Chamber to Charles II, who was banished from the king's presence as "an evil instrument and bad counsellor of the king."

In an upper room of the gatehouse four of the seven ages of man are depicted in wall paintings. The first represents a boy hawking, and is inscribed "Thus doe I all the day." The second shows a man wooing, and is inscribed "Thus doe I while I may." On the third a middle-aged man points to the young couple with the words "Thus did I while I might." And the fourth shows an old man tottering to the grave saying "Good Lord! Will this world last for ever?" With that pious reflection we return to Bury St. Edmunds.

CHAPTER XVIII

WEST TO NEWMARKET

BURY ST. EDMUNDS is completely encircled by seats, or former seats, of the Suffolk nobility. In approaching the town from south or east, no less than from north or west, the effects of their pride and pleasure are manifest. The land is highly cultivated and the villages are cared for. Throughout the last four hundred years or more, most if not all these villages have been associated with a well-known family, and the records of their cultivation go back as far as any in the land. These were the fields where the flocks of the lord abbot grazed. Some of the oaks still standing were planted to provide acorns for his pigs. The arable land was first ploughed by the abbot's oxen. It was because this land was so fertile and productive that it was coveted by the king's favourites at the Dissolution, who built their houses upon it and established their families.

Hardwick, where, during the last hundred years the heads of the Cullum family built up their fine library and collection of marbles, was granted by King Edmund to the cellarer of the abbey in 945, and at the Dissolution by Henry VIII to Sir Thomas Darcy. The Cullum family settled there in 1656. Hawstead Place near by, of which practically nothing now remains, was the seat of the Drurys, who were visited there by Queen Elizabeth in 1578. There is a pleasant story told of this occasion—the owner, William Drury, it is related, was knighted by the queen on restoring to her a silver-handled fan she had dropped into the moat.

Many fine memorials to the Drurys are to be seen in Hawstead church; but their best memorial is in the perpetuation of their name in Drury Lane Theatre, London, a building so named because the town house of the family formerly occupied its site. Another interesting London association is in the familiar plane trees, which are said to have been introduced into England by Lord Bacon. Near Hawstead Place some very old specimens are still to be seen, and as the Bacons were related to the Drurys, it does seem possible—and perhaps probable—that the plane tree reached London by way of Suffolk.

West of Hardwick lies Ickworth, the seat of the Marquess of Bristol. Soon after Domesday this estate was given by Abbot Baldwin to one named Ulward in exchange for Elveden, to be held in return for services to the abbot. When the line of inheritance failed at the death of the widow of Thomas de Ickworth in 1437, the reigning abbot claimed the estate and gave it to Sir William Drury. The Hervey family, who have owned it ever since, acquired it by the marriage of John Hervey of Thurleigh in Bedfordshire with the daughter and heiress of Henry Drury in the first half of the fifteenth century. It has, therefore, been the home of the Herveys for five hundred years.

The present Ickworth House was built by Frederick, fourth Earl of Bristol and Bishop of Derry, virtuoso and patron of artists, who had it specially designed to house the vast collections he accumulated, principally in his Continental travels, on which he always travelled in his own coach, accompanied by a suite of attendants. The architect was commissioned to construct a round house—which in this case meant an oval one—with curved corridors leading to two wings built with large skylights and intended to serve as galleries. The rooms in the middle part were also to be unusually lofty, because the bishop-earl said that low rooms depressed his spirits whereas lofty rooms elevated them. The outside of the house was to be decorated with reproductions in relief of Flaxman's illustrations to the *Iliad* and the *Odyssey*. All these unusual and carefully planned features required time for completion, so it was not until 1830 that the house was ready for occupation, by which time the bishop had been dead for twenty-seven years. It is not surprising, therefore, to find that in the later stages the original design was modified and adapted to uses other than those originally intended.

Frederick Augustus Hervey, fourth Earl of Bristol, fifth Baron de Walden, and Bishop of Derry, was a distinguished man and in Ickworth House he has a worthy memorial. But in the church on the estate there is a memorial with a stronger

appeal to the romantic. It is a few lines written by Horace
Walpole to the memory of Mary Lepell—"Sweet Molly
Lepell," whose wit and charm were celebrated in English
verses by Voltaire, and who was the darling and favourite
toast of the Jacobites. She married John, Lord Hervey, son
of the first Earl of Bristol, a man of considerable ability, the
author of *Memoirs of the Court of George II*, but one whose
character was not conducive to domestic happiness. He
was savagely attacked by Pope, because he was a friend
of Lady Mary Wortley Montagu, the lady Pope wished to
marry.

Another character from livelier days than ours is recalled
at Little Saxham, west of Ickworth, the home of "mad-cap
Croftes," a favourite of Charles II, who visited him there on
at least four occasions. On the second of these, Pepys was
present, and in his diary entry for the 23rd October, 1668, we
read "That the King was drunk at Saxam with Sedley, Buck-
hurst, &c. the night that my Lord Arlington came thither,
and would not give him audience, or could not; which is true,
for it was the night that I was there and saw the King go up
to his chamber, and was told that the King had been drinking." It was, as Pepys concluded on that occasion, "a mad
world; God bless us out of it!"

Beyond Ickworth and the Saxhams there is little to think
of except the Newmarket road. We are again on one of
Suffolk's historic highways; and if this one has none of the
tales of smuggling and daring escapes from the king's officers
that are told on the Yarmouth road, it has been no less a place
of hazard and adventure. The lonely heaths of Breckland,
which come down to this road, held secret lairs of highwaymen and desperate characters driven to reckless methods of
making good their losses at Newmarket. The region was also
a great place for gipsies, and it is these who lay flowers on the
Boy's Grave, a solitary mound where the road from Moulton
to Chippenham crosses the Newmarket road. Dark-coloured
flowers laid here on Derby Day are believed to foretell that a
dark-coloured horse will carry away the prize money at that
day's race. This is not, as it is sometimes said to be, a gipsy's
grave, but that of a shepherd boy who was so afraid of his
master that when he lost a sheep he hanged himself rather

than report the loss. For this he was buried in a suicide's grave at the cross-roads, with a stake driven through his heart. On Kesgrave Heath, in the east of the country, there is—or was—another mysterious mound called Dobb's Grave. Some years ago the rector of Brightwell had the grave opened and found a skeleton with a stake driven through it.

Mr. Leonard P. Thompson, in his lively book, *Old Inns of Suffolk,* has an exciting account of a highway robbery on this road. He relates how a Mr. Macro of Barrow Hall, near Bury St. Edmunds, was returning home on the first Monday evening of January 1783, when he was stopped near his own gate by a highwayman, who "with an oath demanded his money." Mr. Macro struck out with his stick, but failed to knock the pistol out of the assailant's hand. When the highwayman fired, grazing Mr. Macro's cheek, the shot was heard by the family indoors, who ran out and put the highwayman to flight without the coveted money-bags, which were heavy with the parish tithes.

The following morning Mr. Macro carefully examined the place where he had been attacked, and on finding the shoe-prints of a horse he followed them. They led, he discovered, into the stable-yard of the "Bell" at Kentford. In the kitchen of the inn he recognised his assailant, whom he was able to overpower and secure, and in due course to bring before the justices at Bury St. Edmunds on a charge of attempted robbery and murder. The name of the highwayman was James Steggles. His pistols, and also the bob-wig he had used for disguise, were traced by the astute Mr. Macro and produced in evidence at the trial. Steggles was hanged at Bury St. Edmunds on the 2nd of April, 1783, after making a full confession. His curious request that a mourning coach should convey him to the place of execution was refused, and an account of the last act in the drama relates that he was "executed in a suit of white baize, made in one entire piece from his neck to his feet, trimmed with black, and tied with black ribands round his arms."

Kentford, on the river Kennet, is an attractive village and a joy to discover on this monotonous Newmarket road, of which the only good thing to be said is that its fourteen miles can be traversed at record speed. Perhaps this in itself is a useful preparation for the celebrated town at the Cambridge-shire end of it.

Newmarket sits in the saddle with one leg in Suffolk and one in Cambridgeshire. It is a town that, like its votaries, likes to have something "each way," and the balancing of topographical odds here is more than a man who has not had a bookmaker's training can be expected to calculate. The High Street, a broad, breezy thoroughfare, with a more alert air about it than is to be found anywhere else in Suffolk out-side Ipswich, divides the town between its two counties. Geographically, two of its parishes are in Suffolk, one in Cambridgeshire; but for administrative and ecclesiastical pur-poses the whole of the urban district is in Suffolk. The con-stitution of the town is thus as tricky as the racing by which it lives and prospers. It is even possible that before these words find print the whole of Newmarket will have been transferred to Cambridgeshire. It will not go without a con-test. West Suffolk derives at least fifteen per cent of its rate revenue from Newmarket, and if it lost the town its popula-tion would fall to less than 100,000.

South-west is a long rampart called the Devil's Dyke, which in the days when it was built as a defensive earthwork had fens and marshes on the east of it and forest on the west. At that time it divided East Anglia from Mercia. To-day it is intersected by the race-course and the London road; but along the top is the so-called chariot-track, and it is interesting to learn that the Jockey Club has no authority over this ancient road along which a coffin is wheeled each year to preserve the right of way.

Newmarket has a singularly youthful appearance. Its High Street might be the broadway leading to the sea in one of the smarter modern resorts. But on the outskirts, especially in the mornings, when strings of horses can be seen cantering from their stables towards Warren Hill, there can be no mis-taking its identity. It has, I believe, about forty training establishments, and a tour of these would quickly convince anyone that it is all that it claims to be as "the headquarters of the Turf."

The town is not an ancient settlement. It is believed to have been built when Exning, a neighbouring village, was stricken by plague. But it is much older than its trim, up-to-date appearance at first sight suggests. Its prosperity dates from the reign of James I, who first visited Newmarket on the 27th of February, 1605; but the Heath had been used for racing—and by kings—long before James and his Scottish nobles made horse-racing popular in England. Richard II, when Prince of Wales, raced there against the Earl of Arundel, owners up, and on two occasions Edward II expressly forbade racing on the Heath at Newmarket, fearing the result of a large gathering of his nobles. Henry VIII, so far as we know, was never there, which seems strange, because he was intensely interested in horses and did much to improve their size and stamina.

Of the Newmarket of the Stuarts little remains. Something of it is to be seen in Market Street, in Drapery Row, in what was formerly the "Three Tuns," and in a few isolated houses. The "Bushel" Inn was once the scene of unrecorded royster-ing in the days when Buckingham and Rochester, in the company of ladies of charm and wit—if not of virtue—paid tribute to Bacchus and other gods the Puritans had neglected. In 1683 half the town was destroyed by fire, the Palace itself escaping. It was this disaster that forced Charles II to return to London earlier than he had planned. Chance was never so much in his favour, for if he had returned as intended his way would have been barred at Hoddesdon by a cartload of hay while the Duke of Monmouth's supporters crept from their ambush to kill him. This was the Rye House Plot. Another Newmarket inn associated with the lively but licentious days of the Restoration, the "White Hart," was destroyed by a Nazi bomber on the 15th February, 1941.

James is said to have written his *Religio Regis, or the Faith and Duty of a Prince* at Newmarket. In it he praises the manly sports to be enjoyed on horseback, which he not un-naturally favoured, as he cut a poor figure out of the saddle. His legs were so weak that he usually leaned on one or two of his courtiers when compelled to walk. In old age he retired to Newmarket when in need of its invigorating air to restore his spirits rather than for sport, though he would sometimes be carried out in a litter to see the hawks fly.

Both James I and Charles I entertained on a lavish scale in the town they had practically made. With the Commonwealth its fortunes declined. Cromwell was afraid that under cover of a race-meeting the Royalists would plot against him. During the years of the Parliamentarian revolt the eastern counties were almost completely united against the king, but by 1648 Royalist sympathies were again finding spirited expression. There was a disturbance at Chelmsford in March of that year. In the June following there was the siege of Colchester, towards the end of which several cavaliers met at the " King's Arms" at Newmarket, an inn no longer standing and issued a proclamation that "all gentlemen whatsoever that had desire to serve his Majesty . . . should repair to the King's Arms, there to receive present entertainment and money." Colonel Thornton of Soham and Sir Bernard Scudamore were two of four colonels issuing this appeal, and their promise of advance rewards drew a number of impecunious followers to their standard. But their little party was quickly broken up when Captain Pickering rode in from Cambridge to investigate.

In Charles II's reign Newmarket was well and truly established. Charles rebuilt the Palace, the name of which is perpetuated in Palace Street, and made the town a rendezvous for all the reckless gamesters and courtesans of Europe. Audley End in Essex he bought—though he never fully paid for it—as a convenient place to leave the queen and her ladies while he proceeded to enjoy the dangerous delights of Newmarket unhampered by the presence of a wife. Numerous capital stories are told about Charles and his companions in their wildest escapades. Some of them read like tales from Boccaccio, and though the king was no better than his friends in most respects there is usually an engaging quality about his words, and not a few of his deeds, that endears him to all except the most prudish. He could exchange compliments with scholars as neatly as with courtiers. There is a particularly pleasant story of a conversation between Charles and Bishop Stillingfleet that illustrates this well. The bishop had preached before the king on one occasion at Newmarket, and had read every word of his sermon.

"How does it come to pass," asked the king, "that you

always read your sermons before me, when, I am informed, you always preach without book elsewhere?"

"The awe of so noble an audience," the bishop replied, "where I see nothing that is not superior to me; but chiefly, the seeing before me so great and wise a prince, makes me afraid to trust myself."

Seeing the king was pleased with this reply, the bishop himself ventured to ask a question:

"But pray," he said, "will your Majesty give me leave to ask a question too? Why do you read your speeches in Parliament, where you can have none of the same reasons?"

"Why, truly, doctor, your question is a very pertinent one," replied the king, "and so will be my answer. I have asked them so often, and for so much money, that I am ashamed to look them in the face."

Much of the money the king required was to pay the debts contracted in the Newmarket gambling-houses by his mistresses, such as the Duchess of Mazarin—who kept a gambling-house herself, but was frequently in debt—and the notorious Lady Castlemaine, afterwards the Duchess of Cleveland. In 1668 Pepys recorded: "I was told to-night that my Lady Castlemaine is so great a gamester as to have won £15,000 in one night, and lost £25,000 in another night, at play; and hath played £1,000 and £1,500 at a cast." Her debts could only be paid by the king, who does not appear to have been a heavy gambler himself.

The easy-going monarch was on friendly terms with everyone who frequented the Heath, mixing freely with the crowds and ready to share a joke with the poorest. On one occasion he stood by while a snuff-box was taken from Lord Arlington's pocket. When the thief saw that the king's quick eye had caught him in the act he winked at His Majesty and put his fingers to his nose at Lord Arlington. Charles enjoyed the joke so much that he allowed the thief to escape. A few minutes later, when Lord Arlington fumbled for his snuff-box, the king laughed and said: "You need not give yourself any more trouble about it. Your box has gone, and I own myself an accomplice. I could not help it; I was made a confidant."

The Palace, which stood in the centre of the town, has

gone; but the merry monarch continues to be associated with the Turf at Newmarket through his nickname, "Old Rowley," from which the famous Rowley Mile takes its name. The story goes that the name was originally borne by a stallion owned by the king, and was transferred after an incident that occurred in the women's quarters. Charles was passing through them one day when he heard a maid of honour singing an indecent song about Old Rowley. His Majesty knocked at the door.

"Who's there?" asked the maid.

"'Tis Old Rowley himself, ma'am," replied the king.

The Rowley Mile is included in "The Flat," the course on which six of the eight annual race-meetings at Newmarket are run. These six are the Craven, which is the first important race of the year in England, the First and Second Spring, the First and Second October—the first of these two is usually misnamed, for it occurs as a rule in September— and the Houghton. The First and Second July Meetings are on the course known as "Behind the Ditch," the Ditch being the Devil's Dyke. The Two Thousand Guineas, first run in 1809, which is run at the first Spring Meeting along with the One Thousand Guineas, is also misleading in its name. The stakes for it are very much higher to-day, as they are also for the One Thousand Guineas. At the First October Meeting the Jockey Club Stakes is the chief event. The Houghton is run for the Cambridgeshire and the Dewhurst Plate; the Princess of Wales' Stakes is run for at the First July Meeting.

A small cluster of trees on the Rowley Mile course, known as "The Bushes," are commonly accepted as the testing point. In passing these the stamina of the horse becomes apparent. Either it begins to lose speed from exhaustion here, or shows itself capable of the final spurt that carries the owner's colours past the winning-post a quarter of a mile away.

The racing Newmarket of modern times developed in the reign of Queen Victoria under the patronage of the Prince of Wales, afterwards Edward VII. Egerton House was built to train his horses, and continued as a royal establishment until sold in 1943 by the Princess Royal, to whom it was bequeathed by George V. Lord Marcus Beresford, King Edward's manager, and his trainer, Richard Marsh, both of whom continued in the service of King George V, were great personalities in the Newmarket of a generation ago. Lord Lonsdale and Lord Derby, the most popular sportsmen of their day, were then in their prime, and the latter may prove to be the last of the grand old sporting aristocrats of England. There are young representatives of many old families who lack neither character nor sporting instinct, but taxation has crippled them. In 1930 Lord Derby himself was compelled to cut down his establishments, and it is enlightening to learn that at the time he estimated that each of the horses he had in training cost him £650 a year.

No small part of Edward VII's enormous popularity sprang from his success as a sportsman. He won the Derby twice while Prince of Wales, with Persimmon in 1896 and with Diamond Jubilee in 1900. His third win, with Minoru in 1909, was the first occasion on which the race had been won by a reigning sovereign, and the enthusiasm of the crowd on this occasion was greater than anything ever witnessed at a Derby Meeting. The king led in his third winner to shouts of "Good old Teddy!" Then someone began to sing "God Save the King," and in a moment, as a recorder of the incident said, "the National Anthem had been caught up far and wide till it seemed to shake the very downs."

George V was a keen race-goer, and those who knew both say that he was a far better judge of a horse than ever his father had been. We think of Edward VII rather than George V as the sporting king of modern England, but George V was probably never happier than at Newmarket, where he is remembered with great affection for the simple kindness that is always remarked upon by those who knew him. His daughter, the Princess Royal, inherited her father's love for Newmarket, and both our present king and Princess Elizabeth have shown that with them the long association of the Royal Family with the Turf will be maintained.

Newmarket is proud of being known as "Royal New-market," and bears itself accordingly. There is more polish and paint about it than about any other East Anglian town. Every bit of metal shines; every house and shop is well kept. The racehorse keeps the town prosperous. It has no poor streets or mean houses. The centre is reached along mag-

nificent avenues of beech trees or across open fields where
racehorses are to be seen being put through their paces,
watched by their owners and trainers.   In the racing seasons,
life here is probably more elegant than anywhere else outside
the West End of London.

Of the inns of fashionable Newmarket the most prominent
is the "Rutland Arms," built at the beginning of the nineteenth century to replace an old house on the same site called
the "Ram." This is the inn associated with the eccentric
Lord Orford, who, about the middle of the eighteenth century, drove a team of four stags from Houghton Hall, his
Norfolk home, to Newmarket. The Essex hounds happened
to be in the neighbourhood that day, and they caught the
scent of stags, with alarming results that may readily be
imagined. The worst, however, was avoided by the presence
of mind of the ostler at the "Ram," who heard the baying of
the hounds in pursuit of the terrified stags, followed by cries
of alarm from the townspeople as Lord Orford's carriage
swerved into the High Street. The inn yard offered sanctuary,
and into it the stags bounded with his lordship clinging to
the reins, almost paralysed by fear. Like a flash the ostler
slammed the doors, and Lord Orford and his strange team
were rescued.

Inevitably Newmarket has had many distinguished visitors
—far more than any other town in Suffolk during the past
three hundred years—and it has not been neglected by writers
of fiction. Jorrocks himself was there on a well-known occasion, when he differed from Mr. Pickwick arriving at Bury
St. Edmunds in that he failed to recognise the place. He
enquired, you may remember, "if they were sure they had
not stopped at some village by mistake." He differed from
Mr. Pickwick still more in showing the most commendable
prudence—a quality not commonly found in Newmarket.
On retiring for the night he stuffed his bank-notes into the
toes of his boots, slipped his silver into the wash-hand stand,
and put his watch in a more usual place—under the pillow.
Having taken these preliminary precautions for the security
of his property he next turned his attention to the security of
his person, about which Mr. Pickwick was so careless. Mr.
Jorrocks did not climb into his large four-poster bed until he

had drawn a chest of drawers across the door. In this he showed himself a canny North Country man, and the conversation at that door the following morning was a veritable bit of Yorkshire transplanted into Suffolk—if the inn was in fact in Suffolk and not in Cambridgeshire! The Yorkshireman tried to open Mr. Jorrocks's door, and when he failed sang out: "Jorrocks, my man! Mr. Jorrocks! Jorrocks, old boy! Holloa, Jorrocks! "

"Wot? " replied the worthy person addressed.

"Jorrocks! " the Yorkshireman called out in rousing tones, "it's time to be up. . . . The morning's breaking."

"Let it break," muttered Jorrocks from his feather pillows; "it owes me nothing."

CHAPTER XIX

SUFFOLK FAME

To the man who is born and bred in it, Suffolk is home and needs no commendation. To the man of another county, it may appeal for a hundred different reasons, some of which may be shared by thousands while others may be as personal as the choice of a wife. To the bookman it is the land of many good companions. There is Dickens at Ipswich, Bury St. Edmunds, Sudbury, and Blundeston—and who could be a better companion than Dickens? There is Borrow at Long Melford and Lowestoft, Gainsborough along the Stour and the Orwell. And if the irrepressible high spirits of Dickens or the temperamental vagaries of Borrow and Gainsborough become too much for his tired nerves, there is Crabbe to tell a crusty tale, or Fitz to smoke a pipe with. Best of all, perhaps, there is Constable, a kindly, understanding man, not hag-ridden by genius as so many painters have been, but enjoying the pleasures that appeal to normal men and sharing their sorrows. This quality of being normal in experiencing life, and at the same time so much above normal in power to express it, is rare, though much less rare in England than in France. It is pre-eminently an East Anglian characteristic. Chaucer himself, who among English writers possessed it in unrivalled measure, is believed by many scholars to have been the son of an Ipswich vintner. His merchant, it may be recalled, wished the sea could be kept free for the passage of merchandise "Betwixe Middulburgh and Orwelle."

East Anglia's remarkable record of genius has several times been the subject of scientific enquiry. In *A Study of British Genius*, Havelock Ellis found that three districts in England had been more favourable than others to its production. These were East Anglia, the extreme south-west of England, and the Welsh border. Sir Arthur Conan Doyle found Suffolk among the first three English counties in the production of intellectual ability on the basis of population, remarking that its record was "quite phenomenal."

A number of factors have contributed to this noteworthy characteristic. The most important of these has been the settlement in the eastern counties of so many enterprising foreigners. Roman, Scandinavian, Norman, Flemish, Dutch, and other virile stocks settled here from earliest recorded times till the revocation of the Edict of Nantes at the end of the seventeenth century.

In thinking of Suffolk's record of fame the names of its most eminent families come first to mind. To record a few where so many have claims to recognition may be invidious, but the Bigods, Uffords, de la Poles, Wingfields, Bacons, Howards, Herveys, and others already mentioned have stood so high in the nation's councils throughout its history that we cannot fail to recall them. If individuals are in mind, we have Grosseteste, Tybald, Sancroft, and Wolsey in the Church, Thomas Howard—the victor of Flodden—and Lord Kitchener as soldiers, with the seamen whose stories have been told, and others of equal rank in many spheres. The county's pride in its offspring is fully justified.

But the picture is still incomplete. Suffolk is primarily an agricultural county, and I have no quarrel with the farmer who has thrown down this book several times because in dealing with one village after another I have omitted to state that in this a famous prize stallion was reared, or in that a Red Poll bull with half a dozen championships to his credit. Breed is a popular subject in Suffolk, and one on which a Suffolk man speaks with authority, for if the beneficent results of racial cross-breeding already mentioned came by national rape and seduction rather than by any union comparable with matrimony, in the breeding of animals, where ethical considerations are less restrictive, the Suffolk stock-breeder has shown himself a master. The three principal Suffolk breeds—the Suffolk punch, the Red Poll cow, and the Black-faced sheep —are among the county's best achievements and a lively part of the Suffolk scene. No one with an eye for a beautiful animal can travel along its roads without stopping to admire those sleek-coated chestnut horses cropping the grass at the

Little Wenham
Mellis

end of their day's work, or a fine herd of cattle grazing along a river bank.

The handsome Suffolk punch of to-day is a very different animal from the one described in the eighteenth century as "half horse, half hog," because of its short legs and barrel belly. Camden's *Britannia* informs us that the Suffolk horse dates back to 1506, which, I suppose, means that by that date the breed had achieved a recognised distinctive character. Arthur Young referred to " the old breed " of horse peculiar to the county. But no one appears to be certain about its origin. It is the only English cart-horse that shows no sign of Spanish ancestry. As it has a distinctly Scandinavian appearance it seems probable that it was brought over by Norse conquerors. But if the remote forerunner of the Suffolk horse cannot be recognised indisputably, the history of the punch as we know him to-day is definite enough. Every animal now recognised as being of the breed traces his descent in a direct male line to Crisp's Horse of Ufford, foaled in 1768.

Those who are accustomed to seeing taller breeds usually remark that the punch's body looks too heavy for its legs. The average height is sixteen hands and the weight may be as much as two thousand pounds. Another apparent fault from the point of view of appearance to those who know other cart-horses better is the lack of " feather " on the legs. Both these characteristics, however, increase the punch's usefulness. The lack of " feather " keeps the legs cleaner in working on heavy Suffolk clay, and the low withers, the short, thick neck and straight shoulders, the strong buttocks and the sharp movements of the sturdy legs give the punch tremendous pulling power. It has been bred principally as an agricultural draught horse, and as such it has no superior. It was also in great demand for artillery work during the First Great War, where it surpassed all others as a Heavy Battery horse. In watching a Suffolk punch at work we may not marvel at its grace of movement or be impressed by its pride and power; but we can hardly fail to be stimulated by its brisk, cheerful energy and determined action. It gives the impression of intelligently applied strength rather than of sheer brute force, and it appears to be a tireless worker.

U

Wortham
Columbyne Hall, near Stowmarket

The Suffolk Horse Society, which has its headquarters at Woodbridge, dates from a meeting held in Ipswich town hall on the 19th June, 1877, when the Earl of Stradbroke, father of the present Lord Lieutenant of the county, was elected patron. It was formed to compile a history of the punch and to trace the genealogies of all known animals of the breed as far as authenticated evidence could reach. Mr. Herman Biddell of Playford was the first editor, and after he had spent nearly three years tracing pedigrees he produced the first volume of the *Suffolk Stud Book* in 1880. When this was published it was the most exhaustive record of its kind ever produced in England.

The Suffolk polled cow, claimed by the Red Poll Cattle Society to be probably Britain's oldest breed of cattle, seems to be indigenous to East Anglia, though like the horse it has been much improved since the beginning of last century. If we refer again to Arthur Young we find him claiming that as a milk producer the Suffolk Dun Cow, from which the Red Poll is descended, "much exceeds on an average that of any other breed in the Island, if quantity of food and size of animal are taken into account." The statement would be more valuable if we knew how much reduction in milk yield he allowed for the medium size and sparing appetite of the animal! It is, however, certain that the Dun was a remarkably good milker and it is interesting to find that then as now the Suffolk cow was less greedy as a feeder than most breeds. The great advantage of its moderate appetite is that its milk yield falls less than that of most when winter sets in. There are several breeds with a higher seasonal yield, but few that maintain so high a yield consistently, not only in winter as well as summer, but also throughout a longer period of years.

Milk yield, however, is not to be taken alone when considering the merits of the Red Poll. It is bred for beef no less than for milk, and competes with the Lincolnshire Red Shorthorn for the honour of being Britain's best dual-purpose cow. With its value as beef in mind, the Red Poll breeder is well satisfied with an average milk yield of between eight and nine hundred gallons a year, especially as this is found to have a butter-fat content averaging nearly four per cent.

The production of a hardy, dual-purpose cow has been in

mind throughout the history of the breed. The climate of Suffolk would have made the breeding of a cow likely to reach the highest class as a milker difficult. Rainfall is low in East Anglia, and in consequence its grass crops do not equal those of the south-west of England. Its vegetation is affected also by the east winds that sweep across the coastal heaths and the High Suffolk plateau in severe winters. With these and other points in view, Mr. John Reeve, a Norfolk farmer, crossed Norfolk and Suffolk breeds at the beginning of last century in order to combine the milk yielding capacity of the Suffolk Dun with the beef producing capacity of the Norfolk cow. His experiment was entirely successful, and it is from this crossing that the present Red Poll has been evolved.

The third of the famous Suffolk breeds, the Black-faced sheep, was obtained by crossing the Norfolk horned ewe with the Southdown ram, and it has been recognised as a pure breed since 1880. Its flocks are widely distributed. Like the other Suffolk breeds it is a hardy animal, lambing in January during the coldest weather, and in consequence commanding high prices at spring sales. Perhaps the most interesting thing about the Suffolk sheep is its popularity in the United States of America and Canada. Its head and legs are clean, which gives it a great advantage over other breeds in countries liable to snowstorms, where woolly-headed sheep are often blinded. In the western states of America it finds favour for another reason. Suffolk lambs, it has been found, mature so rapidly that they are ready for killing before the native grass seeds—similar to our wild oats—are ripe. These seeds are apt to pierce the skin and set up an irritation that prevents the lambs fattening. For these advantages the breed is rapidly becoming the favourite in America.

With these three breeds to their credit it is not surprising that Suffolk farmers should still have the reputation they had in Cobbett's day. It was he who wrote of them: "I have always found Suffolk farmers great boasters of their superiority over others, and I must say that it is not without reason."

Besides many successful breeders, Suffolk has produced several eminent writers on agriculture, including Arthur Young himself. The first of its farmer-poets, Thomas Tusser, was an Essex man by birth, but he was a farmer at Cattawade, on the estuary of the Stour, when he wrote his *Hundreth Good Pointes of Husbandrie*, which was later amplified into *Five Hundreth Pointes of Good Husbandrie*. Fuller said of Tusser that he "traded at large in oxen, sheep, dairies, grain of all kinds, to no profit" and that he "spread his bread with all sorts of butter, but none would stick thereon." No doubt he was giving an honest report of what he had been told about Tusser. Fuller was no cynic; but on this occasion he did less than justice to his subject. Tusser's will shows that he practised thrift as successfully as he preached it. Doubtless it was as common in the sixteenth century as it is in the twentieth to suspect anyone who tries to teach others how to prosper of being a poor economist in managing his own affairs. It is certain that to know what should be done and to be able to do it are two qualities that are not always found together. Tusser was also subject to suspicion as a professed gatherer of the proverbial moss of profit because he was a rolling stone. Perhaps it would be more interesting to know how much profit others were able to get from his advice than to know how much he was able to get from it himself, for it is doubtful whether the wisest treatise such as Tusser's Dialogue of *Wyvynge and Thryvynge* can help two who do not agree to walk together in love, or a fool to stick to his money. Those who are able to profit by good advice seldom need it, and those who need it are seldom able to profit by it. Tusser's usefulness is not so much in his advice, sound as that may be, as in the information he gives about the conditions that he thought called for his prudent treatment. We find, for example, how little provision there was for wintering cattle in his day. There were no field turnips for fodder then, and by the time the grass was ready again the cows were half dead from starvation. Still more dangerous, he tells us, were the effects of over-eating in early summer:

> From Christmas till May be well entered in,
> Some cattle wax faint, and look poorly and thin;
> And chiefly when prime grass at first doth appear,
> Then most is the danger of all the whole year.

The remedy is somewhat crude:

Take verjuice and heat it, a pint for a cow,
Buy salt, a handful, to rub tongue ye wot how;
That done with the salt, let her drink off the rest;
This many times raiseth the feeble up beast.

Many proverbs are traceable to Tusser's work, and it is worth
noting that East Anglian authors figure prominently in all
dictionaries of quotations. Many of them have been masters
of a terse, epigrammatic style. The bite of the salt marshes is
to be found in their English. Francis Bacon, who excelled
so greatly in this style, was the son of Sir Nicholas Bacon of
Redgrave, himself an uncommonly shrewd man. Arthur
Young, also, is an eminently quotable author, with authentic
East Anglian astringency in his writings. It was he who
wrote: "The magic of property turns sand into gold," and:
"Give a man the secure possession of a bleak rock, and he
will turn it into a garden; give him a nine years' lease of a
garden, and he will convert it into a desert."

Young farmed land in Essex and Hertfordshire as well as
in Suffolk—and nowhere with any success. He was the greatest writer on agricultural subjects England has produced; but
he was temperamentally unsuited to the patient drudgery
that must always occupy a great part of the successful farmer's
time. He was a careful observer and he had a keen brain.
He could sow the seeds of fruitful practice in other minds,
even though he was too restless to tend them in his own. His
Suffolk home was at Bradfield Combust, on the main road
from Sudbury to Bury St. Edmunds. The hall he occupied
has been replaced by another, but the village itself, where his
father was both squire and rector, is little altered.

Young was a born writer rather than a born farmer. Whatever his official employment was supposed to be, reading and
writing filled his days. They brought him fame, but little
profit. "I have worked more like a coal-heaver, though without his reward," he wrote when nearly fifty, and he might
have written the same just before his death thirty years later.
Perhaps the coal-heaver would reply that Young did it from
choice, for he was certainly a hard master to himself. At sixty
he wrote: "The ground white with snow and wind cutting.
I am up every morning at four and walk into the garden

pond. . . . I do not mind it at all and sometimes stand in the wind till dry." On the other hand, there are hints in his diary of the pleasure he found in female society, which may or may not have been the cause of his domestic unhappiness. He was probably as little suited to marriage as he was to farming.

Young's work became as familiar on the Continent as it was in England. After publishing an *Agricultural Survey of France* he became so highly esteemed in that country that in 1801 the French Directory ordered the translation of all his agricultural writings. These appeared in twenty volumes entitled *Le Cultivateur Anglais*. When the English Board of Agriculture was established in 1793 he became its first secretary. He was consulted by experts from every part of the world, and worked with the same feverish intensity until in old age blindness brought him to a pathetic dependence on others. Even then his work went on; dictating and being read to during the week; preaching and teaching on Sundays, for he was a profoundly religious man. He died in London, but was buried at his own Bradfield Combust, where the noble trees he planted are a living tribute to his memory.

Other East Anglian writers have followed Young's example by writing reports on the state of English agriculture in their day, notably Sir H. Rider Haggard, who made a detailed examination of farming conditions in the first years of the present century, and Mr. J. Wentworth Day, a Suffolk man who has been described as "a modern Cobbett," the author of challenging books on East Anglian farming at the present time. All have been severely practical, and have seasoned their chapters with political as well as agrarian opinions. They have gone about the land on horseback, and whatever they have disagreed about they have all had one sound principle in common, namely that "it is a quietness to a man's mind to live upon his own and to know his heir certain."

It is easy to be deceived by sentimental descriptions of the rural scene. Nowhere is life more stern and exacting than on the land, and in no industry have conditions fluctuated more alarmingly. Rider Haggard reported that land which sold at £60 an acre in 1870 sold at £7 10s. an acre in 1900. Julian Tennyson, whose death in action during the Second Great

War was so great a loss to Suffolk, said he knew a farm that sold for £2,500 in 1920, £1,500 in 1927, £750 in 1934, and £400 in 1938. In the depression at the beginning of the century thousands of acres, particularly in the Bury St. Edmunds district, were given up to sport. Food production was unprofitable even with wages at twelve shillings a week. Between the two Great Wars taxation was already too heavy to allow more than a few wealthy men to buy large estates for sport, and many farms were in a deplorable state when the drive for home-grown produce during the last war again forced the nation to pay the farmer his due. To-day he lives well and carries himself with dignity. The recurring periods of farming depression are a thread in the tapestry of English history that must be cut out for ever.

The Suffolk of recorded history was first St. Edmund's county. Its heart was in the great abbey at St. Edmundsbury. Later it was the home of powerful barons. In Tudor England it was Wolsey's county. At the end of the Middle Ages it was a thriving centre of industry, and later again a county of large estates and proud families. But it was always farmers' country —the tune of the Suffolk Regiment is *Speed the Plough*. Its shepherds and ploughmen have known many masters and have outlived them all. Little is left to-day of St. Edmund's noble abbey. The great churches of the fifteenth century remain, but with dwindled villages about them. No new cities have spread themselves across this Suffolk ploughland. No famous centres of learning have been established in its ancient towns. So when we turn from the study of history to the contemplation of its present scene many of the brighter lights go out and we are left with the steady glow of sunset on widespread farmland, cottage homes, and tangled hedgerows. Suffolk has no popular "beauty spots."

If I were asked why this county appeals to me so strongly, I should reply that above all else Suffolk holds me because it is inscribed so nobly with the story of man's pilgrimage. It abounds with interest for the social historian. Its churches must always come first to mind in this connection; but no less than has been read into the story of its churches might be read into its manor-houses. They are not so obvious to the eye. You do not see Little Wenham Hall, for example, a dozen miles away, as you see Stoke-by-Nayland or Kersey church towers. But this only enhances the joy of discovery to the man who wanders down the byroad that branches off the main Ipswich to Colchester road and finds it where it has stood for nearly seven hundred years. Little Wenham Hall, or Castle, was built about 1260 and restored by the de Brewse family in either the fifteenth or sixteenth century. In its walls we see Flemish bricks being used for the first time to our knowledge in England. These replaced the flat Roman bricks, more like roofing tiles, to be seen at Burgh Castle in Suffolk and more extensively at Colchester Castle in Essex. Part of the walls appear to be constructed of material similar to that used in Orford Castle, which was probably taken from the sea-shore. The banqueting hall, now reached by an outer staircase, has a tiled floor, once strewn with rushes, and a great open hearth with a recess where the gold and silver plate would be washed. Tapestries would hang upon the grey walls, and the eyes of guests would wander up them to admire the fine oak ceiling. Over the small eastern room or recess is the chapel, entered through a doorway between two arched windows divided by an octagonal shaft.

The Flemish settlers developed brick-making in East Anglia, and it was from them that the English learnt the art of moulding brick for use in chimneys and gatehouse decorations, still so prominent a feature of Tudor manor-houses. This is but one instance of what I mean in saying that Suffolk is inscribed so nobly with the story of man's pilgrimage. For anyone who has an eye for curious marks on castles, churches, farm-houses, or cottages, the influence of each succeeding race of settlers may be traced by something that denotes that a Roman, a Dane, or a Dutchman once passed that way.

In books and buildings the life of the past is still plain to us. Suffolk remembers its worthies and preserves its homesteads. Many of the fifteenth- and sixteenth-century manor-houses for which the county is justly famed have been mentioned already. Others I shall be reproached for having missed include Gifford's Hall at Wickhambrook, Gedding Hall, with its fine Tudor gatehouse, Erwarton Hall near the mouth of the Stour, and Playford Hall, where Thomas Clarkson the abolitionist lived, and where he died in 1846 at the age of eighty-five. In visiting the houses these men once occupied we come as near as we can to their living presence. We can see the rooms they once sat in and kneel in the churches where they worshipped. I felt this yesterday at Wetheringsett, while leaning over the wall of the rectory where Richard Hakluyt lived. He was rector of Wetheringsett from 1590 to 1616, settling in the village the year after he published his *Principall Navigations, Voiages, and Discoveries of the English Nation,* which he enlarged and reissued in three volumes in 1598-1600, while living in that same house, where the only water he could see was a tiny rivulet, one of the sources of the Dove, which flows from his rectory garden and along his churchyard wall. From this quiet retreat, where a group of cream-washed cottages bask in the sunshine, their walls diapered with the shadows of tall elms —"huge homestead elms"—Hakluyt dispatched the final edition of what has been called the "prose epic of the modern English nation." A few miles away, across a sparsely populated countryside, is Stradbroke, where Robert Grosseteste was born, and a few miles farther, Fressingfield, where Archbishop Sancroft lived and died. It is more than two hundred and fifty years since anyone saw him walking in its lanes, but Ufford Hall has many features that were there in his day.

Perhaps the most curious feature of the Suffolk scene in general is the mingling of apparently conflicting elements. Not only is the wild and lonely east different from the serene and cultivated west, in every part of the county the homely and familiar is found alongside the mysterious. It is as though the sentences of a story by Hardy had got mixed up with the sentences of a story by de la Mare. Most of the plateau we call High Suffolk has neither mystery nor surprise until we run into one of its quiet towns, where the cottages and shops are built round the churchyard so that every time the townsfolk open their doors or peer through their windows they are reminded of man's mortality. The visitor who sees for the first time these clusters of cottages round a massive church tower, like a ring of flowers round the gnarled stump of a giant oak, often remarks that he has difficulty in believing that what he sees is actually there. This sense of the incongruous is much stronger near the coast, particularly at Blyth-burgh, where the great church appears to rise from the barren heath with only a few houses near it. We expect to see a town beyond, but when we have passed the church we find only a wilderness of marshland with a scattered herd of cattle cropping its coarse grass. At Dunwich it is not the seen but the unseen that confuses the mind. In humble cottages we hear tales of a noble city that lies in ruins below the waves that wash the bare shingle. We are told of bells that have been heard ringing in shattered belfries, or homelier tales of how the tailors of Dunwich could sit in their shops on the vanished cliffs and watch the shipping in the Yarmouth roads.

But when the surprise of these incongruous elements in the Suffolk scene has faded, its aspect becomes more friendly. Its church towers are no longer overwhelming in their solemn grandeur. Other things are noticed besides their size and splendour—the red valerian, perhaps, that so often grows against their black flint walls. Names on the mossy grave-stones are the names of friendly people we have met in shop or inn. Suffolk is the land of the cats that walk by them-selves; but it is also the land of genial, companionable men. Its countryside remains fresh and lovely. It will certainly attract more visitors in the future than it has done in the past, though never, perhaps, the multitudes who have dis-figured so much of the English coast. It has no glamour, and for that reason may be saved for those who prefer a homely face, with lines of character, good humour, and kindness upon it—and a sparkle of roguish fun—to the sophisticated lure of more fashionable and populous counties.

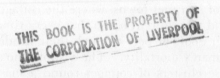

INDEX

INDEX

Benedictines, 11
Benhall, 170, 172
Beorn, King Edmund's huntsman, 217
Beresford, Lord Marcus, 283
Betham-Edwards, M., 45
Bible in Spain, The, Borrow, 201
Bicknell, Maria, 65
Bigod, Earl of, 104; family, 288; Hugh, 164, 223–4; Roger, 164, 223
Bigod's Hill, 222; Castle, 223
Blackburne, E. L., 189
Black Heath, 162
Blacklands Hall, 31
Blackman's Head, 119
Black monks, Eye, 11
Blackmore, R. D., 95
Black Shuck, 120–2; Breckland, 263; Bungay, 221; wild man of Orford, 160
Blaise, Bishop, 69
Bloomfield, Robert, 16, 260–2
Blyth, river, 180; valley, 181–95
Blythburgh, 8, 180, 181–5; isolation, 298; shipping, 181
Bocking, Dean of, 80
Boleyn, Anne, 43, 103, 104
Borley Rectory, 108
Borough, The, Crabbe, 159, 211
Borrow, George, 201–3, 287
Boundaries, 2, 3
Box, river, 55, 64
Boxford, 56; Lion, 63
Boy's Grave, the, 277
Bradfield Combust, 293, 294
Bradley, Little, 21
Bradshaw, Mrs., 162
Bramfield, 185
Brandeston, 137
Brandeston Hall, 137
Brandon, 264–6, 271
Brandon, Charles, Duke of Suffolk, 103; Huntingfield, 188
Breckland, 9, 259–74; beeches, 12; Bloomfield, 260; flint-knapping, 265; flora and fauna, 269–71; ghosts, 262; heaths, 264, 277; history, 268; Laken-heath Common, 268; Mildenhall, 272; prehistoric remains, 274; timber, 266; wild-fowling, 259
Brett, river, 64, 67; villages, 83
Breydon Water, 212–13
Brice's Farm, 136
Brightwell, Rector of, 278
Bristol, Frederick, fourth Earl of, 276
Bristol, Marquess of, 256, 258, 276
Britannia, Camden, 289
Britten, Benjamin, 159
Broke, Captain, 94
Broke Hall, 117
Broke, Sir Philip, 115–18

Bromeswell Heath, 133
Brontë, Emily, 130
Brooke, Captain, 143
Broughton Hall, 106
Brown, Baldwin, 229
Bruisyard, 163
Buck, Rev. James, 237
Bull-baiting, 42, 86
Bungay, 11, 221–7; Mr. King's Baths, 225–6
Bures, 3, 4; Constable, 59; Guildhall, 58; St. Edmund's Chapel, 56; Stour, 57
Burgh Castle, 213
Burr, Margaret, 41
Burroughs, Rev. Humphry, 40
Bury St. Edmunds, 3, 243–58; Abbey, 235, 243, 246, 248–9, 250–5, 258; Angel Hill, 35, 244, 245; Catchpole, Margaret, 96; Cullum Library, 215, 257; Dickens, 243; Dissolution, 253–5; fairs, 244–5; geology, 9; James I, 256; John, 255; libraries, 257; Louis Philippe, 257; John Lowes, 137; monasteries, 251; Moyses Hall, 245, 257–8; parliaments, 255; relics, 253; Richard I, 254; roads, 8, 9; Abbot Samson, 214, 247–51, 258; Shake-speare, 238, 240; St. James's, 253; St. Mary's, 253; white bull, 253–4; "white" brick, 37; Jack Straw, 244; Arthur Young, 4
Butley, 160; river, 162; priory, 173

Cadogan, Lord, 256
Caister, 216
Calais, siege of, ships for, 150
Caldwell, Daniel, 47
Callender, Sir Geoffrey, 115, 117
Cambridgeshire, 2
Cambridge University Press, 177
Camden, William, 140
Campanology, 38, 40; East Bergholt, 65; Dr. J. J. Raven, 230
Canute, 67, 251, 252
Capel, Sir William, 61
Carlyle, 247, 248
Carriers' Cosmographie, Taylor, 78
Carter, George, 120
Carter, Thomas, 38
Carthagena, 117
Castel of Love, Grosseteste, 235
Castlemaine, Lady, 282
Castles: Bigod's, Bungay, 223, 224; Burgh, 213; Caister, 216; Clare, 28; Framlingham, 164, 224; Haughley, 104; Mettingham, 240; Norwich, 224; Orford, 161, 296; Walton, 128, 224; Wingfield, 239

300

INDEX